D1643709

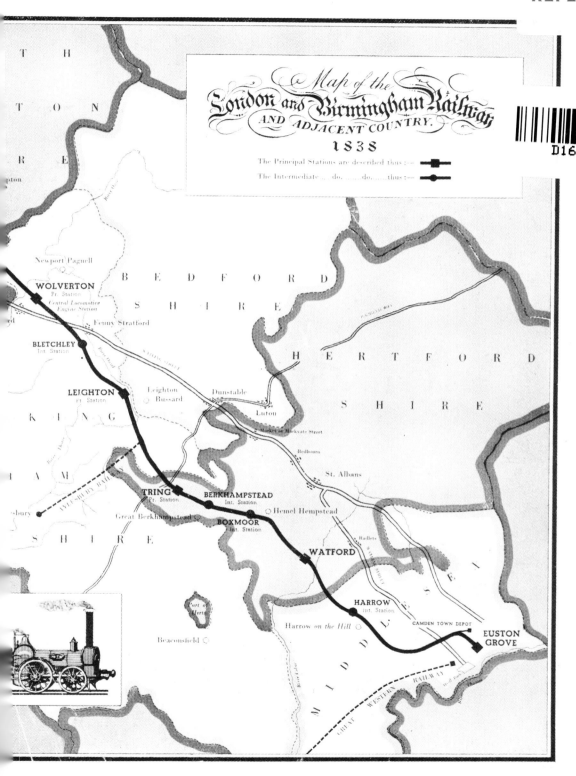

Map of the
London and Birmingham Railway
AND ADJACENT COUNTRY.
1838

The Principal Stations are described thus :—
The Intermediate do. do. thus :—

Town of Trains 1980
has been published as a Limited
Edition of which
this is

Number   3

A complete list of the
original subscribers is
printed at the back of the book

A. E. Grigg

TOWN OF TRAINS

FRONT COVER: *Hardwicke* at Fenny Stratford, with a guard of the
1890s, surrounded by scenes from Oxford, Cambridge, Banbury and the
Oxbridge Line countryside. (Designed by Alan Walker)

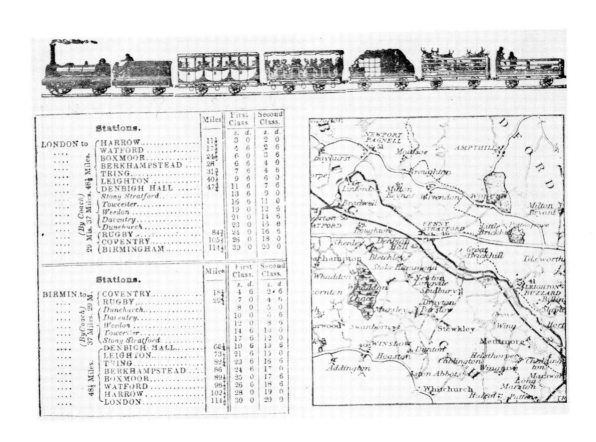

	Stations.	Miles	First Class. s.	First Class. d.	Second Class. s.	Second Class. d.
LONDON to	HARROW	11¼	3	0	2	0
....	WATFORD	17½	4	6	2	6
....	BOXMOOR	24½	6	0	3	6
....	BERKHAMPSTEAD	28	6	6	4	0
....	TRING	31¾	7	6	4	6
....	LEIGHTON	40½	9	6	6	0
....	DENBIGH HALL	47¾	11	6	7	6
....	*Stony Stratford*		13	6	9	0
....	*Towcester*		16	6	11	0
....	*Weedon*		19	0	12	6
....	*Daventry*		21	0	14	6
....	*Dunchurch*		23	0	15	0
....	RUGBY	84¾	24	0	16	6
....	COVENTRY	105¼	26	0	18	0
....	BIRMINGHAM	114½	30	0	20	0

(48¾ Miles. (By Coach) 37 Miles. 29 Mls.)

	Stations.	Miles	First Class. s.	First Class. d.	Second Class. s.	Second Class. d.
BIRMIN. to	COVENTRY	18¼	4	6	2	6
....	RUGBY	29¾	7	0	4	6
....	*Dunchurch*		8	0	5	0
....	*Daventry*		10	0	6	6
....	*Weedon*		12	0	8	6
....	*Towcester*		14	6	10	0
....	*Stony Stratford*		17	6	12	0
....	DENBIGH HALL	66¾	10	6	13	6
....	LEIGHTON	73¾	21	6	15	0
....	TRING	82¾	23	6	16	6
....	BERKHAMPSTEAD	86	24	6	17	0
....	BOXMOOR	89¾	25	0	17	6
....	WATFORD	96¾	26	6	18	6
....	HARROW	102¾	28	0	19	0
....	LONDON	114½	30	0	20	0

(29 M. (By Coach) 37 Miles. 48¾ Miles.)

From Drake's Railroad Map, 1838.

TOWN OF TRAINS

1838- -1980

BLETCHLEY AND THE OXBRIDGE LINE

A.E. GRIGG

BARRACUDA BOOKS LIMITED
BUCKINGHAM, ENGLAND
MCMLXXX

PUBLISHED BY BARRACUDA BOOKS LIMITED
BUCKINGHAM, ENGLAND
AND PRINTED BY
BOWMAN—ROCASTLE LIMITED
HERTFORD, ENGLAND

BOUND BY
BOOKBINDERS OF LONDON LIMITED
LONDON N5

JACKET PRINTED BY
CHENEY & SONS LIMITED
BANBURY, OXON

LITHOGRAPHY BY
SOUTH MIDLANDS LITHOPLATES LIMITED
LUTON, ENGLAND

TYPE SET IN 11pt TIMES ROMAN
WITH DISPLAY TYPE BY
BRIAN ROBINSON
NORTH MARSTON, ENGLAND

© A. E. Grigg 1980

ISBN 0 86023 115 1

CONTENTS

ACKNOWLEDGEMENT

I would like to thank the many older railwaymen who told me stories of long ago, and filled the blank spaces in my memory of events that I have been directly or indirectly concerned with during my footplate career at Bletchley.

Thanks to the many people who gave or loaned me illustrations: to the *Bedford Times* for the photo of the 1938 streamlined train, to Leslie Bowler for the 1881 map of Bletchley Station, and to Leonard Grigg for the drawing of Jonas Sinfield's 'Jimmy'.

I am also grateful to my daughter-in-law, Mrs Eileen Grigg, for typing the manuscript, and to the staff at Bletchley Library, who were always helpful.

BIBLIOGRAPHY

Various issues of the *Milton Keynes Gazette, Jackson's Oxford Journal, Bedford Times, Bucks Flying Post,* and the *Bucks Herald;* also J. K. Fowler's *Echoes of Old County Life* and many other publications to which frequent reference has been made, too numerous to list.

FOREWORD

The Railway and the countryside have been bound close together for 150 years. They say that the wayside station has all but gone and yet I know of just such a station, presided over by two 'old retainers,' who know their village, who are impeccable railwaymen and who, jointly with the station pub, welcome the hunt on Christmas Eve.

Railwaymen are often good authors and Mr Grigg, a Bletchley driver, is no exception. One does not escape the railway in a railway town, even today and the author recreates its personality, its railwaymen and above all, the fascination of branch line working, the village station, its station master, porter, signalman, squire and parson.

Go to a retired railwaymen's gathering and you will soon be pinned in a corner. No story is better told than by the old driver who, years before, has had to rise to the occasion with a superannuated express engine in an emergency, who has beaten the odds and come home victorious. Bletchley has many such men, but in all grades, a fascinating mixture of the dramatic and the leisurely. Some of them are there today, doing much the same work in the modern context: countrymen and railwaymen, a splendid and time honoured breed.

Dedication

To my grandchildren Daniel and Laura.
With both grandfathers lifelong railwaymen, this book will no doubt be of great interest to them in years to come.

ENDPAPERS: Map of the London & Birmingham Railway and adjacent country, 1838.

Like my old hometown Northallerton, Bletchley, at least up to a few years ago, was a rural focal point on a main railway line — the London Midland. I was a locoman. Arthur Grigg still is. And he is author of this fascinating book, not simply about Bletchley as a railway junction, but as the home of railwaymen and their families.

As an old colleague of mine — activist for more than a quarter of a century and secretary of our local branch for about 10 years — Arthur and I met several times when he was delegate to our Annual General Meeting.

I remember, too, with some pleasure, the occasion I attended the branch to celebrate our centenary as a union in 1972. At that time, Arthur had already published his first book about the union and his branch. As assistant general secretary then, I applauded his resourceful enterprise. I do so again. There is nothing more authentic than the personal record of active working people and their lives and experiences. When the account is written by a sympathetic and skilful observer who is part of that history, then it is doubly valuable.

THE OLD GUARD'S LAMENT

Eternal Father strong to save
Whose arm is round the fastest train,
Who sees them speeding on their way
Upon the railway lines each day.
Oh hear us when we weep and pray
For those who work them on their way.

O Trinity of Love and Power
Our Trainmen shield in danger hour,
With Maltese Cross and Fitted Trains
Protect them when they're on the main.
Thus evermore we weep and pray
To guide and guard them night and day.

O God of Host whose mighty hand
Dominions hold on sea and land,
With fog and snow our bitterest foe
Protect us where so ere we go.
And when too old to work no more,
Pray keep us from the Workhouse door.

(This poem was written in chalk inside the brake van of a freight train in the late 20s.)

The beginning: ABOVE: The Doric Arch at Euston station, & BELOW: the entrance to Curzon Street station, Birmingham, with INSET ABOVE: George Carr Glynn, later Lord Wolverton, Chairman, London & Birmingham Railway 1837-1846, LNWR 1846-1852 and BELOW: The Marquis of Chandos, later Duke of Buckingham, Chairman, LNWR 1853-1861.

THE PROUD YEARS

A small country town was already developing into surburbia as part of the future Milton Keynes when the last steam engine departed from the black, soot-encrusted loco shed at Bletchley. Diesels were running along the branch lines but the stations were getting shabbier and the staff, like the freight trains, were getting fewer.

Bletchley's branch lines to Oxford and Cambridge looked like a garden whose keeper had ceased to care and the Banbury branch was already being taken over by rabbits and pheasants, while foxgloves and coltsfoot were growing out of the cindery track.

When the endless overhead electric wires and countless structures came through Bletchley and by-passed the branch lines, the optimists spoke of a great future for this commuters' paradise.

This book is about the real paradise, when colourful, majestic engines could be heard giving a distant whistle, then a roar, as they passed under the station's canopied roof, momentarily drowning the noises and perhaps obscuring the activity that makes up a main line junction station.

The story of Bletchley's rural railway beginning, along with the characters who lived in its confines or worked along the branch lines is now slipping into romantic history, along with the lace makers, thatchers and other village craftsmen of long ago.

Gone is the pride and glory felt by Bletchley locomen at the turn of the century when an engine on a classy express failed at Bletchley, quite a common occurrence until the end of steam, and a top link driver took out his engine to couple on to, or perhaps take over from, the failed engine.

He would set off to Crewe or Chester, or perhaps London, with an engine of a lower class than the failure, one that had probably seen express working years before but was now relegated to Bletchley for branch line working, or at the best, main line local train working. Standing on the platform in frock-tailed coat and leather bandolier, the passenger guard haughtily surveying the locomotive changeover would give a dignified wave of his flag and the delayed express was again on its way.

Overloaded, but with a crew determined to show the main line express men of Camden or Crewe just what branch line men could do, they hammered the little engine along to excel itself.

Timepiece incessantly lifted from his waistcoat pocket, the driver checked the minutes gained or lost at various passing points. The fireman was continually up and down his footblock, as six or seven shovels full of coal were quickly placed around the sides of the firebox and the fire hole door immediately closed before cold air could spoil his efforts; back on the block to spy the colour of the chimney smoke and the boiler water level; back again with six or so more precisely placed shovels full of coal into the firebox. Still the stern-faced old driver in the opposite corner lifted his timepiece in and out as the miles and the minutes ticked away and the chimney smoke darkened and lightened.

In LMS days between the wars, named expresses with even larger engines thundered through the station, while the puny little Model T Ford and the boxy Austin Seven were contrasted to the magnificent, powerful steam locomotive going to those gay places displayed on the advertisement posters — to far away Blackpool or perhaps to meet the golfing girl of Gleneagles whose poster clothes changed with the fashions. Still, the mighty

11

engines failed and out from Bletchley shed went a former main line engine, now looking comparatively frail, to haul the express forward, the top link driver in pale blue, well-washed overalls and shiny hat, with a white cloth in hand and a fireman already blackened, and it was right away clear signals through to Crewe.

Although there were such moments of conspicuous glory for locomen, Bletchley men of all grades were essentially rural in character and it was along the branch lines that they usually served. At the small stations the Station Master was generally to be seen, in his dignified, gold braided, peaked cap, or the full dignity of a bowler hat. A fly collar and a fresh flower in the buttonhole completed the image. The long service ticket collector or porter knew the village people well enough to touch his cap to those of local distinction, and respectfully greet the lesser mortals of his village. The wayside checker cared for the local traders' desires and as such had a place in village life.

But the Model T Ford did not stay puny, and with its more practical development, so the branch lines faded like a rose: the war was its autumn bloom and the post-war years the pruning season.

But even in that season of over-pruning, rural characters who had grown old in railway service could remember, or tell from folk memory, stories of the branch line's proudest years.

ABOVE: Before 1838, the line ended at Denbigh Hall Bridge; BELOW: Locomotive No 148, Stephenson's long boiler engine, involved in the Bicester accident, 6 September, 1851.

RURAL INTER-CITY

Few branch lines in Britain could boast such a wide variety of pleasing station architecture and lineside features. The traveller could sit and watch the rustic scene changing along the route, and feel some acquaintance with those who worked in the market gardening area between Cambridge and Bedford, and the farmers of the cattle-grazing countryside from Bletchley to Oxford or Banbury. If interested in railway travel and its history, he would recognise traces of the old London & Birmingham Railway stone sleepers, open signal frames, capacious brick and wood warehouses and low platforms for the short local trains. As darkness fell he could see the flickering gas jets or oil lamps which lent atmosphere to the Victorian railway scene.

When the southern portion of the London & Birmingham Railway passed through Fenny Stratford and abruptly stopped at the London-Holyhead road in April 1838, the temporary station erected there dealt with passengers who virtually all required horse-drawn transport: either to Rugby, where the L & B Railway again commenced, or a stage coach to such diverse places as Newport Pagnell, Stony Stratford, Northampton, Kettering, Boston or Market Deeping.

This station took its name from the nearby, infamous and bawdy inn called 'Denbigh Hall'. Bletchley village itself was nearly two miles away. It was a small village consisting of a cluster of mainly thatched houses around Tree Square where a few roads met. In 1831 the population of 376 were living in 83 houses.

The roaring trade and quick rise to fortune of the landlord of the Denbigh Hall did not last long. A bridge was erected over the London-Holyhead road and on 24 June 1838 the guard on the 9.30 am from Euston Grove waved his flag and the train steamed away from Denbigh Hall, through Sympson Wood, towards Birmingham. By September the line was opened to all trains and the little temporary station at Denbigh Hall was no longer required.

Trains steamed off from Leighton Buzzard to Wolverton, which was roughly half-way from London to Birmingham. This was chosen as the main stopping place, where all trains halted for refreshments, lavatories and changing the locomotives. By 1844 it was described as a 'gigantic station' which 'could be considered one of the wonders of modern times in connection with Railway enterprises'. In those few years, land that was once covered with crops was now overspread with extensive premises and streets. Wolverton, once as insignificant as Bletchley, was now a new town. By July 1844 a new church was consecrated, an infants' school was in existence, attended by 250 children, as well as a weekly evening school for adults and a library. All this was described as 'ample provision for the intellectual and moral improvement of the Company's Servants'.

There was no question of moral improvement for Bletchley or its neighbour, Fenny Stratford. It seems that the L & B Board of Directors did not even want a station near these villages. However, a petition requesting a station was submitted to the Board by the local people. This was considered by a Committee of Administration which reluctantly agreed that a stopping place should be made, where the road from Bletchley to Fenny Stratford was crossed on the level by the railway. The fact that Leighton Buzzard to the south and Wolverton to the north had stations and were 12 miles apart, assisted in the decision. The Board of Directors accepted the recommendation of the Committee of Administration that only one or two trains each way should stop here daily, and in June 1840 Bletchley appeared in the timetables, but as an obviously low category station.

There was no mention of Bletchley in *Bradshaw's Railway Companion* dated 25 October 1839, but information is given about the trains going through Bletchley. There were 'Mixed Classes', 'First Class', 'Mail', 'Mixed Short' and 'Second Class'.

First Class carriages seated four in a car by day and six by night, the fare being about 3d a mile. Second Class carriages were open at the side, without linings, cushions or divisions in the compartments, except at night when they were closed and 'entirely protected from the weather'. Each carriage had a small lamp day and night. Passengers' luggage was placed on top of the coach in which they were riding.

The fares from Euston to Bletchley were first class 13s 6d with four in the car, 12s 6d with six in the car, and second class 10s 6d by night and 8s 6d by day. Children under ten went half price.

There were three trains per day from Euston stopping at Bletchley:-

| Euston | 8.0 am | 2.0 pm | 6.0 pm |
| Bletchley | 10 15 am | 4.15 pm | 8.15 pm |

The 8.0 am and 2.0 pm were 'mixed class' and the 6.0 pm was 'first class'. The Mail trains did not stop at Bletchley.

Bletchley Station was at first just a wooden platform on either side of two running lines, and was actually in the parish of Fenny Stratford, which had a larger population. This point does not appear to have caused any dissension, and the proximity of Bletchley Church may have had some bearing on the naming of the station.

The Mail Exchange Apparatus was erected at Bletchley probably before the station came into use. Denbigh Hall had been disbanded only about five months before trials were taking place with apparatus at Bletchley. Lineside standards were erected at Berkhamsted, Leighton Buzzard and Boxmoor, which came into regular use on 27 October 1838. On 7 November the Postmaster General gave instructions for their introduction 'at all the necessary stations between London and Liverpool', but this was amended because later in the same month the Travelling Post Office was diverted to run to Preston from London. As a result, apparatus was erected at Bletchley, Weedon, Bescot Bridge, Penkridge, Winsford and Preston Brook, and trials took place toward the end of February 1839; regular working appears to have commenced with very little delay, for on 2 March the Post Office wrote to the London & Birmingham Railway 'The new apparatus for the receipt of bags will commence from both ends on Tuesday next 5th March 1839 and in case of failure, the usual signal will be given by turning the white lamp'.

There were failures, and complaints are on record about such problems as the sinking of the rails and the oscillation of the carriages, high winds and loose tarpaulins which knocked bags from the standards. On 25 March 1839, less than three weeks after the date ordered for the working of the additional apparatus, the PO wrote to the L & B to ask '... permission for a small allowance to be given by the Post Office to clerks on the L & BR at stations where the bag apparatus is erected as an inducement to them to see that the apparatus is not improperly interfered with'. It added that the allowance was already being made on the Grand Junction Railway.

Sometime after 1852 the familiar net on the carriages appeared, with a lineside net and leather pouches which held the bags for delivery; the latter innovation was important as there had previously been instances of bags slipping through the wide mesh of the net.

As far as records and memory go, the down side apparatus at Bletchley was situated alongside the down fast line, just south of the station, near the New-Found-Out lake and near a loco pump house. The up side apparatus was alongside the up fast line just north of the station, across the fast line from the loco shed engine gonging off point. There they remained until no longer required.

Passengers for the little station did increase. In 1841 a wicket gate was needed at the level crossing on the Fenny Stratford-Bletchley road, and the Coaching and Police Committee ordered one to be constructed. There was an increasing number of people and cattle using the crossing, some perhaps going to travel by rail. In the same year the population of Bletchley had risen to 418, living in 147 houses, with four more to be erected. Of the population, 48 appear not to have been born in Buckinghamshire. Fenny Stratford had a population of 765 in 1841.

The status of Bletchley Station changed in 1846, but before we come to this, perhaps it is as well to consider how the railway came through Fenny Stratford in the first place and consider what might have been. It is recorded that Richard Creed, Secretary of the London & Birmingham Railway, was broadly in favour of the line going from Tring to just north of Aylesbury, then to Whitchurch, Winslow, Buckingham, Brackley and then Birmingham. This route via Aylesbury is mostly referred to as crossing the Chilterns by the Wendover gap.

At this time Buckingham was the County Town and nearby was Stowe House, home of the Duke of Buckingham, a veritable power-house in national and local politics. The Duke had a thorough dislike of railways and as J. K. Fowler relates in *Echoes of Old County Life,* when a projected line went through the Duke's property, 'he raised a complete posse comitatus of his labourers and dependants to oppose the survey,' and 'there was many a fight and breaking of heads, and every obstacle was raised to prevent a survey being made and the levels taken'.

George Stephenson's original plan of the L & B via the Wendover Gap, was bitterly opposed by almost every landowner along the projected line. Much of this projected route later became the New Metropolitan Railway.

Robert Stephenson was commissioned for a second report for the route of the L & B Railway, which was eventually adopted. The route via Watford, Tring and Bletchley was not without opposition from Lord Essex, Clarendon and others, which drove Stephenson to the other side of Watford, necessitating the viaduct at Bushey, the long Watford Tunnel, the heavy Boxmoor embankment and the deep chalk cutting at Tring.

It is possible that the Duke of Buckingham and the squirearchy under his influence prevented Buckingham from taking the role of Bletchley or Wolverton on the L & B Railway; had this happened, it would probably never have lost its position as the County Town.

It is some consolation that the Duke's son did not have the same dislike of railways, and his grandson was an enthusiast who took the top job on the successor to the L & B, the London & North Western Railway.

When the L & B opened throughout in 1838, none of the main lines touched the county town of Bedford, 16 miles east of Bletchley. The station nearest to Bedford was Leighton Buzzard, which was actually in the parish of Linslade in Buckinghamshire. A coach ran daily to meet trains there.

There was an obvious need for a railway into Bedford and as early as 1836 people were discussing the possibility of a railway from Cambridge via St Neots, Bedford and Newport Pagnell to join up with the L & B Railway.

It was in 1844 that George Stephenson came to Bedford, to discuss with a group of businessmen the possibility of a branch line to the London & Birmingham main line. By the next year, a Bedford Railway Company had negotiated with the L & B not only to have a branch line from Bedford joining the main line at Bletchley, but that the larger company would take over and run it.

15

The Chairman of the Bedford Railway Company was T. J. Green, Mayor of Bedford 1843-44 and also County Treasurer. As a local coal merchant, he urgently needed a railway for his business. Others included Robert Newland, a brewer, and T. A. Green, while investors probably included Thomas Barnard, Isaac Elgar, Henry Littledale and George Watt. One of the auditors was a well known county figure, W. B. Higgins.

On a Saturday afternoon in December 1845, the first turf was cut for the new 16 mile railway, and Brogborough Hill, about halfway along the new railway route, was selected for the occasion.

The Duke of Bedford, who lived about four miles away, had been engaged to preside at the ceremony, but was suddenly summoned to London on public business; the Duchess, to avoid disappointment, consented to officiate, assisted by Lord Alford.

A large crowd of people from Bedford, Woburn, Ampthill and all the surrounding villages gathered at Brogborough Hill, and a profusion of flags and standards marked the direction of the proposed line.

The Duchess arrived in a carriage and four with postillions in scarlet livery, and was greeted by a band and a cannon salute. With a beautifully ornamented silver spade, she dug the ceremonial sod, then Lord Alford, to the crowd's cheers, threw off his coat and hat and filled an ornamental barrow with earth.

Now the navvies could start on the real work. Wages for these men from 1843-69 were anything from 15s to 22s 6d a week, higher than those of farm workers. Often local men joined the gangs and then migrated with them. Lawlessness was common, as the navvies lived in wooden shanties with little or no comforts, and would occasionally break out and indulge in excessive drinking. Rev George Maclear tried to help those working on the Bedford-Bletchley line by reading the Bible with them, and there were evidently Irishmen in the gangs, as the Roman Catholic register at Shefford began to show Irish names at this time.

The Directors of the Bedford Railway Company reported difficulties with the Brogborough Cutting. In a cutting the waggons might be waiting above while barrows, connected by rope with a horse-drawn pulley, were wheeled up planks laid up the side of the cutting; a slip might cause a man to fall from a muddy plank with his load on top of him. Even if the waggons were below, it was a long haul for the unwanted earth. A normal day's work for each pair of navvies was usually 14 sets; that is, they filled a horse drawn waggon 14 times by shovelling earth and rock over their heads — a total of 20 tons.

The advent of the railway affected most people's lives. The Duke of Bedford's heavily timbered estate became a compensation for any loss of land to the railway. The agent, a Mr Bennett, noted in 1836 that the recent prices for wood sales were the highest he had ever known, and in this year the income from the Duke's Beds and Bucks estate was £9,000. It reached a record figure in 1846 with £26,446, then dropped, but from 1858 to 1860 rose again to over £10,000. By the 1880s it was on average £4,500.

Plans were made for a ceremonial opening of the line on 19 October 1846 and a public opening on the following day, but a heavy rainstorm caused a subsidence between Bletchley and Fenny Stratford and the opening had to be postponed.

On 17 November the line opened to the ringing of church bells. The Bedford Brass Band played and a large crowd watched 600 people leave for Bletchley in 30 carriages drawn by two locomotives. The passengers inspected the work in progress to enlarge, for the first time, Bletchley's little, mainly wooden, station.

The locomotives appear to have been turned, ready for the return journey, on a turntable invented by a man named Hancock. This was probably on the north side of the Bedford line as it curves round into Bletchley Station, where it remained until about 1909.

On returning to Bedford, the passengers were received by the Duchess of Bedford, who congratulated Mr Jackson, the contractor, on the ample accommodation at Bedford Station and the excellent execution of the work. She then entered the refreshment room, most tastefully and elegantly arranged by Mr Brashier on the orders of the directors.

What was described as a 'brilliant company' then dined in the Bedford Assembly Rooms, the 200 guests including Sir Harry Verney Bart, Chairman of the Bletchley & Oxford Railway Company, which, although it had obtained its Act authorising construction of a line from Bletchley to Oxford, was four years away from being completed.

The speeches were congratulatory and optimistic, the Chairman proposing a toast 'Success and Prosperity to the Bedford Railway', to enthusiastic cheers. He described the line as 'the master link in this magnificent chain, the very foundation stone of the structure, the basis on which the whole scheme rests', while the Recorder of Bedford, M. Prendergast, said he looked on it as a 'Magna Carta upon the inhabitants'. They were certainly all happy and satisfied.

An announcement in the *Bedford Times* three days before the opening, proclaimed 'At length we are enabled to make an authorised announcement of the opening of the Bedford Branch of the London & North Western Railway. Many unforseen circumstances have arisen to prevent the opening; but at length all obstacles appear to have been removed and we are really to have a trip to Bletchley on Tuesday. Fresh tickets for the passage and fresh invitations to the dinner have been issued, and there is every possibility of the affair going off with spirit. A memorial has been got up by the young men in the town, requesting that shops may be closed on that day in order that all classes may participate in the holiday. There is no doubt the steam is really up this time and that like Hood's light porter, the train will 'draw lot' for the first journey to Bletchley'.

On 18 November the line opened to the public and life changed for many Bedford inhabitants.

Bedford had its holiday and crowds swarmed along the lineside and around the station. It was a great step into the future for Bedford and its leading citizens were full of self-congratulations; but there were casualties.

After the London & Birmingham opened throughout in September 1838, the innkeeper at the George in Woburn found there was so little demand for posting horses, that in the following year he gave up this side of his business. But the most lamented casualty, and a very early one, was the *Bedford Times* coach. In an announcement in the newspaper on 17 November, the railway's opening day, Messrs Higgins & Horne begged 'to inform inhabitants of Bedford and the neighbourhood, that the Coach will perform its last journey to London on the first Saturday after the opening of the London & North Western and Bedford Railway, and they take this means of thanking them cordially for the liberal patronage bestowed upon it for so many years'.

On the same page, Mr Higgins of the Swan Hotel informed 'the Gentry and Inhabitants of Bedford and its vicinity' that he had undertaken the agency of the LNW and Bedford Railway and that 'Omnibuses will meet every train to and from Bedford, taking up and setting down passengers as required. Post Horses and Flys are in readiness at the station'.

Agency or not, Mr Higgins had a competitor; George Hills, Postmaster and livery stable keeper, advertised on the same page his regret that he was unfortunate in not getting the agency for the railway, but he would have conveyances to meet all trains and would provide *Omnibus Sociable*. Convenient Flys, Gigs etc, by which the public might be accommodated at his usual moderate charges, were available. Orders would be received at the Horse and Jockey Inn, St Mary's, or at the livery stables, Mill Street.

There was some genuine nostalgia at the passing of the *Bedford Times* coach, a handsome vehicle and only 20 years old. It was in the late 1820s that W. H. Whitbread started it as a sporting diversion, and it quickly made a name for itself by virtue of its speed, (timed at 10½ mph) its regularity, its comfort and its irreproachable turn-out. It was held second to none on the London Road, and Bradford Rudge's well-known painting of the coach shows why. The body was painted claret and blue and a contemporary description mentions an undercarriage and wheels of vivid scarlet and a splendid four in hand with glossy coats, shapely heads and clean and powerful legs. Inside passengers had a luxurious ride, for the interior was richly cushioned and padded, mostly with rose-coloured silk, the windows hung with green curtains in summer and scarlet in winter.

There were plenty of others ready to adapt themselves to the new era, and profit from it. The next week the *Bedford Times* announced the new timetable with four trains to and from Euston each day. Conveniently below the annoucement was a notice of building ground for sale by auction in the Swan Hotel by Messrs Pulley and Son: 'two pieces of Leasehold building ground containing together 2A 3R 35P in the parish of St Mary, Bedford, on the East side of the London Road, nearly opposite the Bedford Station, held by Lease from the Master and Co — Brethren of St John's Hospital, Bedford, for three healthy male lives of the respective ages of 56, 59 and 41, by the yearly reserve rent of £2 6s 6d in the following convenient Lots ...'

The most cheerful news item came in January: 'It is with considerable pleasure that we are enabled to announce the cheering intelligence that should no unforseen circumstances arise, on the first of February, coals may be purchased in Bedford at 11 pence per cwt. Messrs Stephenson & Co have 1000 tons at Fenny Stratford ready for railway transit. When it is remembered that this element of comfort is now selling in Bedford at 1s 9d a cwt, the vast reduction will be hailed by all classes as one of the greatest boons a railway could confer'.

The *Illustrated London News* found nothing unduly interesting along the line until near Bedford, where it reminded the traveller that 'At a little distance may be seen the village where the celebrated John Bunyon was born, and a short line of rail which leaves the main terminus at Bedford is carried down to the banks of the Ouse — a stream which will recall to the visitors the memory of the hapless poet Cowper'.

A little engine shed was built near the station and other buildings to accommodate the goods for a county town. Five stations were built along the line — Marston (later renamed Ampthill), Lidlington, Ridgmont, Woburn and Fenny Stratford — and Bedford had its first rail service direct to London in about 2½ hours at a cost of £16,000 to £17,000 per mile.

The opening day was a holiday at Bletchley and Fenny Stratford, but while the Church bells were rung and a band was out, there is no local record of any prominent local gentry involved in the promotion of the line or the festivities. Nevertheless in his *History of Fenny Stratford,* Dr Bradbrooke records that a W. Hanscombe of Apsley Guise did all the 'quicking' and fencing and supplied more than 27,000 sleepers. A Mr Hanscombe, senior, provided all the decorative and other plant at festivities at a three day cricket match which was held at Denbigh, an All England Eleven appearing.

The first railway into Bedford prospered as it charged half the stage-coach fares, and passengers reached London in half the time.

In 1846, when the Bedford line to the east of Bletchley Junction was nearly completed, a company called the Oxford and Bletchley Junction Railway Company obtained an Act authorising them to construct a line from Oxford to the LNWR to form a junction to the west of Bletchley.

At a board meeting of the company on 19 August 1846, £200 was voted for the moral and religious instruction of the workmen to be engaged to build the new railway.

In the same year, the Buckingham and Brackley Railway Company also obtained an Act to construct a line from a junction near Claydon on the projected Oxford and Bletchley line to Buckingham and Brackley. After some negotiation, the two companies entered into an agreement with the result that in 1847 they became amalgamated by Act of Parliament under the title of the 'Buckinghamshire Railway Company'. The Act also contained powers for an extension of the Buckingham and Brackley line to Banbury, also an extension on the other end of that line at the junction near Claydon, southward to Aylesbury. This latter extension was abandoned during the panic of 1846-47.

A prospectus listed the patronage of the following local dignitaries: the second Duke of Buckingham, Lord Nugent, Sir Harry Verney of Claydon, Sir John Chetwode of Chetwode Manor, Messrs Aubrey of Oving, Pierrepoint of Evenly, Dayrell of Lillingstone, Morgan of Biddlesden, Bracebridge of Chetwode Priory, Price of Westbury, Bailey of Shenley, Horewood of Stean Park, Lowndes of Winslow, and Parrot, Dewes, Humphreys and Stowe, all of Buckingham.

The contract for the whole of the Buckinghamshire lines was awarded to Brassey and Co, who appointed Samuel Horn as their agent with offices in Castle Street, Buckingham.

In February 1847 the *Bucks Herald* contained a notice under the heading 'Oxford, Bicester and Bletchley Railway': 'Owners of land required for the above railway in the neighbourhood of Bicester have been served with requisite notices of purchases by the projector. It is understood that the line will commence in the neighbourhood of Bletchley in about a fortnight; that Messrs Brassey, the contractors, do not intend to allow any payment by 'truck' and that ere long there will not be less than 2,000 men employed on this and the Brackley and Claydon Junction line. It will be seen that application for the extension, amalgamation and deviation at Oxford, has passed the standing orders in the Commons, unopposed'.

By the time work on the Buckinghamshire lines commenced, railway mania was over. The overwhelming demand for railways to be built in Britain was now just a trickle, and even those viable schemes waiting to be built were finding it hard to obtain the necessary capital. The badly bitten investors were acting shy.

For Thomas Brassey and Co, their contracts were coming to an end and despite efforts on their behalf, many of the men were unemployed and starving. The first turf was cut by Mr Field of Rugby, Brassey & Co's head physician, in the presence of many spectators on Tuesday, 20 April 1847 on a spot at Buckingham, near the Cross Keys Inn; it must have been welcome work for his company.

The incursion of so many labourers into the area brought troubles, anticipated by the Board at its second meeting on 20 August 1846, when a resolution was passed that the contractors were to provide huts and lodgings for their work people, pay weekly on Fridays in cash and not pay out in beershops or public houses. There would be no work on Sundays and local magistrates required policemen to be placed on the line.

On 10 August 1847, the Superintendent of the Buckingham Borough Police reported to the Buckingham Watch Committee that he received no assistance from the Railway Police and was obliged to have the whole of his force in the town on Saturday nights, because of the number of labourers about. A further complaint was made about the obstruction of the road bridge over the River Ouse by the railway water cart. Mr Horn undertook to have this obstacle removed.

The building of the whole of the Buckinghamshire lines brought work to many villages which would otherwise have been seeing lean times. Many men went hackle carting — one man who probably owned only his horse and cart found work with the various contractors. It was announced in the Oxford *Jackson's Journal* of 10 April 1847 that the enterprising Mr

Bugden, contractor for the formation of brickworks between Oxford and Winslow, intended to have a brickworks near the line not far from Bicester; digging for clay had already commenced. The same week the contractor for earthwork started more labourers between Launton and Marsh Gibbon.

According to F. W. Bennett, a local historian, Tom Betts of Freeman Cottages, Bletchley, was enterprising enough to sell beer from a tent to the men working on the line.

In 1847 there was a national financial crisis, so by November, the Board made the decision to stop work on the Oxford line for seven months, and delay starting work on the Banbury extension from Brackley until the new year. In 1849 more economies were made, by laying only a single track from the junction near Claydon to Oxford and to Banbury, and by selling surplus rails to the LNWR Company.

By October 1849, work on the Buckinghamshire lines had progressed so far that the contractors had orders to hold themselves in readiness for Bicester and Oxford Stations: in fact Fox, Henderson and Company eventually won the contract to build Oxford Station near Botley Road, on the site of the old Rewley Abbey. The contract was not made until January 1851 and the specification stipulated that the station was to be constructed on the same principle as the building of the Great Exhibition: it was to be completed in three months so that the line to Bletchley could be opened on 1 May 1851.

At the half-yearly meeting of the Company held in London on 14 February 1850, Sir Harry Verney reported that the total receipts amounted to £941,880 and the expenses for the purpose of the railway were £933,567, leaving a balance in hand of £8,283. Work on the Banbury line was progressing rapidly and nearing completion, and but for some unexpected delay in obtaining land for Banbury Station, the line might be opened for traffic in March. Work on the Oxford line had been proceeding vigorously and it might be opened as far as Islip early in the spring. The Chairman further added that a Bill for improvement of the line had been brought in and read a second time in the House of Commons, and the directors hoped it would pass without opposition. The retiring directors were re-elected and a vote of thanks recorded for the gratuitous service of the Rev Freemantle of Claydon who ministered on the line.

It had not been all plain sailing in the Buckingham area. Charles Whitehall, a local poet, records the Bath Lane railway bridge collapsing soon after a train-load of spoil had passed over it, and Harrison, in *Leisure Notes on Buckingham,* mentions that Bent Hill bridge over the railway collapsed during construction.

The numerous cases of damage to railway property that came before the Bucks Petty Sessions did not unduly delay progress. The *Bucks Herald* was constantly reporting cases such as that of John Tant of Stratton Audley, charged by Charles Haynes of Marsh Gibbon, a constable of the Buckingham Railway, with 'braking a bucket the property of the above railway company and injured it to the amount of one shilling'. Tant was ordered to pay 6d damage and 9d costs.

Sometimes the Duke of Buckingham sat on the Bench, but at this time he was having problems himself. In 1847 a great crash came in his affairs and the world held the opinion that the family's fortunes would never recover. Venison was being sold and the leverets killed and sent to the London sales from his estates at Stowe and Wotton. Soon that earthly paradise of Stowe would lose many of its treasures.

By the end of April, all was ready for the opening of the line from Bletchley to Banbury. On the 25th, after an experimental trip on the line, Thomas Brassey, the contractor, provided a dinner at Winslow for 130 invited people.

On 1 May 1850 the line from Bletchley to Banbury opened. Trains covered with flags and bunting carried local celebrities along the line to open each station in turn.

The first message to flash along the wires to Banbury Station announced the birth of the Duke of Connaught. Winslow, Buckingham, Brackley and Banbury were the earliest stations to open.

The first train left Banbury Station at 6.30 am and, although the morning was keen and cold, a large crowd congregated to witness the event which, however, did not attract many passengers. The first train out and into the station was driven by Henry Warriner. The second train left at 9.45 am, when the number of spectators, as well as passengers, had increased. At 1.50 pm the third train made its departure, by which time the bustle and excitement was at its height and the station had a festive appearance, complete with the Banbury Brass Band, booths and stalls. The fourth and last train departed at 5.00 pm.

The celebrations were arranged under the management of Mr McConnel, Superintendent of the Locomotive Department, Southern Division of the LNWR, and nothing occurred to mar the harmony or the regularity of the departures.

The big civic celebration at Banbury was not held until well after the official opening. Then in early August the Mayor of Banbury presided at a dinner in the Red Lion Hotel, where railway officials and local gentry celebrated the new means of transport, which was now transmitting the town's mail to London and Birmingham.

After the usual loyal toasts, Sir Harry Verney proposed the health of Mr Glyn of the LNWR Company and said the Buckinghamshire Railway Directors were glad to have such a town as Banbury as their terminus; he also saw the town as a great agricultural centre where they could buy at the good shops and sell their produce. A Mr Francillon thought Banbury, Brackley, Buckingham and Winslow might be considered as one town for commercial purposes. He then proposed the health of Mr Brassey and others until there were very few whose health had not been mentioned.

At this time Buckingham Station was just a little wooden building on the Lenborough Road side of the line. Despite a Buckingham Borough Council minute in 1849 recording that the contract for Buckingham Station had been let to Mr Dunckley of Bletchley for £20,000, as late as 1854, the Council was still urging the Railway Company to build a 'new and sufficient station now that an excellent road had been formed at no expense to the company'. The road referred to was promoted by the Marquis of Chandos and named Chandos Road.

The *Bedford Times* summarised the facts and aspirations of the Buckinghamshire lines within a few days of the opening of the first section to Banbury. The total length would be 53 miles and the total cost was expected to be £1,120,000, an average of £20,300 per mile. It was expected eventually to be a double line throughout, although at the opening it was only double as far as Claydon Junction, with the exception of a double track near each station where trains could pass. The rails weighed 85lbs per yard, the sleepers were large and creosoted or Burnetised and a heavy jointed sleeper was used. The ballast was two and a half feet deep. The counties of Oxford and Bucks, intersected by the Buckinghamshire railway, contained about 680,000 inhabitants with a surprising number on the Banbury line. Winslow area contained 3,800 inhabitants, Buckingham 7,000, Brackley 2,300, and Banbury 21,000. It was estimated that 65,000 tons of coal would be used annually in these four towns and the district around, almost the whole of which had to be bought by the railway. This would certainly be a boon to these country districts, but was a higher price than paid in London, although only 40 miles as the crow flies from a good coalfield. The revenue to the company from this source on the Banbury line alone would be little short of £10,000 per annum.

The London and North Western Co leased the lines from the Buckinghamshire Co and their administration commenced as it ended under British Rail over 100 years later, with economy and cuts for both staff and trains. Their immediate policy was for no separate goods and passenger staff, one set of hands attending to both duties. There would be few trains, but large carriages holding a large number of passengers running at moderate speeds. They intended to have no night staff and to reduce working charges to the minimum. Almost the whole staff to be employed was drafted from the older line and they announced 'no vacancies will be filled up'. This arrangement also applied to the locomotive department, from which some old hands were taken. This no doubt meant that Wolverton and Bletchley supplied the drivers.

On 1 October the single line from the junction near Claydon reached Islip, and Bicester made it a holiday and celebrated. Twelve days later the Verneys at Claydon House celebrated benevolently. Some 280 ragged school chlidren and their teachers from Westminster were conveyed at reduced fares from London to Islip, then taken to Claydon House to be entertained. Here the children were given a dinner of meat, plum pudding and apple pies. Beer was also available, but a great number of children were apparently teetotallers and declined it, preferring water. One little cockney boy is reported to have found a frog and excitedly thought he had caught a monster. After spending the afternoon playing games and wandering over the grounds of Claydon House, they returned to London on a train at five o'clock after a marvellous day.

When the line reached Islip on 1 October, it was almost immediately the end of the line for the old driver of the coach *Civility* from Northampton to Oxford. Buckingham lamented its passing in *Jackson's Oxford Journal* of 5 October 1850.

'The opening of the Buckinghamshire Railway from this place to Islip, has driven off the road the Northampton coach, which passed through our streets daily for more than 20 years; and the coachman made his final bow to his passengers on Monday last after having driven the coach upwards of twenty years without intermission, except from occasional illness which exposure to bad weather would sometimes come on in spite of temperate living and ordinary care. The distance from Oxford to Northampton is above 40 miles and reckoning only 300 working days in the year, the distance travelled would be 80 miles per day or 24,000 miles yearly, just about the circumference of the globe we inhabit; and again, multiplying these by 20 for the number of years, we have the amazing amount of 480,000 miles which *Civility* traversed, almost without accident, as far as our recollection serves. We hope that one who has been so long the servant of the public, may be able to retire on his hard earned competence, if he has attained one, and we are quite sure he will carry with him the good opinion and good wishes of all who ever travelled with him'.

This lament at the passing of *Civility* was followed by a reminder that the journey by rail from Buckingham to Oxford was not so impressive: there was first a train journey from Buckingham to Winslow, where one had to change for a further train to Islip, where the line ended. Then there was an hour's journey by omnibus for the six or so miles into Oxford.

On 2 December the line reached the Oxford-Banbury turnpike road 2½ miles nearer to Oxford, but although only three miles to Oxford itself, a tunnel at Wolvercote and a canal (cutting between two rivers) to be crossed near the new station on Botley Road, no doubt caused major problems.

The line was opened throughout to Oxford on 20 May 1851, when the first train to leave the new station was a special passenger train to the Great Exhibition in London, and ran the 78 miles to Euston in 110 minutes.

Although the station was officially opened on Tuesday, 20 May, the real celebration was deferred until the following Monday so that it could be commemorated in a suitable manner. The Directors gave a banquet at the Star Hotel, to which members of the County, City and University bodies, magistrates, heads of colleges, clergy, Corporation, professional gentlemen and principal tradesmen, numbering upwards of 420, were invited. Even more would have been invited, but the Star Room could not accommodate them, and even so, some had to content themselves with an adjoining room.

The Directors arrived at Oxford on a special train and were greeted by a great concourse of people at the flag-decorated station. The bells of St Thomas' church poured forth a merry peal and such a scene of bustle and excitement had never before been seen in the locality.

The humbler classes were not forgotten. So that they could participate in the celebration, a cheap excursion was announced to leave at 7.30 am in the morning to give 'persons of faculty' the chance of visiting the Great Exhibition on the first day of its opening, at one shilling admission. Free tickets were given to workmen and others who had contributed their 'mite', in aid of the funds of the Great Exhibition.

The liberality of the Directors did not stop there; they asked many college servants to join this excursion, but found it impossible to tear them away from their duties in the midst of term.

At the Star Hotel, tables were elegantly decorated, and held what was described by the press as 'handsome collation, including soups, fish, etc'. Wines including champagne, moselle, and claret of the finest quality were supplied with profuse liberality.

Sir Harry Verney MP presided, grace was said by the Chaplain to the Buckinghamshire Railway Co, Rev W. R. Freemantle, and Gimmetts' Band played many appropriate and popular airs during the meal and between toasts.

Numerous speeches were made by the leading dignitaries. Mr McConnell, Locomotive Superintendent at Wolverton, considered it no slight honour to conduct the communication between two great seats of learning — Oxford and Cambridge — to promote intercourse between places that before were separated, and to afford their inhabitants the facility of obtaining coal at a price far below that to which they had hitherto been accustomed. There were loud cheers for all the speeches.

At 7.30 pm a train conveying the Directors, their friends, London press reporters and others, left the station, and in just over 40 minutes its arrival at Bletchley was telegraphed to Oxford; by 9.20 pm it reached Euston Square and Oxford knew of its arrival minutes later.

It was to be another 11 years before the extension from Bedford to Cambridge was opened to make the two University Cities directly joined by rail.

The construction of the Bedford and Cambridge Railway was understandably viewed with great interest by the people of Bedford and villages along the line. The *Bedford Times* described it as 'an occasion which has put the crowning stroke to their railway communication to the four points of the compass, and has placed their ancient borough in the enviable position of a convenient central point of departure'.

But before that great crowning stroke, a little private railway on the projected route was already giving local service in its 3½ miles of track.

The little Sandy — Potton Railway was no ordinary railway, for it had no statutory authority and no Act of Parliament called it into being. It was built as a hobby at the expense of Sir William Peel CB, VC, KCB, the third son of the famous Sir Robert Peel.

After the Crimean War 'Captain' Peel returned to England and worked to build his railway, for which by 1852 he had already purchased 1,400 acres of land between Sandy and Potton. The details of the work he left to his agents, Mr Tilcock and Mr Brundell, a railway engineer of Doncaster. An engine built by George England & Co, of Hatcham Iron Works, was purchased for £800.

In March 1857 Peel sailed in command of the steam frigate *Shannon* for service in China, but at Singapore his ship was diverted to Calcutta, for the Sepoy Mutiny had broken out. He fought at the second relief of Lucknow in 1858, but on 9 March was severely wounded and died at Cawnpore on 22 April. Capt Peel VC was commemorated by statues in Calcutta and

LONDON & NORTH-WESTERN RAILWAY.

BEDFORD AND BLETCHLEY TIME TABLE, FOR JANUARY.

FROM BEDFORD.	TRAINS DAILY, (except on Sundays.)					On SUNDAYS.	
To London via Bletchley	Morning.			Afternoon.		MORN	AFT
Trains Leaving	h. m.	h. m.	h. m.	h. m.	h. m.	h. m.	h. m.
BEDFORD Arrive at	7.30	9.45	11.45	2.5	3.45	8.20	3.43
Marston	7.45	9.50	12.0	2.20	6.0	8.35	4.0
Lidlington	7.46	—	12.1	2.31	6.1	8.39	4.1
Ridgmount	7.48	—	12.3	2.23	6.8	8.34	4.3
Woburn Sands	8.5	10.15	12.20	2.40	6.20	8.55	4.20
Fenny Stratford	8.13	—	12.24	2.44	8.38	9.3	4.28
Bletchley (Joins main line	8.20	10.28	12.85	2.55	6.35	9.10	4.35
Leighton	8.35	10.38	1.7	3.15	7.7	—	4.55
Tring	8.55	—	1.33	3.38	7.32	—	5.18
Berkhampstead	9.15	—	—	3.48	—	—	—
Boxmoor	9.3	—	—	3.54	—	—	—
Kings Langley	9.22	—	—	—	—	—	—
Watford	9.30	11.26	2.2	4.15	8.2	—	5.5
Harrow	—	—	—	4.25	—	—	—
LONDON	10.10	12.0	2.45	5.1	8.45	—	6.44

DOWN TRAINS.

TO BEDFORD.	TRAINS DAILY, (except on Sundays.)					On SUNDAYS.	
From London via Bletchley.	Morning.		Afternoon.			MORN	AFT
Trains Leaving	h. m.	h. m.	h. m.	h. m.	h. m.	h. m.	h. m.
LONDON Arrive at	7.30	11.0	3.45	5.30	7.30	—	—
Harrow	7.52	—	—	—	—	—	—
Watford	8.0	11.57	4.18	6.7	8.0	—	—
Kings Langley	8.15	—	—	—	—	—	—
Boxmoor	8.20	—	—	—	—	—	—
Berkhampstead	8.30	—	—	—	—	—	—
Tring	8.48	12.14	—	6.37	8.46	—	—
Leighton (Joins Bedford Line)	9.8	12.34	5.6	6.57	9.8	—	—
Bletchley	9.28	12.45	5.15	7.10	9.58	4.50	
Fenny Stratford	9.35	1.5	3.20	7.20	9.83	4.55	
Woburn Sands	9.43	1.15	5.30	7.30	9.45	5.5	
Ridgmount	9.51	1.21	3.38	7.38	9.51	5.11	
Lidlington	9.58	1.23	3.8	—	9.58	5.18	
Marston	10.8	1.33	3.46	7.48	10.3	5.23	
BEDFORD	10.15	1.45	4.0	6.0	10.15	5.55	

LONDON AND NORTH WESTERN RAILWAY.

OPENING OF THE BRANCH LINE TO BEDFORD.

NOTICE.

THE Public are informed that the repairs of this railway having been completed, it was opened throughout to Bedford on WEDNESDAY, the 18th instant, and that trains are dispatched

FROM EUSTON STATION AT

¼ past 7 a.m., { arriving at Bedford at about } ¼ past 10
¼ before 11 a.m., ... ¼ past 1
¼ past 4 p.m., ... ¼ past 6
¼ past 5 p.m., ... 8 p.m.

AND FROM BEDFORD AT

¼ past 7 a.m., { arriving at the Euston Station about } 20 m. p. 10 a.m.
10 a.m., ... ¼ past 12
10 m. past 2 p.m., ... 5 p.m.
50 m. past 6 p.m., ... ¼ past 8 p.m.

By Order,
R. CREED, Secretary.

Office, Euston Station,
November 20th, 1846.

BEDFORD AND LONDON AND BIRMINGHAM RAILWAY.

BUILDING GROUND

ON THE

LONDON ROAD,

NEARLY

OPPOSITE THE BEDFORD STATION.

24

Locomotive No 34 of the London & Birmingham Railway with train,, about 1839. (Watford Corporation)

FROM BEDFORD.

To London via Bletchley.	TRAINS DAILY, Except on Sundays. Morning. h.m. h.m.	Noon. h.m. h.m.		On Sundays Morn. h.m.	Noon
Trains Leaving arrive at					
BEDFORD	7.10 10.15	3. 0 5.55		7.30	
Ampthill (Marston)	7.23 10.37	3.13		7.43	
Lidlington	7.24	3.14		7.44	
Ridgmount	7.28	3.16 6.13		7.40	
Woburn Sands	7.41 10.40	3.31 6.22		8.04	
Fenny Stratford	7.59	3.55 6.30		8.15	
Bletchley——Leaves	8.13 10.53	4.12 7. 5		8.28	
Leighton	8.27 11.10	4.84 7.25		8.48	
Tring	8.49	4.47		8.58	
Berkhampstead	9. 0	4.57		9. 9	
Boxmoor	9. 9			9.17	
King's Langley	9.17			9.25	
Watford	9.30	5.15 7.52		9.46	
Harrow	9.43	5.30 8. 5		9.51	
Bushey				9.55	
Willesden					
LONDON	about 10. 5 12.15	6. 0 8.30 10.20			

BEDFORD to OXFORD.—A train leaves Bedford at 1h. 30m calling at Ampthill, 2h. 3m.; Woburn, 2h. 18m.; Bletchley 2h. 30.; and arriving at Oxford at 4h. 15m.

DOWN TRAINS.

TO BEDFORD.

From London via Bletchley.	TRAINS DAILY, Except on Sundays. Morning	Afternoon		On Sundays. Morn. h.m.	Noon
Trains leaving arrive at					
LONDON	7.30 10.15	3.30 5.30		7.30	
Willesden					
Sudbury					
Harrow	7.53			8.10	
Watford	8.10 10.30	5.54 6. 8		8.10	
King's Langley	8.17				
Boxmoor	8.24				
Berkhampstead	8.38	5.57		8.49	
Tring	8.48 11.22	6.15 6.40		8. 8	
Leighton	9. 0	6.30 7. 0		9.23	
Bletchley——Leaves	9.45 11.55	6.45 7.15		9.45	
Fenny Stratford					
Woburn	9.38 12.15	4.56 7.20 7.30		9.41	
Lidlington					
Ampthill (Marston)					
BEDFORD					

OXFORD to BEDFORD.—A train leaves Oxford at 1h. 0m calling at Bletchley, 1h. 0pm.; Woburn, 1h. 50m.; Ampthill 3h. 0m.; and arriving at Bedford at 3h. 30m. afternoon.

turning by the afternoon Train, the First Lot will be put up PUNCTUALLY AT HALF-PAST TWELVE.

TWO pieces of Leasehold Building Ground containing together 2A. 3R. 35P. in the Parish of Saint Mary, Bedford, on the East side of the London Road, nearly opposite the Bedford Station, held by Lease from the Master and Co-Brethren of St. John's Hospital, Bedford, for three healthy male lives of the respective ages of 56, 59, and 41, by the yearly reserved Rent of £2 6s. 6d. in the following convenient Lots:—

	Frontage.	Depth.
Lot 1. Nearest the Town	50ft.	200ft.
Lot 2. Adjoining Lot 1	50ft.	200ft.
Lot 3. Adjoining Lot 2	50ft.	200ft.
Lot 4. Adjoining Lot 3	50ft.	200ft.
Lot 5. Separated from Lot 4 by an intended occupation road	84ft.	200ft.
Lot 6. Nearest the Station and adjoining Lot 5	84ft.	200ft.

Lot 7. On the East side of Lots 1, 2, 3, 4, (including the soil of the intended occupation Road of the width of 25 feet) and containing 1A. 1R. 10P. or thereabouts.

Lot 8. On the East side of Lots 5 and 6, and adjoining Lot 7, containing 0A. 1R. 28P. or thereabouts.

The Reserved Rent of £2 6s. 6d. to be borne by the Purchaser of Lot 7. The Occupation Road to be for the joint use of the Purchasers of Lots 4, 5, 7, and 8, and to be formed and kept in repair by the Purchaser of Lot 7.

Further Particulars, with Plans and Conditions, may be obtained of Messrs. PULLEY and SON, Auctioneers; Mr. James Tacey Wing, Architect, and Messrs. Pearse and Son, Solicitors, Bedford.

LONDON AND NORTH WESTERN RAILWAY.

LEFT: The opening of the branch line to Bedford, 1846; RIGHT: Bedford-Bletchley timetables, January and May 1847.

the one in Sandy church is still there, but he never saw his little railway.

By early June 1857 the line had been completed and a committee met in the Crown Inn, Potton, to arrange the official opening celebrations. The railway ran from Potton to Sandy with one cutting and a curve and formed a junction with the Great Northern Railway on the Biggleswade side of Sandy (opened 1850). Before the official opening, the line had been carrying some goods, then on 19 June it was reported that No 19 up train on the Great Northern would be specially stopped at Sandy on the day of the opening.

On the brilliantly sunny Tuesday morning of 23 June 1857, Lady Peel named the little engine *Shannon,* after the frigate her son commanded, his death ten months away. Sandy and Potton were excited, gaily decorated places on this lovely summer day; Sandy bedecked with banners and evergreens, while Potton had silk flags with patriotic mottos, such as 'The Queen God Bless Her'. A triumphal arch was topped with the royal arms, and underneath, the slogans 'Captain William Peel and Progress', 'Perseverance and Industry will join Potton and Cambridge' and 'In remembrance of the Live Shell October 1854'.

Even the *Illustrated London News* noted 'the little and truly English town of Potton was hung with banners, and the woods around had contributed whole trees, which were also spanned with triumphal arches of evergreens'.

The Bedfordshire Militia Band was out bright and early. It stopped to play 'Rule Britannia' outside Swiss Cottage, the centre of a large estate belonging to Capt Peel at Stratford, near Sandy, and then conducted guests from the station to the Market Place. On the south side of a place called the Shambles, a giant marquee, 126 feet long by 30 feet wide, had been erected. Over 400 people sat down in the marquee to lunch for 2s 6d each, including a pint of beer. Luncheon was also served in the grounds for the Executive Committee: the Sun and the Swan Inns were pressed into service too for a further 150 guests and there was a special lunch for 44 of the labourers who worked on the line.

The cost of the celebrations is reported to have amounted to £96 2s 6d, which included dinners for guests, six guineas to the Glee Singers, £5 to the Beds Militia Band, and £2 12s 11d for illuminations and advertising by printed bills in Potton, Sandy, Gamlingay, Everton and Wrestlingworth. It was truly a great day for Potton and Sandy.

For almost a year — until April 1858 — traffic on the Sandy — Potton line was limited to goods, then for the next four years it also carried passengers. The line's entire stock consisted of *Shannon* and another tank engine, a brake van, two wagons and one trolley. The signalling consisted principally of waving a red flag when a would-be passenger from one of the farmhouses wished to embark.

While *Shannon* chugged along in her own little domain, the landowners and businessmen of Bedford and such men as Sir Harry Verney, who lived outside the County but visualised an east to west railway as a social need as well as financially advantageous, were struggling against powerful odds to gain powers to build a Bedford to Cambridge Railway.

Various abortive attempts had been made from time to time to achieve a direct communication from east to west. A Bill for a Bedford, Potton and Cambridge Railway was promoted in 1859, but rejected mainly because of the opposition of the Great Northern, who still hoped to reach Cambridge by way of their ally, the Royston and Hitchin Railway. The Royston line had been leased to the Eastern Counties Railway for 14 years from 1852, but they did not intend to renew their lease. The Bedford and Cambridge Company then negotiated an agreement whereby the Great Northern agreed not to oppose the re-introduction of a bill, in return for running powers over the proposed line from a crossing over the river Cam — where it was proposed a line from Shepreth would join — into Cambridge.

The Bedford and Cambridge Railway Bill for a slightly amended line was introduced in the 1860 session and received the Royal Assent on 6 August. The promoters found it difficult to raise the required capital of £240,000 and had to appeal to the LNWR, who were to work the line, for a contribution of £70,000. In return, the LNWR insisted on the right to appoint three directors to a board whose maximum strength was 15. The LNWR also imposed a condition that a joint committee, comprising their three directors and two others, should supervise the construction of the line. The agreement also bound the LNWR to run four trains with passenger carriages each way on weekdays between Bedford and Cambridge and not less than two daily between Cambridge and Oxford; it bound the LNWR, after the expiration of the first year, to keep the line in good repair, exempting the shareholders of the Bedford and Cambridge Co from all penalties and loss caused by accidents in working the line; it required the LNWR at any time after three years, to lay a second line of rails (this was estimated at £80,000). Several conditions were laid down to guarantee dividends and sale of lands and some would obviously later cause considerable acrimony.

The Chairman of the Bedford — Cambridge Co and also of the joint committee was William Henry Whitbread of Southill Park who, according to the *Bedford Times,* had worked energetically to carry the Company to a successful conclusion. It also seems that his 20 odd years of sporting diversion with the *Times* Coach had not produced nostalgia for the 'four in hand' and dimmed his vision to the need for the new means of transport. The engineer was Charles Liddell and the contractor, Joseph Firbank.

The Act incorporating the Bedford and Cambridge Co provided for the compensation of the owners of the Sandy — Potton line and in 1861, when the line closed, the whole of the rolling stock was valued at £960. It was bought by the Contractor, Joseph Firbank, and the little engine *Shannon* used to build the new railway, which absorbed the former track. The Potton terminus near the Biggleswade Road was abandoned; the cutting about half a mile to the west was deepened and the level at Deepdale bridge raised, though the sharp curve at this point was not altered. Sandy station had already been built by the Great Northern.

The fortunes of *Shannon* are worth a reverent mention. From Potton to Crewe it moved to the Wantage Tramway, where it was later viewed by the public with the affection reserved for old pioneers; after 100 years a preservation society would claim to have the oldest engine still under steam.

Work began about April 1861 and proceeded with considerable speed. The directors, anxious that the line should take advantage of traffic engendered by a Great Exhibition in London, opened it for passengers on Monday, 7 July 1862. This was about three months earlier than the expected date. On the grand opening day at Bedford, passengers were given free rides on gaily decorated trains. A young porter on the station that day was George Crane, who afterwards came to Bletchley station, and about 70 years later recalled the day in an interview with the local newspaper.

Once more Bedford celebrated and the *Bedford Times* exalted the town's achievement, extolling the value of railways and the momentous results, both material and intellectual. 'A stride in civilisation, surpassing that of a thousand years past, is taking place before the eyes and in the life time of a single generation ...'.

It seems that many hundreds travelled to Cambridge on those opening days. The Directors and their friends had two trains in each direction on the previous Friday, and the representative of the *Bedford Times* described the 'gratifying' trip, and 'the well spent day — engaged in the exploration of those venerable college chapels, libraries, halls and gardens, so rich in time-honoured associations ...'.

The 77 miles east to west link was complete, joining two famous University Cities and with connections with five main line companies, and Bedford was justifiably proud.

There had been considerable strides made towards safer rail travel since the Bedford to

Bletchley line opened in 1846 and in the 11 years since the Bletchley to Oxford line opened. The line was single from Bedford right through to Cambridge, except for a short double length at stations for trains to pass. There was no telegraph system along the line, but what was described as an 'ingenious staff system' was in operation, which was the 'most perfect method devised for rendering collisions impossible'.

The workings of the system are worthy of mention. The staff for each section of the line had a distinguishable and different colour. Before a train could start from its first station on the single line, a small staff, perhaps red, had to be handed by the Station Master to the guard, who waved it to the engine driver to proceed. On arrival at the next station, the guard was bound on pain of immediate dismissal without hope of appeal, to give up the staff to the Station Master. Before he could start afresh, he received another staff — blue — and the train again proceeded. This was given up at the next station and exchanged for red again, and so on alternately until the journey's end. There was only one staff for each length of line and no train could leave without it. Special regulations were made for emergencies or ballast trains where more than one might be required in a section of line, and provision was made for Excursions or special trains. The staff fitted into a little box in the Station Master's Office and was placed in it by way of a small orifice at the side, when it acted upon a catch and opened the lid. This released a pass ticket with the words 'staff to follow by next train' printed on it, and the train received this ticket of leave to go from each station as it passed. The line had to be clear, for the simple reason that the staff was in the Station Master's possession, for without the staff he could not open the box to give out a pass-ticket. To further guard against mistakes, a red staff would not open a blue box.

This appears to have been successful until 1871 when the line was doubled between Sandy and Cambridge. From Bedford to Sandy remained single line throughout its lifetime, but in 1888 it was altered to the Electric Train Staff System, without tickets being issued. This was the first time the Electric Train Staff was operated on the LNWR and it had considerable advantages in guarding against human error.

The stations between Bedford and Cambridge on that opening day were Blunham, Sandy, Potton, Gamlingay, Old North Road and Lords Bridge.

Goods traffic did not commence until 1 August because the goods sheds at the stations were not completed and not all the cranes were set up and ready for work, but the five trains each way daily were filled beyond anticipation. So great was the pressure of traffic on the line, that one day carriages were borrowed from the Eastern Counties Railway, and on the same day a long train of passengers and horseboxes was dispatched from Newmarket via Bedford and Bletchley for the Worcester Races July Meeting.

[162]

London and Birmingham Railway.

TIME TABLE.

NOTICE. The time is that of the **Arrival** of the Trains, and Passengers, to ensure their being booked, should be at the PRINCIPAL STATIONS **five minutes** earlier, and at the INTERMEDIATE STATIONS **ten minutes** earlier.

Carriages intended to receive Passengers who are expected by the Trains at the London or Birmingham Stations, should be on the Arrival Side of such Stations, a quarter of an hour, at least, before the time specified in the Tables.

Distance from Euston Station	LONDON to BIRMINGHAM. STATIONS.	Down Trains. 6 A.M. Mixed *†‡‖	7 A.M. Third Class	8 A.M. Mixed	8¾ A.M. First Class *§†	9¼ A.M. Mixed to Rug. ‖‡	9¾ A.M. Mail 1st Cl *§	11 A.M. Mixed *‡‖	2 P.M. Mixed †	3 P.M. Mixed to Aylesbury	5 P.M. Mixed ‖	6 P.M. Mixed to Wolverton	8½ P.M. Mail Mixed *§	9 P.M. Mail ‖‡	Sunday Trains. 8 A.M. Mixed ‡‖	9¾ A.M. Mail 1st Cl. *§	6 P.M. Mixed to Wolverton	8½ P.M. Mail Mixed *§	9 P.M. Mail ‖‡
Miles		H. M.	H. M.	H. M.	H. M.	H. M.	H. M.	H. M.	H. M.	H. M.	H. M.	H. M.	H. M.	H. M.	H. M.	H. M.	H. M.	H. M.	H. M.
—	Leave LONDON at	6. 0	7. 0	8. 0	8.45	9.15	9.45	11. 0	2. 0	3. 0	5. 0	6. 0	8.30	9. 0	8. 0	9.45	6. 0	8.30	9. 0
11½	Arrive at HARROW	—	7.42	8.29	—	—	—	—	2.29	3.29	5.29	6.29	—	—	8.32	—	6.29	—	—
17½	WATFORD	6.46	8. 2	8.47	—	—	—	11.47	2.47	3.47	5.47	6.47	—	—	8.51	—	6.47	—	—
21	KINGS LANGLEY	—	8.17	8.57	—	—	—	—	—	3.57	—	6.57	—	—	9. 1	—	6.57	—	—
24½	BOXMOOR	—	8.32	9. 7	—	—	—	—	3. 7	4. 7	—	7. 7	—	—	9.12	—	7. 7	—	—
28	BERKHAMPSTEAD	—	8.47	9.19	—	—	—	—	3.19	4.19	—	7.19	—	—	9.25	—	7.19	—	—
31¾	TRING	7.21	9. 1	9.31	10. 8	10.36	11. 3	12.24	3.31	4.31	6.21	7.31	9.49	10.11	9.36	11. 3	7.31	9.49	10.11
43¼	AYLESBURY	—	—	10.15	—	—	—	—	—	5.15	—	8.15	—	—	10.15	—	8.15	—	—
41	LEIGHTON	7.41	9.36	9.51	—	—	—	12.44	3.51	—	6.40	7.51	—	—	9.56	—	7.51	—	—
46¾	BLETCHLEY (& Fenny Stratford)	—	9.58	10. 6	—	—	—	—	4. 6	—	—	8. 5	—	—	10.12	—	8. 6	—	—
52½	WOLVERTON	8. 7	10.10	10.20	10.55	11.22	11.47	1.11	4.20	—	7. 6	8.30	10.35	10.55	10.25	11.47	8.30	10.35	10.55
60	ROADE	—	10.40	10.49	—	—	—	—	4.49	—	7.34	—	—	—	10.55	—	—	—	—
62¾	BLISWORTH	8.42	12.30	10.58	—	11.55	12.20	1.48	4.58	—	7.42	—	11. 8	11.25	11. 7	12.20	—	11. 8	11.25
69¾	WEEDON	8.59	12.49	11.17	11.51	12.12	12.36	2. 7	5.17	—	8. 1	—	11.26	11.42	11.26	12.36	—	11.26	11.42
75¾	CRICK (and Welton)	—	1. 9	11.35	—	—	—	—	5.35	—	—	—	—	—	11.46	—	—	—	—
83	RUGBY (Mid. Co. Jn.)	9.30	1.28	11.56	—	1. 0	1. 8	2.43	5.56	—	8.38	—	11.58	12.15	12. 5	1. 8	—	11.58	12.15
89	BRANDON	—	1.48	12.13	—	—	—	—	6.11	—	—	—	—	—	12.25	—	—	—	—
94	COVENTRY	9.57	2. 2	12.26	12.52	—	1.34	3.12	6.26	—	9. 2	—	12.27	—	12.40	1.34	—	12.27	—
103	HAMPTON (Derby Junc.)	10.25	2.36	12.55	1.21	—	—	—	6.55	—	—	—	—	—	1.15	—	—	—	—
112½	BIRMINGHAM about	11½	3½	1½	2	—	2½	4½	7½	—	10½	—	1½	—	2	2½	—	1½	—

Distance from Birmingham	BIRMINGHAM to LONDON. STATIONS.	Up Trains. Mixed from Wolverton	7 A.M. Mixed	Mixed from Aylesbury	8½ A.M. Mail 1st Cl. *§	10 A.M. Mixed †‖	12 NOON Mixed *	1½ P.M. Mixed *†	Mixed from Rugby ‡‖	2½ P.M. Third Class	4 P.M. First Class *§	6 P.M. Mixed ‖‡	12 P.M. Mail Mixed *§	1 A.M. from Rugby ‖‡	Sunday Trains. Mixed from Wolverton	8½ A.M. Mail 1st Cl. *§	1½ P.M. Mixed ‡*‖	12 P.M. Mail Mixed *§	1 A.M. from Rugby ‖‡
Miles		H. M.	H. M.	H. M.	H. M.	H. M.	H. M.	H. M.	H. M.	H. M.	H. M.	H. M.	H. M.	H. M.	H. M.	H. M.	H. M.	H. M.	H. M.
—	LEAVE BIRMINGHAM at	—	7. 0	—	8.30	10. 0	12. 0	1.15	—	2.20	4. 0	6. 0	12. 0	—	—	8.30	1.30	12. 0	—
9½	ARRIVE AT HAMPTON (Derby Junc.)	—	7.20	—	—	10.20	12.20	1.35	—	2.54	4.20	6.19	—	—	—	—	1.51	—	—
18½	COVENTRY	—	7.47	—	9.12	10.47	12.47	2. 4	—	3.29	4.47	6.45	12.47	—	—	9.12	2.17	12.47	—
23½	BRANDON	—	8. 5	—	—	—	1. 5	—	—	3.47	—	7. 3	—	—	—	—	2.35	—	—
29½	RUGBY (Mid. Co. Jn.)	—	8.23	—	9.43	11.17	1.23	2.35	4. 0	4.13	5.17	7.18	1.23	1. 5	—	9.43	2.53	1.23	[illegible]
37	CRICK (and Welton)	—	8.50	—	—	—	1.50	—	—	4.41	—	7.42	—	—	—	—	3.20	—	—
42¾	WEEDON	—	9. 4	—	10.18	11.54	2. 4	3.11	4.31	5. 4	5.54	7.56	2. 4	1.40	—	10.18	3.34	2. 4	1.40
49¾	BLISWORTH	—	9.27	—	—	12.16	2.28	3.35	4.55	5.28	6.16	8.17	2.28	2. 0	—	—	3.58	2.28	2. 0
52½	ROADE	—	9.35	—	—	—	2.38	—	—	5.37	—	8.27	—	—	—	—	4. 8	—	—
59¾	WOLVERTON	6.45	9.55	—	11. 5	12.40	3. 0	4. 0	5.20	6.15	6.40	8.45	2.55	2.30	6.45	11. 5	4.30	2.55	2.30
65¾	BLETCHLEY (& Fenny Stratford)	6.58	10.21	—	—	—	3.26	—	—	6.37	—	9.11	—	—	6.58	—	4.56	—	—
71½	LEIGHTON	7.14	10.37	—	—	1.16	3.42	—	—	6.58	7.16	9.26	—	—	7.14	—	5.12	—	—
	Leave AYLESBURY for LONDON	7. 0	—	11. 0	—	—	—	—	—	—	7. 0	—	—	—	7. 0	—	5. 0	—	—
80¾	TRING	7.41	11. 4	11.26	12. 6	1.42	4.11	5. 0	6.21	7.30	7.42	9.51	4. 1	3.35	7.41	12. 6	5.41	4.1	3.35
84½	BERKHAMPSTEAD	7.54	11.16	11.39	—	—	4.25	—	—	8.12	—	10. 3	—	—	7.54	—	5.54	—	—
87¾	BOXMOOR	8. 4	11.25	11.49	—	—	4.34	—	—	8.27	—	10.12	—	—	8. 4	—	6. 4	—	—
91½	KINGS LANGLEY	8.12	—	11.57	—	—	—	—	—	8.37	—	—	—	—	8.12	—	6.12	—	—
94½	WATFORD	8.21	11.40	12. 7	—	2.11	4.49	—	—	8.47	8.11	10.27	—	—	8.21	—	6.21	—	—
100¾	HARROW	8.39	11.55	12.24	—	—	5. 7	—	—	9. 7	—	10.42	—	—	8.39	—	6.39	—	—
112½	LONDON about	9½	12½	1½	1½	3½	6	6½	8	10	9½	11½	5½	5	9½	1½	7½	5½	5

N.B.—The times of the Trains conveying the Mails are fixed by the Postmaster General, under the powers granted by Act of Parliament, Act 1 & 2 Vic. cap. 98.

* Trains in conjunction with the Grand Junction, Liverpool and Manchester.

† Trains in conjunction with the Birmingham and Derby Junction.

‡ Trains in conjunction with the North Midland.

§ Trains in conjunction with the North Union, and Lancaster and Preston Junction.

‖ Trains in conjunction with the Midland Counties, Leicester, Nottingham, and Derby.

Waiting Rooms, with Female Attendants, are provided at the Euston, Watford, Wolverton, Rugby, Coventry, and Birmingham Stations: Refreshments at Wolverton and Birmingham.

Private Carriages and Horses cannot be booked unless they are at the Stations fifteen minutes before the time above specified; nor can they be conveyed by the Night Mail Trains up or down, nor by the down Day Mail Train.

Carriages, Trucks, and Horse Boxes are kept at all the Principal Stations; but to prevent the possibility of disappointment, it is requisite that one day's previous notice be given whenever they are required.

The Company will only hold themselves responsible for Luggage when it is booked and paid for, according to its value; and they strongly recommend to Passengers to have their Name and Destination in all cases distinctly marked thereon, and to satisfy themselves that it is deposited on the Company's Carriages.

Post Horses, for the conveyance of Carriages arriving at the Euston Station, are always in readiness, at a charge of 10s. 6d., including Post-boy, to any part of London.

1st JUNE, 1841.

[See over.]

Smith and Ebbs, Printers, Tower-hill, London.

The London & Birmingham Railway timetable for 1 June, 1841.

Bedford and Cambridge Railway.

ON FRIDAY, JULY 4,

A Train for the Directors and Shareholders of the Line, will run as under:—

MORNING.

Leave	Bedford	9. 0 a.m.	Leave	Cambridge ...11. 0 a.m.
Arrive at	Blunham	9.13 ,,	Arrive at	Lord's Bridge 11.14 ,,
,,	Sandy............	9.22 ,,	,,	North Road ...11.31 ,,
,,	Potton	9.34 ,,	,,	Gamlingay ...11.45 ,,
,,	Gamlingay......	9.42 ,,	,,	Potton ....11.52 ,,
,,	North Road ...	9.58 ,,	,,	Sandy ....12. 3 noon
,,	Lord's Bridge ..10.14	,,	,,	Blunham ......12. 9 ,,
,,	Cambridge......10.30	,,	,,	Bedford ....12.30 ,,

AFTERNOON.

Leave	Bedford	3.30 p.m.	Leave	Cambridge ... 5.30 p.m.
Arrive at	Blunham	3.43 ,,	Arrive at	Lord's Bridge 5 44 ,,
,,	Sandy............	3.52 ,,	,,	North Road ... 6. 1 ,,
,,	Potton	4. 4 ,,	,,	Gamlingay ... 6.15 ,,
,,	Gamlingay......	4.12 ,,	,,	Potton .... 6.22 ,,
,,	North Road ...	4.28 ,,	,,	Sandy .... 6.33 ,,
,,	Lord's Bridge	4.44 ,,	,,	Blunham ...... 6.39 ,,
,,	Cambridge......	5. 0 ,,	,,	Bedford .... 7. 0 ,,

Euston Station, *1st July*, 1862.

LEFT: Opening of the Bedford-Cambridge line, 4 July 1862.   ABOVE: George Stephenson; CENTRE: Sir Harry Verney; BELOW: Sir Herbert Leon.

30

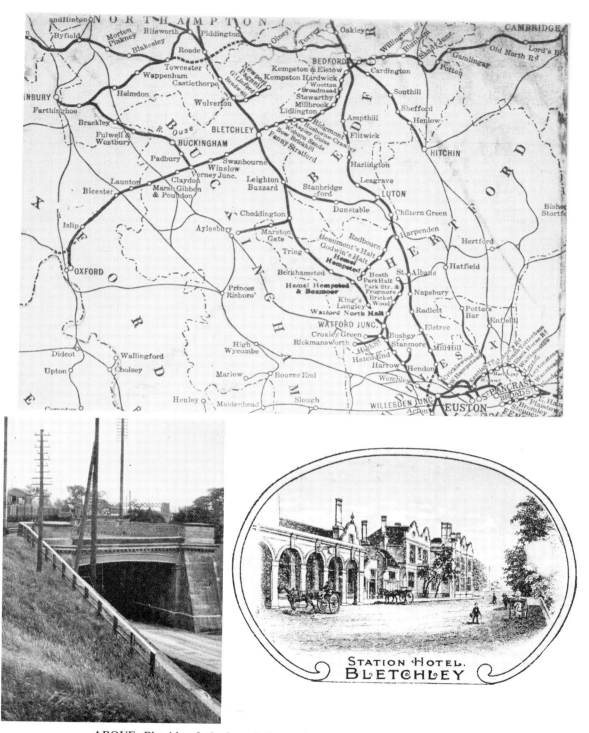

ABOVE: Bletchley & the branch lines, 1938. LEFT: Denbigh Hall Bridge
c1900 and RIGHT: Station Hotel, Bletchley from an early c1910 London &
North Western and Caledonian Railway map.

31

SUPPLEMENT TO THE "LEIGHTON BUZZARD OBSERVER."

RAILWAY TIME-TABLES FOR FEBRUARY, 1879.

We do not hold ourselves responsible for any errors that may occur in these Time-Tables. Information respecting inaccuracies which may be found in the Tables will be gladly received.

LONDON AND NORTH-WESTERN LINE.

DOWN. — WEEK DAYS.

DOWN.																	
LONDON	6 0	7 15	7 30	7 20	9 0	9 15	10 10	10 15	11 0	12 0	12 16	12 30	1 45	2 45	3 0	3 10	4 15
Kilburn	6 8	...	...	7 30	...	...	...	...	...	...	...	12 40	...	...	...	3 20	...
Willesden Junc.	6 16	7 27	7 42	7 36	9 12	9 25	10 22	10 25	11 12	12 12	12 22	12 46	1 57	2 57	3 12	3 28	4 27
Sudbury	6 23	...	...	7 52	...	...	...	...	...	...	...	12 56	...	...	...	3 34	...
Harrow	6 30	...	...	8 0	...	9 38	...	10 35	...	...	...	1 5	2 9	...	...	3 42	4 38
Pinner	6 37	...	...	8 8	...	...	...	...	...	...	...	1 13	...	...	...	3 49	...
Bushey	6 44	...	...	8 16	...	...	...	...	...	...	...	1 21	...	...	...	3 56	...
Watford	6 50	...	...	8 22	...	9 50	...	10 47	...	...	...	1 27	2 24	...	...	4 1	4 51
King's Langley	7 2	...	...	8 34	...	...	...	10 56	...	...	...	1 37	...	...	...	4 10	...
Boxmoor	7 12	...	...	8 44	...	10 4	...	11 5	...	...	...	1 47	2 38	...	...	4 19	5 5
Berkhampstead	7 21	...	...	8 54	...	...	...	11 13	...	...	...	1 57	2 48	...	...	4 28	5 15
Tring	7 31	...	...	9 4	...	10 19	...	11 22	...	...	...	2 8	2 58	...	...	4 38	...
Cheddington	7 43	...	...	9 15	...	10 27	...	11 32	...	...	...	2 19	3 8	...	...	4 49	5 51
LEIGHTON	7 57	...	...	9 29	...	10 36	...	11 42	...	...	...	2 30	3 18	...	...	5 0	5 41
Bletchley	8 42	8 23	8 37	10 6	10 12	10 49	11 21	12 20	12 11	1 8	1 26	2 48	3 30	3 54	4 11	5 18	6 30
Wolverton	8 53	...	...	10 11	...	10 56	...	12 32	...	...	...	3 0	...	...	...	5 31	6 42
Roade	9 8	...	...	10 37	...	...	...	12 47	..	...	...	3 21	...	...	...	...	6 57
Blisworth	9 19	...	9 1	10 45	10 36	11 17	11 44	12 55	..	1 36	1 48	3 29	...	...	4 34	5 48	7 5
N'thamp Br arr	9 35	...	9 15	11 10	11 0	11 35	12 0	1 15	...	...	2 10	3 50	...	...	4 58	6 15	8 4
,, dep	8 40	...	8 40	10 30	10 10	11 20	11 26	...	...	1 15	1 15	3 5	...	...	4 15	5 16	...
Weedon	9 30	...	...	10 57	...	12 2	...	...	...	...	...	3 44	...	...	...	6 5	...
Crick	9 44	...	...	11 10	...	12 15	...	...	...	...	...	4 0	...	...	...	...	...
Rugby	9 58	9 15	9 30	11 25	11 5	12 30	12 14	...	1 0	2 8	2 17	4 15	...	4 45	5 10	6 30	...
Coventry	...	...	10 2	...	11 36	...	12 43	...	1 43	...	2 44	...	...	5 17	...	...	...
Birmingham	...	...	10 35	...	12 15	...	1 20	...	2 45	...	3 20	...	..	6 0	...	...	...

DOWN.												Sundays.						
LONDON	4 50	5 0	5 15	5 40	6 0	6 10	...	7 0	9 0	9 25	12 0	9 0	10 0	2 45	5 0	6 45	9 0	12 0
Kilburn	...	...	...	...	...	6 21	...	...	...	9 35	...	...	...	2 54	...	6 55	...	...
Willesden Junc.	5 1	5 12	5 27	5 51	6 12	6 28	...	7 12	9 12	9 41	12 12	9 12	10 12	3 0	5 12	7 2	...	...
Sudbury	...	...	...	...	...	...	...	...	...	9 47	...	...	...	3 6	...	7 9	...	...
Harrow	5 11	...	...	...	...	6 39	...	7 27	...	9 54	...	...	...	3 12	...	7 18	...	...
Pinner	5 17	...	...	...	...	...	...	...	...	9 59	...	...	...	3 17	...	7 26	...	...
Bushey	...	...	...	...	...	...	...	...	...	10 5	...	...	...	3 24	...	7 34	...	...
Watford	5 26	...	...	6 9	...	6 52	...	7 48	...	10 10	...	9 35	10 34	3 31	...	7 41	...	...
King's Langley	5 36	...	...	6 17	...	7 1	...	7 51	...	10 18	...	9 42	...	3 38	...	7 50	...	...
Boxmoor	5 45	...	...	6 25	...	7 10	...	8 0	...	10 27	...	9 51	...	3 47	...	7 59	...	...
Berkhampstead	5 54	...	...	6 33	...	7 19	...	8 10	...	10 36	...	10 0	...	3 56	...	8 8	...	...
Tring	6 5	...	...	6 41	...	7 29	...	8 21	...	10 47	...	10 9	...	4 5	...	8 19	...	...
Cheddington	...	...	...	6 49	6 56	...	...	8 30	...	...	...	10 19	...	4 15	...	...	...	...
LEIGHTON	...	...	...	...	7 5	7 47	...	8 39	...	11 5	...	10 28	...	4 28	6 0	8 37	...	...
Bletchley	...	6 9	6 26	...	...	8 5	...	8 53	...	11 20	...	10 42	11 14	...	...	8 54	...	...
Wolverton	...	...	...	...	...	8 18	...	9 4	...	...	...	10 54	...	...	...	9 5	10 16	...
Roade	...	...	...	...	...	8 33	...	...	...	...	...	11 8	..	...	...	...	...	...
Blisworth	...	...	6 49	...	7 40	8 43	...	9 20	10 22	...	...	11 18	11 41	...	...	...	10 32	...
N'thamp Br arr	...	...	7 5	...	8 4	9 15	...	9 35	10 50	...	...	11 35	11 55	...	...	...	10 50	...
,, dep	...	...	6 30	...	7 18	..	...	8 45	10 15	...	...	11 6	11 25	...	...	...	10 15	...
Weedon	...	...	...	...	...	...	...	9 35	10 43	...	...	11 32	...	...	...	...	10 43	...
Crick	...	...	...	...	...	...	...	...	...	...	...	11 45	...	...	...	...	...	...
Rugby	...	7 0	7 19	...	8 13	...	...	10 0	11 3	...	2 10	12 0	12 12	...	7 0	...	11 3	2 10
Coventry	...	...	7 44	...	8 38	...	...	..	11 33	...	2 32	...	12 53	...	7 31	...	11 33	2 32
Birmingham	...	...	8 20	...	9 15	..	...	...	12 10	...	3 15	...	1 50	...	8 10	...	12 10	3 15

UP. — WEEK DAYS.

UP.																
Birmingham	...	...	...	7 35	...	...	9 36	...	11 10	8 2	12 0	...	...	2 10	...	...
Coventry	...	...	...	8 4	...	...	10 2	...	11 42	9 15	12 34	...	...	2 39	...	...
Rugby	...	...	...	8 26	8 30	...	10 28	10 45	12 15	9 45	1 8	...	2 4	3 5	3 15	3 36
Crick	...	...	...	...	8 45	...	...	...	...	10 13	...	...	...	...	...	...
Weedon	...	...	...	...	8 51	...	...	...	...	10 27	1 27	...	...	...	...	...
N'thamp Br arr	...	...	...	9 15	9 35	...	...	11 35	...	11 0	2 10	...	...	...	4 0	4 30
,, dep	...	...	7 30	8 40	9 0	...	...	10 53	...	10 53	1 15	1 15	...	...	3 30	3 50
Blisworth	...	...	7 42	8 54	9 17	...	10 58	11 14	...	11 25	1 41	1 45	...	...	3 45	4 8
Roade	...	...	7 50	...	9 23	...	...	...	...	11 34	...	...	...	...	...	...
Wolverton	...	...	8 0	...	9 33	...	...	...	...	11 50	...	2 3	...	...	...	...
Bletchley	7 5	...	8 30	9 20	9 45	9 50	11 19	11 38	1 5	12 6	...	2 15	...	...	4 14	...
LEIGHTON	7 18	...	8 45	...	9 55	10 5	...	...	...	12 18	...	2 27	...	...	...	4 40
Cheddington	7 29	...	8 59	...	...	10 19	...	...	...	12 30	...	2 36	...	...	...	...
Tring	7 40	8 40	9 8	...	...	10 30	...	...	...	12 42	...	2 45	...	...	...	...
Berkhampstead	7 50	8 50	9 16	...	...	10 43	...	...	...	12 52	...	2 53	...	...	...	...
Boxmoor	7 59	8 58	9 24	...	...	10 52	...	...	...	1 1	...	3 1	...	...	...	...
King's Langley	8 8	9 6	...	...	...	11 1	...	...	...	1 10	...	3 9	...	...	...	...
Watford	8 18	9 16	...	...	...	11 11	...	...	...	1 20	...	3 15	...	...	...	5 14
Bushey	8 24	...	...	...	...	11 16	...	...	...	1 31	...	...	...	...	...	...
Pinner	8 31	...	...	...	...	11 24	...	...	...	1 39	...	...	...	...	...	...
Harrow	8 36	9 28	...	...	...	11 30	...	...	...	1 46	...	3 26	...	...	...	...
Sudbury	8 45	...	...	...	...	11 38	...	...	...	1 55	...	...	...	...	...	...
Willesden Junc.	8 51	9 40	9 51	10 15	10 42	11 44	12 25	12 36	2 0	2 5	3 0	3 37	3 45	4 55	5 15	5 35
Kilburn	8 57	...	...	...	...	11 54	...	...	...	2 14	...	...	...	...	...	...
LONDON	9 10	9 57	10 5	10 30	10 55	12 10	12 30	12 50	2 15	2 30	3 15	3 50	4 0	5 10	5 30	5 50

UP.												Sundays.						
Birmingham	...	1 0	...	...	4 0	...	3 30	6 0	...	7 15	...	...	8 40	...	12 50	...	...	6 28
Coventry	...	...	...	...	4 32	...	4 38	6 29	...	7 47	...	...	9 32	...	1 39	...	...	6 48
Rugby	2 10	3 10	4 22	...	4 55	5 9	5 15	6 58	8 32	8 15	7 10	...	10 2	2 11	2 31	4 39	...	7 28
Crick	2 26	...	...	...	...	...	5 30	...	...	...	7 25	...	10 18	...	...	...	...	...
Weedon	2 39	...	...	...	...	...	5 43	...	...	...	7 37	...	10 31	...	2 52	...	...	...
N'thamp Br arr	3 10	...	...	...	...	5 55	6 15	...	9 15	...	8 4	...	11 5	...	3 20	...	...	...
,, dep	2 25	...	...	...	...	5 15	5 40	...	8 45	...	7 18	...	10 30	...	2 45	...	...	...
Blisworth	2 54	3 45	...	...	...	5 39	5 56	...	9 0	...	7 49	...	10 45	...	3 4	...	...	...
Roade	3 3	...	...	...	...	...	6 7	...	...	...	7 59	...	10 57	...	...	...	...	...
Wolverton	3 19	...	...	...	...	...	6 20	...	...	...	8 15	...	11 13	...	3 24	...	...	...
Bletchley	3 32	...	...	4 35	...	6 4	6 40	7 50	...	9 4	8 45	7 30	11 30	3 1	3 36	...	5 40	...
LEIGHTON	...	...	...	4 50	5 57	...	6 52	...	...	...	8 55	7 42	11 43	...	3 48	...	6 5	...
Cheddington	...	...	...	5 3	...	...	7 7	...	...	...	9 6	7 53	11 57	...	...	...	6 15	...
Tring	...	...	...	5 16	...	...	7 19	...	...	...	9 18	8 5	12 10	...	4 3	...	6 26	...
Berkhampstead	...	...	...	5 26	...	...	7 28	...	...	...	9 27	8 15	12 20	...	...	...	6 36	...
Boxmoor	...	...	...	5 36	...	...	7 37	...	...	...	9 36	8 24	12 30	...	...	...	6 45	...
King's Langley	...	...	...	5 46	...	...	7 46	...	...	...	9 45	8 33	12 40	...	...	...	6 54	...
Watford	...	4 52	...	5 57	...	...	7 55	...	10 5	...	9 55	8 42	12 50	...	4 30	...	7 4	...
Bushey	...	...	...	6 2	...	...	...	...	...	...	10 15	8 50	12 55	...	...	...	7 10	...
Pinner	...	...	...	...	...	...	...	...	...	...	10 22	8 57	1 3	...	...	...	7 17	...
Harrow	...	...	...	6 10	...	...	6 9	...	...	...	10 29	9 3	1 10	...	4 42	...	7 23	...
Sudbury	...	...	...	...	...	...	...	...	...	...	10 36	9 11	1 18	...	...	...	7 31	...
Willesden Junc.	...	5 13	6 10	6 23	6 42	6 57	8 22	8 47	10 20	10 0	10 42	9 18	1 25	...	4 55	6 30	7 38	9 15
Kilburn	...	...	...	...	...	...	8 32	...	...	...	10 51	9 26	1 31	...	...	...	7 50	...
LONDON	...	5 30	6 25	6 35	6 55	7 10	8 45	9 0	10 35	10 15	11 5	9 40	1 50	4 5	5 10	6 45	8 10	9 30

BRANCH LINES.

TO AYLESBURY.

											Sundays.	
LEIGHTON	7 18	8 45	10 5	...	12 18	2 27	4 50	6 52	...	...	7 42	4 40
LONDON	6 0	7 20	9 15	10 15	...	1 45	4 15	...	7 0	9 0	...	2 45
Tring	7 31	9 4	10 16	11 22	...	2 58	...	...	8 21	10 9	...	4 5
Cheddington	7 50	9 25	10 35	11 40	12 40	3 15	5 35	7 15	8 35	10 25	7 55	4 50
Marston Gte	7 56	9 31	10 41	11 46	12 46	3 21	5 41	7 21	8 41	10 31	8 1	4 56
Aylesbury	8 5	9 40	10 50	11 55	12 55	3 30	5 50	7 30	8 50	10 40	8 10	5 5

FROM AYLESBURY.

										Sundays.		
Aylesbury	7 5	8 35	9 55	11 10	12 10	2 0	4 25	6 30	8 10	7 30	10 0	5 15
Marston Gte	7 14	8 44	10 4	11 19	12 19	2 9	4 34	6 39	8 19	7 39	10 9	5 24
Cheddington	7 20	8 50	10 10	11 25	12 25	2 15	4 40	6 45	8 30	7 45	10 15	5 30
Tring	7 40	9 8	10 30	...	12 43	2 45	5 16	7 19	9 18	8 5	12 10	6 26
LONDON	9 10	10 5	12 10	...	2 30	3 50	6 35	8 45	10 35	9 40	1 50	8 10
LEIGHTON	7 57	9 29	10 36	11 42	...	2 30	5 0	7 5	8 39	...	10 24	5 40

TO BEDFORD.

										Sun.
LONDON	7 15	9 0	10 10	12 10	1 45	3 0	5 0	...	6 10	10 0
LEIGHTON	7 57	9 29	10 36	11 42	3 18	3 18	5 41	...	7 47	10 28
Bletchley	8 25	10 20	11 28	1 30	3 50	4 20	6 15	...	8 10	11 35
Fenny Strat.	8 27	10 23	...	1 33	3 53	...	6 19	...	8 14	11 38
Woburn	8 33	10 30	...	1 40	4 0	4 27	6 26	...	8 21	11 46
Ridgmount	8 37	10 38	...	1 4[illegible]	4 8	...	6 35	...	8 30	11 53
Lidlington	8 44	10 44	...	...	4 14	...	6 41	...	8 36	11 58
Ampthill	8 48	10 50	...	1 55	4 20	4 38	6 46	...	8 41	12 3
Bedford	8 59	11 5	11 56	2 6	4 3[illegible]	4 49	7 0	...	8 55	12 15

FROM BEDFORD.

										Sun.
Bedford	7 30	8 55	10 44	11 20	12 24	3 0	5 0	5 42	8 3	9 51
Ampthill	7 40	9 5	10 55	11 30	12 34	3 10	5 10	5 54	8 13	10 2
Lidlington	7 46	9 11	...	11 35	...	3 16	5 16	...	8 19	10 8
Ridgmnt	7 51	9 15	...	11 40	12 41	3 21	5 21	...	8 24	10 14
Woburn	7 59	9 23	...	11 47	12 47	3 28	5 29	6 5	8 31	10 21
Fny. Strat	8 5	9 30	...	11 53	...	3 34	5 35	...	8 37	10 27
Bletchley	8 10	9 35	11 13	11 57	12 55	3 40	5 40	6 15	8 43	10 31
LEIGH	8 45	9 55	12 18	12 18	2 27	4 50	...	6 52	8 55	11 43
LONDON	10 5	10 55	12 30	2 30	2 15	5 30	...	8 45	10 15	1 50

TO DUNSTABLE, LUTON, & GREAT NORTHERN

													Sun	
LEIGHTON	...	8 2	9 0	10 10	...	12 25	...	2 40	...	5 10	7 10	...	9 0	...	...
Dunstable arr.	...	8 17	9 15	10 25	...	12 40	...	2 55	...	5 25	7 25	...	9 15	...	...
,, dep	7 10	8 22	...	...	10 5	12 45	1 26	3 35	5 5	5 50	7 45	8 30	10 15	...	...
,, Ch. St.	7 15	8 27	...	...	10 10	12 50	1 33	3 40	5 10	5 55	7 50	8 45	10 20	7 40	5 50
Luton arr.	7 25	8 37	...	...	10 20	1 0	1 43	3 50	5 20	6 5	8 0	9 0	10 30	7 49	6 0
,, dep.	7 32	8 40	...	...	10 25	1 10	...	3 54	5 28	...	8 5	...	...	7 50	6 5
Harpenden	7 44	8 54	...	...	10 37	1 24	...	4 7	5 40	...	8 18	...	...	8 2	6 18
Wheathampstead	7 50	8 59	...	...	10 42	1 29	...	4 12	5 45	...	8 23	..	...	8 7	6 23
Hatfield	8 7	9 15	...	...	10 57	1 45	...	4 28	6 0	...	8 39	...	...	8 26	6 47
King's Cross	9 5	9 54	...	...	11 30	2 45	...	5 14	6 45	...	9 15	...	...	9 35	7 35

TO OXFORD.

								Sun.
LONDON	7 15	9 0	11 0	12 10	3 0	5 15	7 0	10 0
Bletchley	8 30	10 15	12 20	1 25	4 20	6 30	9 10	11 40
Swanbourne	8 41	...	...	...	4 31	6 41	...	11 51
Winslow	8 47	10 32	12 38	1 41	4 36	6 54	9 26	11 57
Claydon	9 0	10 44	12 50	1 50	4 47	7 2	9 30	12 3
Launton	9 11	...	...	...	...	...	...	...
Bicester	9 16	10 58	1 5	2 4	5 1	7 16	9 51	11 19
Islip	9 28	11 11	1 18	2 17	5 12	7 28	10 3	12 33
Oxford	9 40	11 25	1 38	2 30	5 25	7 40	10 15	12 45

GREAT NORTHERN TO LUTON AND DUNSTABLE

												Sun.	
King's Cross, G. N.	...	...	...	7 45	8 45	...	12 0	2 45	4 20	...	5 35	8 32	7 30	6 50
Hatfield	...	...	...	8 30	9 45	...	12 33	3 18	4 53	...	6 11	9 10	8 45	7 50
Wheathampstead	...	...	...	8 46	10 0	...	12 48	3 34	5 9	...	6 2[illegible]	9 26	9 0	8 5
Harpenden	..	...	...	8 55	10 5	...	12 53	3 39	5 14	...	6 32	9 31	9 7	8 10
Luton arr	...	...	...	9 8	10 18	...	1 5	3 52	5 27	...	6 45	9 44	9 23	8 25
,, dep	6 35	8 0	...	9 13	10 23	...	1 8	3 58	5 32	7 23	6 48	9 47	9 26	8 30
Dunstable, Ch. St	6 45	8 10	...	9 23	10 33	...	1 18	4 8	5 42	7 35	6 57	9 57	9 35	8 40
L. & N.W. arr	6 50	8 15	...	9 27	10 38	...	1 23	4 13	5 47	7 40	7 3	10 2	...	...
,, dep	6 55	8 25	...	9 30	11 15	...	2 8	4 20	6 30	8 15	...	...	...	...
LEIGHTON	7 10	8 46	...	9 45	11 30	...	2 23	4 35	6 45	8 30	...	...	...	...

FROM OXFORD.

								Sun.
Oxford	7 50	8 40	10 0	12 0	2 30	4 35	6 30	9 15
Islip	...	8 50	10 11	...	2 40	4 45	6 40	9 26
Bicester	8 13	9 3	10 24	12 19	2 53	4 58	6 54	9 41
Launton	...	...	...	...	2 58	...	7 2	...
Claydon	8 30	9 18	10 39	...	3 9	5 14	7 16	9 59
Winslow	8 43	9 28	10 52	12 42	3 13	5 25	7 24	10 11
Swanbourne	8 55	...	10 58	...	3 26	5 33	7 34	10 21
Bletchley	9 18	9 50	11 19	1 5	4 11	6 2	7 48	10 35
LONDON	10 30	12 10	12 30	2 15	5 30	7 10	9 0	...

TO BUCKINGHAM & BANBURY.

LONDON	7 15	11 0	9 0	3 0	5 15	...	7 0	10 0	...	...	...
Bletchley	8 30	12 20	10 15	4 20	6 30	...	9 10	11 40	...	...	...
Swanbourne	8 41	...	...	4 31	6 41	...	...	11 51	...	...	...
Winslow	8 47	12 38	10 32	4 36	7 0	...	9 26	11 57	...	...	...
Buckingham	9 11	1 4	11 40	5 0	7 3	...	9 51	12 16	...	...	...
Brackley	9 25	1 20	11 50	5 13	7 16	...	10 4	12 33	...	...	...
Farthinghoe	9 37	1 36	...	5 25	7 29	...	10 16	12 50	...	...	...
Banbury	9 44	1 45	...	5 3[illegible]	7 40	...	10 25	1 0	...	...	...

FROM BANBURY & BUCKINGHAM.

Banbury	7 45	...	9 55	...	...	2 20	4 25	6 25	4 15	...	...
Farthinghoe	7 53	...	10 3	...	...	2 28	4 33	6 34	4 26	...	...
Brackley	8 5	...	10 15	...	...	2 40	4 45	6 49	4 41	...	...
Buckingham	8 18	...	10 28	...	...	2 53	5 0	7 2	4 57	...	...
Winslow	8 42	...	10 52	...	...	3 13	5 25	7 24	5 17	...	...
Swanbourne	8 55	...	10 58	...	...	3 26	5 33	7 34	5 25	...	...
Bletchley	9 8	...	11 11	...	...	4 11	6 2	7 48	5 40	...	...
LONDON	10 30	...	12 30	...	..	5 30	7 10	9 0	8 0	...	...

GREAT WESTERN. — DOWN.

DOWN.												Sundays.			
London	...	8 15	11 0	...	1 5	...	...	4 50	...	...	8 10	...	8 30	...	8 10
High Wycombe	...	10 0	12 39	...	2 33	...	...	6 4	...	...	9 32	...	10 25	...	9 41
West Wycombe	...	10 10	12 44	...	2 40	...	...	6 9	...	...	9 37	...	10 31	...	9 47
Risborough, arrival	...	10 22	12 57	...	2 54	...	...	6 21	...	...	9 48	...	10 42	...	9 59
Risborough to Aylesbury	8 45	10 33	1 6	...	2 59	3 45	...	6 25	...	7 20	9 50	...	10 45	...	10 3
AYLESBURY, arrival	9 3	10 51	1 20	...	3 11	4 3	...	6 40	...	7 38	10 5	...	11 0	...	10 18
Risborough, for Thame	7 30	10 25	1 0	..	2 57	...	...	6 30	...	...	...	...	10 45	...	10 2
Bledlow	...	10 30	1 5	..	3 3	...	...	6 38	...	...	...	...	10 50	...	10 8
Thame	8 5	10 42	1 17	...	3 18	...	...	6 57	...	...	...	...	10 59	...	10 30
*Wheatley	8 55	11 2	1 36	...	3 35	...	...	7 15	...	...	...	...	11 13	...	10 40
Oxford	9 25	11 22	1 55	...	3 55	...	...	7 35	...	...	...	...	11 33	...	11 0

*Littlemore about 10 m. before & after Wheatley.

GREAT WESTERN. — UP.

UP.													Sundays.			
Oxford	...	...	...	8 25	...	11 15	...	...	2 35	...	6 0	...	6 10	...	5 35	...
*Wheatley	...	...	...	8 55	...	11 33	...	...	2 58	...	6 20	...	6 30	...	5 58	...
Thame	...	...	...	9 23	...	11 55	...	...	3 23	...	6 50	...	6 53	...	6 22	...
Bledlow	...	...	...	9 35	...	12 5	...	...	3 33	...	7 0	...	7 2	...	6 32	...
Risborough, from Thame	...	...	...	9 40	...	12 10	...	...	3 38	...	7 10	...	7 7	...	6 38	...
AYLESBURY, departure	6 46	...	7 55	9 20	9 20	11 50	...	2 35	3 25	6 7	6 50	...	6 45	...	6 20	...
Risborough, from Aylesbury	6 55	...	8 10	9 35	9 35	12 8	...	2 50	3 37	6 20	7 5	...	7 0	...	6 36	...
Risborough, departure	...	...	8 12	9 45	...	12 15	...	...	3 43	...	7 15	...	7 9	...	6 43	...
West Wycombe	...	...	8 24	9 57	...	12 26	...	...	3 55	...	7 27	...	7 21	...	6 55	...
High Wycombe	...	...	8 31	10 8	...	12 37	...	...	4 7	...	7 37	...	7 29	...	7 7	...
London	...	...	10 0	11 20	...	2 20	...	...	5 38	...	9 5	...	9 20	...	9 0	...

* North Western Passengers from AYLESBURY wishing to stop at any of the Stations between Tring and London should see by the main line the time the Train is due at Euston, and then ascertain whether such Train calls; but in travelling to the North they will notice the time the Trains arrive at Cheddington or Tring, and then refer to the Down Trains.

LNWR timetables for February 1879.

TOWN OF TRAINS

The development of Bletchley into a railway junction of importance with all the attendant sidings, signalboxes, locomotive shed, and of course, the enlarged station, was a gradual process.

Why should an insignificant, isolated little wooden station between the small village of Bletchley and the larger one of Fenny Stratford, have been chosen as a junction for the Bedford line? When the railway came in 1838, Mr Franklin was Station Master of the temporary station at Denbigh Hall, and there were two men responsible for loading passengers' luggage on and off the trains.

Wolverton had a fine station, (even described as one of the Wonders of the World by a contemporary writer), where all trains stopped for refreshment and to change engines, and appears to have been a more convenient place. But it seems that the Radcliffe Trust at Wolverton would not release any more land to the London & Birmingham Railway (it became the London North Western in 1846) whereas land was available at Bletchley. Bletchley was also nearer Woburn than was Wolverton and no doubt proved more suitable for the Duke of Bedford.

When the Bedford line opened in 1846, Bletchley station was enlarged for the first time, but was still a station of little importance. Trains from Bedford continued through to Euston and returned to Bedford. There were a few sidings to accommodate the exchange traffic from the LNWR for Bedford, but as there was an engine shed at Bedford, there was little need for one at Bletchley.

Before the coming of the Banbury line in 1850 and the extension right through to Oxford in 1851, there was the gradual formation of a loco shed ready for the two new branch lines, although small loco sheds were built at both terminus stations.

On the main line, Wolverton was of supreme importance: not only was there a loco shed but locomotives were actually built there and J. E. McConnell, the Locomotive Superintendent of the Southern Division, was in charge at Wolverton.

The minutes of the LNWR Committee of Administration of these branch lines, dated 15 November 1850, recorded the opening of the Buckinghamshire lines and the necessity of a new engine shed at Bletchley: 'it was decided to provide a shed on the principle adopted by Fox, Henderson & Co., for the Great Exhibition Room, provided that the cost be not more than that of an ordinary wood shed with brick foundation'. In the event it was built of wood and galvanised iron containing three roads and capable of stabling about 12 engines.

In 1866 some extensions were made and early in 1872 the minutes record that '... during the great gale on Sunday night, the old portion of the shed was blown down and is now a complete wreck'. The Committee decided that this part should be rebuilt.

A plan of the loco shed and yard in 1878, when application to the 1879 session of Parliament for additional land was made, shows the loco shed with three roads, which continued through the shed, converging into one road near the old lodging house and former loco office, where an engine could take water from the tank above the building. The land then being acquired was on the east side of the station. The section on the south side of the Bedford branch belonged to Sir Philip Duncombe Pauncefort of Great Brickhill, that on the north side belonging to Samuel Liscombe Seckham, the then owner of Bletchley Park.

The shed came in for further extensions when the station was rebuilt in 1881, and by 1904 was listed as having six roads of 250 feet in length, with total capacity for 24 tender engines or 36 tank engines. The width of the shed was 100 feet.

The large open expanse on either side of the station was broken when Railway Terrace was built in 1853. This was the first street to be built in the vicinity of the railway and ran parallel with the line on the west side, on the way to the village of Bletchley.

The terrace was at first called Drivers' Row and its earliest inhabitants would have been engine drivers. Later it was called Company's Row until it officially became Railway Terrace.

On the east of the railway line opposite the Terrace, it was just wide open space as far as the little market town of Fenny Stratford. The first house was built here about 1870 and became known as the Half Way House. About 1879 this was converted into the New Inn public house and the road became Station Road. By 1877 houses were being built nearer to the railway on the east side in what was named Duncombe Street, after the Lord of the Manor. The street ran parallel with the railway line opposite to Railway Terrace. By 1880 houses were appearing on this same side, but to the north of Station Road, and became Park Street, East Street and South Terrace; soon Bedford, Oxford and Cambridge Streets were also built.

But on the west of the railway it was a different story. Right alongside the railway from the station up to Denbigh Hall, were the grounds of Bletchley Park. The Harrisons inhabited the mansion when the railway came, but Herbert Leon took over from Samuel Seckham in 1883 and remained for 43 years as a local squire. A thick belt of trees skirted the railway bank and conveniently screened the railway smoke from his mansion and its grounds.

In November 1851 the LNWR Co authorised tenders to be placed for gas fittings for its own gas works at Bletchley. The building of a Gas Works for railway premises can be seen as the beginning of Bletchley as an important railway centre. In 1858 the station was again enlarged. Part of the platforms were covered with architectural embellishments. The roof end gables were vertically glazed over delicately carved transoms.

In 1859 a third line from Bletchley to London appeared. The second bore of Watford Tunnel in 1874 enabled two fast lines and two slow lines as far as Willesden by 1876, and by 1879 the four lines reached Euston.

A plan submitted in 1879 for extending the bridge carrying the Oxford line over the Bletchley-Watereaton Road in the 'Parish of Bletchley and the Township of Fenny Stratford,' showed the four lines from London to Bletchley coming into three lines just south of the station.

In 1881 the station was rebuilt to the design that was to remain, other than some modernising in 1952, until the bulldozers moved in and razed it to the ground in 1965.

The railway architect of that period wanted to give his design a sense of importance and dignity. Bletchley had an elaborate and sturdy arched portico with a horse mounting stone at the foot of one of the pillars. The tunnel under the station for passengers was replaced by an overbridge. Separate double lines were laid on the east and west sides of the station for the departure of Oxford and Cambridge trains.

On No 1 platform, the Oxford arrival platform, near the station entrance, a refreshment room and small hotel graced the new station. Other buildings along this platform included the Telegraph and Post Office.

The sidings, with further signalboxes, developed over many years, reaching their peak by the Second World War, when Swanbourne Sidings were built to cope with the varied traffic that required remarshalling. The rebuilding of the station continued long after 1881, then in 1887 the great Richard Moon, Chairman of the LNWR, opened the new Coffee Tavern for Railway Staff.

In the years after 1881 a large building was erected at right angles to the station frontage, obscuring the loco shed. This building was taken over by the Post Office, which had previously occupied a smaller building near the portico. The associations connected with railwaymen — the Railway Servants Coffee Tavern Company and the United Kingdom Railway Temperance Union — took over the vacated premises. The UKRTU had periodically held meetings and the Coffee Tavern Company was in business, but they were awaiting suitable premises.

The Coffee Tavern consisted of a large, comfortable room with facilities for preparing temperance beverages and a committee room at the back. Upstairs, a recreation room had tables for games such as chess or dominoes, a harmonium which had been presented to the Bletchley Branch of the UKRTU, and books given to them. The Tavern was decorated throughout with moral wall mottoes such as 'Lessened drink brings double bread', or 'As ye sow so shall ye reap', although a little vice was catered for in the provision of a smoking room.

The secretaries of the two societies, H. J. Piper of the Coffee Tavern and W. Daniels of the Temperance Union, were hopeful of furthering the education of railwaymen; the books already in their possession were the nucleus of a library and they sought its enlargement.

The opening ceremony commenced soon after 11.0 am when Richard Moon, Rev W. G. Barry and Rev H. S. Smith, Mr Hubbard MP, Capt Verney RN, Doctor McGachen and others inspected the premises.

Mr Moon, Mr Thomas the Station Master, and Mr Coxon the night Station Master all spoke of their hopes for the new venture; Mr Moon's warning that *The Whitehall Review* should on no account be allowed in the reading room resulted in an angry exchange with the editor of that paper in the pages of *The Bucks Flying Post*.

The old Coffee Nob, as the Coffee Tavern was affectionately known, remained for 78 years. Many railwaymen were fortunate enough to obtain shares and took part in its administration. One of its secretaries was Joe Fennell, who started in the telegraph department at Bletchley in 1872 and was chief in his office when he retired on 31 December 1920: he lived to well over 90 years of age.

The Coffee Tavern was not merely for railwaymen to obtain a cheap cup of tea; postmen, and in later years the public too were welcomed. By World War II Bletchley Park had ceased to be the home of Sir Herbert Leon and the Foreign Office was now the tenant of his mansion. Several hundreds of people did secret work in the grounds and their dispersal for living accommodation meant a regular daily train to and from Bedford, appropriately nicknamed 'The Whitehall'. It was a short walk from Bletchley station through the wicket gate opposite to the Park, and the Coffee Nob became a popular place.

The Temperance Union was less successful with Bible classes after the early years, but later various uses, from railway improvement classes to accident enquiries, were made of the upper rooms

There were many porters on the station smart in appearance with a fresh button hole each morning, who gave courteous service to the public. Some wore stiff high collars with a 'dickie bow' and white shirt front. Some gave long and reliable service and became respected figures in the small community.

One such was John Wright, affectionately known as 'Old John' when he retired in 1879 after 32 years on Bletchley Station. His voice was well known to thousands of travellers, as he called 'Change here for Bedford and Cambridge, Banbury and Oxford — all change here except for London and Willesden Junction'. The *Leighton Buzzard Observer* called Old John a distinguished railway servant, a faithful old porter who had given the Company and travelling public more service than any other porter on the line in his 32 years at the station.

In their praise of Old John, the press were confident that the public who were acquainted with him would liberally assist the committee formed to raise a good sum of money, to place the worthy old man in some small business, where he could earn a respectable livelihood for the remainder of his days.

The press certainly did not exaggerate Old John's popularity. Within a month of his retirement announcement the station committee was formed, consisting of W. Padmore and R. Heydon, Treasurers of Bletchley Station, and T. W. White, Hon Secretary of the bookstall. Soon the committee announced that the fund had presented Old John with a purse containing £80 10s 9d, while other employees at the station had given him a valuable 'Timepiece'. A discreet paragraph in the announcement stated briefly that the 'Company have contributed handsomely'.

Capt Verney from Claydon House frequented the station during the 1880s on his travels to and from London. At a meeting of the Council of the Club and Institute Union at St James and Soho Club, Gerard Street, London, he proposed 'that communication be addressed to the Chairman and Directors of the London and North Western Railway Comany, pointing out the inequality of charging in the second class refreshment rooms, threepence a cup of tea, two pence for a glass of beer and asking them to consider the advisability of supplying refreshments at a cheaper rate'. Within a few weeks Capt Verney was at the grand opening of the Coffee Tavern on the station, giving verbal support to Richard Moon. The Coffee Nob had a reputation for a good, cheap, cup of tea for nearly the next 80 years, but there is no record of the Verney family taking advantage of this facility.

The horse and light waggonette waiting for an alighting train passenger was a familiar sight in 1887, but the noise from a departing train was not always familiar to a horse. Cecil Peake of Stoke Lodge met Mrs and Miss Sinkins at the station. As the party in their light waggonette left, down the approach road slope into Bletchley Road, the noise of a departing train startled their horse. Mr Peake saw the danger and pulled hard on the reins, when the waggonette over-locked, pitched over and threw the occupants into the road. Mr Peake managed to hold the reins and retain some control, Dr McGachin was called and had the passengers removed to the Park Hotel, where the badly injured Mrs Sinkin had to remain for some time.

In this era it was common to see the village boys in the railway approach road holding a horse's head while its owner met an incoming train. The owner generally paid a penny for this essential service. One such boy was Herbert Souster, who became an engine driver and retired as such during World War II. He was a big, strong, and thrifty lad, whose mother joined him into the Penny Savings Bank as soon as he began to earn. Herbert certainly worked for his money. Bletchley Station housed the Post and Telegraph Office, and in those days telegrams were delivered by the first available boy who wanted to earn a few coppers, which meant nearly every boy in the village. When a telegram needed delivering, the clerk came to the office door and gave a loud whistle; the first boy to reach him delivered the telegram. Herbert told how one day he heard the whistle and rushed for the telegram, which was for Selby-Lowndes at Whaddon Hall, about seven miles away. His mission accomplished, he returned to the station and immediately got a telegram for Stoke House, a further three mile walk. On returning to the office again, he was offered another, again for Whaddon Hall. Once again he set off, but by the time he arrived at Whaddon it was getting dark. This time the cook greeted him in surprise, exclaiming 'You must be tired and hungry, lad'. This he could not deny and was promptly taken to the kitchen and given a grand meal. But there was still the long dark walk home. His mother was worried about his long absence, but with the glorious sum of six shillings he was able to give her five and sixpence and keep sixpence for himself.

George Crane was a porter on the station at this time, well-known for his stentorian tones as he called out 'Bletchley — change here for Bedford, Cambridge, Oxford and Banbury'. Later he spent some time as a porter in the London area and several times apparently called out in error 'Bletchley — change here for Bedford ...' George lived to be 89, having commenced his railway career in 1861. He could remember when there was a level crossing over the Bletchley-Fenny Stratford road. Its eventual abolition was due in no small measure to the efforts of Rev Boughton, who used to sit in a horse-drawn cab, often throughout the day and night, taking a census of the people using the crossing. A contemporary of George Crane was Joe Fennell in the Telegraph Office. Both were founder members of the Bletchley Co-operative Society.

Ten or twelve hours, and often more, was the normal day in this period — the eight hour day for all staff did not come until 1919 — and no doubt contributed to many accidents. Then, as now, experienced men broke the rules or became so familiar with their job that they took a short cut to injury or death. In 1896 Henry Franklin was 26 years old and a shunter. At 3.0 am, daybreak, at the end of June, he was knocking wagons off a train from St Helens, intending to ride on the shunting pole by fixing it to the moving wagons after he had uncoupled them. The foreman porter on the station told him that the road was set right for the yard, but he was working on the girder bridge over Bletchley Road and his plan misfired. Franklin had little chance of escape on such a dangerous footway; both his legs were severed and within six hours he died in Bedford Infirmary.

Near the same bridge, in March 1906, two goods trains collided. An up goods train was crossing from the slow line to the Oxford branch. The down Doncaster double-headed goods ran by the home signal and collided with the crossing train. Extensive damage and derailment blocked the running lines, but no-one was hurt. The breakdown worked from the Saturday well into the next day and there was delay to some goods and theatre trains that were booked to run on the Sunday.

A series of accidents followed the mishap. Platelayer E. Jennings, with another railwayman named Barden, was removing a rail among the wreckage, when a wagon lying on its side fell right over; Jennings was trapped beneath the wagon and died an hour later.

Just north of the station another goods train had nine or ten wagons derailed. Later one of the two engines in the crash was derailed while being hauled in to the loco shed, causing further delay.

Signalman Jim Harding of Bletchley No 1 Box admitted at a subsequent enquiry that he failed to warn the Doncaster goods from Stoke Hammond according to regulations: but it seems he warned more trains under the regulation when another train was going over the crossing, than any other signalman in the box, so no action was taken against him. The responsibility and blame rested with the driver on the leading engine of the Doncaster goods.

Mr Cliffe was Station Master and represented the LNWR at the inquest on platelayer Jennings. Mr Cliffe retired after long service on Bletchley station in 1917, but before then he was to see one more major and fatal crash near this same spot.

On 11 August 1916 a soldier and his horse died; a signalmans' error could perhaps be blamed, but unlocked trailing points were the real cause.

Signalman Charter Lavender and porter signalman Teddy Smith were on duty that day in Bletchley No 1 96 lever frame junction signalbox. In the Cambridge Bay stood the 9.10 am local passenger from Euston which had 'four horse boxes attached on the rear at Tring, Cheddington and Leighton Buzzard. Three of these had been detached on arrival at Bletchley, but one was still on the train and was now due to back out of the bay onto the down slow line and then go off to Nuneaton.

Charter gave Teddy Smith instructions to call the 9.10 am local out of the bay. Arthur

Phillips, guard on the local, saw the hand signal from the box and relayed it to driver George Nix. As the train was slowly backing out, Guard Phillips, looking out of his van, was alarmed to see his train going onto the down fast and the signals off for an oncoming express. Arthur managed to stop his own train, jump off and run toward the oncoming express. He saw the signals drop back to danger, but the express came by him with brakes hard on, trying frantically but in vain to stop; then inevitably it ploughed into the rear of the local train, three coaches were turned onto their sides and the horse box completely smashed, killing the ususpecting soldier and horse inside.

The subsequent enquiry found that when the express had been accepted from Stoke Hammond by the signalman at No 1, all points were locked, but No 63 points were unlocked trailing points and were not closed. Had they been interlocked it would have been impossible to have gone on to the fast lines, and the accident would not have happened.

The engine on the express was a George V class No 1799 named *Woodcock* which was later allocated to Bletchley Shed. At the inquest the driver of *Woodcock* told of seeing the signals go back to danger and how he opened the sand valves and applied the brake, but too late. The jury were unanimous in the opinion that death was the result of a pure accident and all concerned did everything possible under the circumstances. Nevertheless, the two signalmen were disciplined by being reduced in grade.

One of the impressive sights at the station ended for ever during the war years. The Slip Coach had drawn many small boys to sit on the fence to see the coach actually slipped.

Few people can remember the Slip Coach. Arthur Beardsmore came to Bletchley from London as a Slip Coach Guard during World War I. He worked the same train every day and his job was to slip a coach off a passenger train from Nuneaton to London. The Slip Coach had a small window in the roof so when the train was approaching Denbigh Hall signalbox the guard could see the Distant Signal for Bletchley No 3. If the Distant was in the 'on' position, the guard would not slip his coach, but allow the train to stop at the station in the normal way, where the coach was detached. If the Distant Signal was 'off', the guard pulled a lever to uncouple the vacuum pipe between his coach and the one in front. Valves in the vacuum pipe on each coach automatically sealed off the pipes, preventing air from getting into the train pipes. A further lever uncoupled the link coupling and the train would speed through Bletchley while the Slip Coach rolled towards the station.

Stopping the coach opposite the bridge stairway was not without problems. Although 21 inches of vacuum were maintained in the train pipe, the guard would gradually destroy the vacuum and not fully apply the brake until the final application was made near the stairway. If the vacuum was destoyed too quickly there was no way of recreating the 21 inches and the coach would stop short of the required spot. If the coach was short of the platform, passengers' heads would be hanging out enquiringly, surveying their apparently stranded coach. Out would come the shunt horse to pull it into the station and then over to the Oxford or Cambridge bay, depending upon where it was routed.

Sometimes the guard would be overcautious with the brake and stop the coach short. Mr Cliffe the Station Master was renowned for his irritation when a precision stop was not made. He admonished Charlie Cope for stopping his coach short and said angrily, 'Tomorrow I will stand near the stairs with a red light and stop right opposite'. Charlie was well-known as a man who, if he had something to say, said it without fear or favour. This time he said very little. As Charlie's Slip Coach rolled towards the station, Mr Cliffe exhibited a red light. Charlie immediately stopped, well short of the station. Out came the horse to pull in the coach, up came the furious Mr Cliffe, but Charlie quoted the rules, which said a red light exhibited by hand is a danger signal, so he stopped his coach immediately. That was also the signal for Mr Cliffe to leave well alone.

The loco shed was unchanged from 1900 until the last steam engine departed in 1965. It was on the west side of the running lines, approached by running into the single line loco siding, at the north end of the station, then setting back into the various roads in the depot. The shed itself had a gabled roof span with numerous chimneys or ducts for carrying off smoke. At the bottom end of the shed were the stores, sand drying room, fitter's shop, mess room and blacksmith's shop with lathe and planing machine, also a drilling machine powered by a 9 hp Crossley gas engine. The foreman's office and clerical office were at the bottom of the shed immediately adjacent to the north end of the passenger station, so that the foreman and his clerical staff overlooked the platforms at that end.

There were two sets of hydraulic pumps used in connection with the hydraulic wheel drop. When installed in 1906 it was one of the latest type, capable of dealing with 7 ft 6 ins wheels.

The depot also possessed a hydraulic accumulator of 700 lbs per square inch and a 4-throw pump to work in conjunction with it. In addition there was a separate 2-throw pump for 2,000 lbs pressure, used to supplement the other pump when extra power was required.

The locomotive water supply came from a reservoir called the 'Newfoundout' situated at the south end of the station. This triangular stretch of water was bounded by the embankments of the main line, the Oxford branch line and the former Worcester Curve, a connecting line from the main line to the Oxford line from 1854-1861. This line was abandoned in that year, and, apart from a section used for a siding into Fletton's Brickworks in 1934, was not used until opened up in 1942 for wartime traffic

In the first quarter of this century, the loco shed was a picturesque spot. Not until 1934 did the nearby Fletton's Brickyards belch out sulphuric smoke from its high chimneys. The Newfoundout was encircled by weeds and rushes and was home to a pair of swans for many years right up to a few years before World War II. The swans were the property of the LNWR, fed by the loco lodging house keeper and their job was to keep the weeds down and thereby save clogging of the pumps in the nearby pump house: the pumps were working 24 hours a day because it was the Company's own water and thus cheaper than the alternative canal supply at Fenny Stratford. In the midwar years that supply was altered to the nearby river. There was a third possible water supply from the wells along the Bedford line, half way to Fenny Stratford Station.

The water tank, which was continually being filled from the places mentioned, was mounted above the coal stage. The 60,000 gallon tank was directly above the coalmen as they laboured in this substantially brick-built building at the north end of the depot. Two lines ran through the opening between the brick piers underneath the tank; the loaded coal wagons were on one road at a higher level than the other. The engines were then coaled by the coalmen from wagons into the bunker or tender of engines on a lower level. There was also an ashpit road alongside the coal stage and until about the end of World War I, engines could be coaled by the coalman filling tubs from his wagon and then tipping them through an opening in the wall onto the engine below.

There was a wide space between the ashpit road and the road leading into and out of the shed, where ashes from the continually arriving engines on the pit were thrown after engine fires had been dropped or cleaned. Over the years there were various methods for disposing of these ashes. Shed labourers would daily empty the pit and then for a few hours in the less busy morning time they would shovel the ashes into a wagon on the ashpit. For many years, after this daily emptying, the ashes would be left for a weekly clean up by a large gang of permanent way men. It was not until the 1950s that a mobile mechanical grab was used to assist here and to give some help to the coalmen.

Almost opposite the coal stage in the depot was the all important turntable which, with a 50 foot table, could turn engines of any class on the LNWR except the Claughton four cylinder express passenger engine. But the table did turn a Claughton in 1913, when No 2222 came on the shed — the original of its class, named *Sir Gilbert Claughton* — by turning engine and tender separately

A longer turntable was installed about 1917 and the old one sent to Banbury loco shed where it remained until the line was forever closed.

The drivers and firemen who kept the depot moving by marshalling engines for servicing and then into the shed, eventually had a hut near the turntable, but before this they made do with a dingy room under the coal stage.

From the turntable to the shed entrance, a retaining wall built of large stone sleeper blocks of the London and Birmingham Railway kept back the higher tree-lined ground of Sir Herbert Leon's estate (he was knighted in 1911). Along the wall was a reserve coal stack, later moved to the Watereaton siding at the south end of the station, to make way for other small buildings, which eventually included a water softening plant.

The shed wall on the Park side was also a retaining wall and No 6 road on that side was the only line that went right through the shed. Once it went right out to the front of the station to the oddest building of the loco department.

The Lodge was older than the portico and hotel which it faced, dating from when the shed was first built. It was a gaunt-looking, square, brick building with a water tank taking up the whole of the flat roof except for a space where a chimney stack rose above the tank. It had two storeys and long chapel-like windows, which gave daylight to both floors. From 1877 it ceased to be used as loco department offices and was used until the end of World War II by enginemen from other depots on lodging turns of duty. The tank crowning this sombre edifice was unused for countless years, but was finally dismantled after 1945. But it was not always a gloomy building. In the first quarter of this century it was surrounded by flower gardens, while the park trees behind softened its drab design. Alfred Bowler was the lodging house attendant in the World War I period and kept the gardens smart and colourful, and fed the swans on the Newfoundout. The top floor was made into sleeping cubicles for about eight men. Down below there were two more cubicles pushed into one corner.

Through many years it housed enginemen from distant places, and as it was only a one night stay, it was tolerated. The last stewardess was Mrs Read, a white-haired lady who came in daily. In about 1938 the young Callboys were detailed to go into the Lodge between calling up men in the town, to wash up, empty chamber pots and clean. When men ceased to lodge in the building, a few Polish shed staff made it their home until better accommodation could be found: later Lou Adney, the Chargehand Cleaner, used it as a uniform clothing store and for miscellaneous storage.

In 1913 the Control Office came to Bletchley and was housed in buildings on what was later No 8 platform. In 1917 T. F. Wenlock came to Bletchley as Station Master and Chief Controller, taking over from Mr Cliffe who had been in charge from the first year or so of this century.

Mr Wenlock moved into the Station Master's house in the Railway Approach opposite the hotel and near the Lodge; he was the last Station Master actually to live in the house. Tommy Wenlock rose from platelayer and later left Bletchley to become a 'top-hatted' Station Master at Euston. At Bletchley Station then, the platforms were numbered 1 to 5, but by the end of the War the same platforms were sensibly renumbered 1 to 8. In those days Nos 1 and 2 were arrival and departure platforms for the Oxford and Banbury passenger trains. Some trains for the north were also scheduled from the north end of No 2. The station entrance, bridge to cross all platforms, hotel and refreshment rooms were on No 1 platform. No 2, being an island platform, was also the down fast platform. Another refreshment room was also on No 2 island platform. No 3, another island platform, was on the east side of the up fast line, and on the west side, the down slow line. No 4, again an island platform, was the up slow line, and on the east of No 4 platform was the departure side for Bedford and Cambridge, but this could also be used as an arrival platform for trains from Euston that were terminating at Bletchley. No 5 platform was for arrivals from Bedford and Cambridge, although arrivals from these places could be switched into No 4. These two roads were not bays, and trains from Cambridge could continue across the junction to Oxford. It was also a slow to fast line junction. A fast to slow line junction was at the north end of the station near to Denbigh Hall.

The down expresses approached from the summit at Tring, 14 miles away and continuously down hill, while the up trains travelled the same distance from Roade along 6 miles down hill, 3 miles level and after 2½ miles up gradient of 1 in 440 approached the station on a down gradient for 2 miles at 1 in 1,100. This made for high speeds through the station, the effect increased by the reverberations of the low roof.

Five signalboxes controlled the whole station area. No 1 Box at the south end of the station was the largest with 80 working levers at that time, and controlled the main line, south end junction and considerable coach shunting; the carriage shed was only a few yards away. No 2 Box controlled the main line engines to and from the shed. Until about 1909 it also controlled the freight shunting yard.

It was at this time that the turntable, which seems to have been in existence in this yard since the Bedford line opened in 1846, was demolished. The loco shed had long had a turntable, but this one seems to have been used by engines returning from Cambridge with a passenger train and having a further return trip to Bedford. The LNWR insisted on as little tender-first running as possible and this table saved crossing the main line to the loco shed. By the turn of the century, the table had its limitations, which is why it was demolished and made into a short siding.

The ground frame was in a hut called No 9 which, after No 5 Box was built, became the Yard Inspector's Office.

When that yard was enlarged and No 5 Box built, that box took over the south end of the shunting yard, the Bedford branch as far as Fenny Stratford and the entrance to the sidings on the opposite side of the Bedford line, called the Top Yard. No 3 Box controlled the main line with its fast to slow line junction and the loop line from Denbigh Hall into the marshalling yard, and trains departing northward from the marshalling yard. No 4 Box came into existence in 1934 when the new sidings were built on the north side of the Bedford line and the box situated at the exit of the sidings about half way to Fenny Stratford on the opposite side, with a cattle underbridge between where the wells used to be that supplemented the engine water supply. The missing No 6 Box has never existed and No 7 was just a pointsmen's box for the north end of the main shunting yard.

The station platforms were roofed for about half of their 600 feet length. No 1 platform was about 100 feet shorter than the others, and although it was an arrival platform for Oxford and Banbury passenger trains, most were turned into No 2 platform, leaving this road as an up and down road for engines going into or from the carriage shed or onto the Oxford branch. The furthermost platform was lined by buildings housing Control Staff, Telegraph Office, Rolling Stock and Traffic Inspectors, Telegraph Linesmen, a lavatory, stores, lamp room, mess room and a Carriage and Wagon Examiner's room.

At the north end of the station were the 10 road sidings which were busy 24 hours a day, and across the Bedford line opposite No 5 Box, the gas works was still in operation, although soon to be replaced by town gas. On this side of the station were saw mills with attendant joiners and other workmen's shops: sidings led southward to the goods shed, passing a horse and cattle landing near the gas works. The goods shed had several 30 cwt handcranes, a horse stable with drinking trough and latrines nearby. The roadway from the goods shed down to Bletchley Road was lined with coal merchants' wharves.

At this south east end of the station another horse dock and a dock for unloading horse-drawn carriages were much in evidence and use. Nearby were signal linesmen, a blacksmith and other shops and huts. Bletchley Road emerges under the railway bridge and becomes visible from here, and between the gate of the goods shed road and to the bridge were two Coal Merchants' Offices and the green tin Railway Institute. This rather unattractive building was well patronised by young railwaymen, the billiard tables being its chief asset, and it played an important part in the leisure time of railwaymen in the first 40 or so years of this century; there were few other places for recreation in what was little more than a village.

The buildings opposite Station Approach Road, from the Station Approach gate to the side garden of the Station Master's house, played an important part in the station's daily life. One part was the stables for the shunting horses, and a wicket gate on the opposite side of the road gave the horses station access. The rest of the buildings were rented to a Mr Hands, the local carrier. Hands' garage dated back to the station's early days when many rail passengers required somewhere for their horses. Hands took over the stables about 1900 in addition to his landlordship of the George Inn, about 200 yards along the Buckingham Road. Previously the stables were used by a Mr Cloud who kept horses for members of the Whaddon Chase.

Cecil Hands, one of the two sons in the business, became a well-known station character. With ten to twelve horses, various kinds of vehicles, and contracts to fulfil, it was a busy life. In the stable yard were a broughton, landau, and a fly. There was a brake, drawn by a pair of horses, which carried 14 people, two up with the driver and 6 seated on either side. This was often hired by a party going to Towcester races or railwaymen going to an Orphan Fund Parade at Wolverton or Newport Pagnell. There was a waggonette for smaller groups often used by a shooting party, and there was also a hearse, hired out to local and sometimes not so local undertakers, complete with sleek black-plumed horses to match.

Before 1914 there was no bank in Bletchley or Fenny Stratford and a regular job for Cecil Hands was to meet the bank clerk at the station when he arrived from Leighton Buzzard. He had to be taken to Fenny Stratford Town Hall, which was used as a bank, and then returned to the station, complete with money.

Just before the war in 1914, the first motor car appeared. After the war there was a gradual progression to motor vehicles until the stables became a garage. Before the Post Office had a motor vehicle, Cecil Hands delivered all the mail from Bletchley to Stony Stratford, Newport Pagnell and other larger surrounding villages. The Hands contracted for the railway passenger parcel delivery. The previous contractor was Mr Richardson of Duncombe Street, whose horse-drawn vehicle resembled a Wild West covered wagon. Hands' motors performed the first motorised mail and the first railway parcel delivery in Bletchley. In the early 1920s the horse had completely gone from the Hands' establishment.

The Prince of Wales was a frequent visitor to Bletchley in the 1920s, for he had his horses schooled and cared for at stables in Great Horwood, convenient for the Whaddon Chase Hunt. He often came in his own coach on the rear of an express, but was known to scorn using it to return and, with his aide-de-camp, would jump into a first class compartment while his empty coach would be returned on the rear of a later train.

In the stables next to Hands' Garage lived the shunt horses, but they also had two small waiting stables, one near the horse dock at the south end and the other at the north end of the station, between the end of No 3 platform and No 2 Signalbox. These two were used as resting places for the horses between periods of shunting.

There was another building near the station that was once the property of the LNWR, but seems to have had little direct use by them. Behind Railway Terrace, fronting onto the Fenny-Bletchley Road, was a spacious brick building that had been stables in the railway's earliest days. A 1915 plan of the railway and its buildings shows them as stables, leased to a Mr Parmeter from 30 December 1865 for 999 years, subject to three months' notice if required, by the LNWR for their own use. At the turn of the century these were certainly stables and no doubt had a flourishing business. Like Mr Clouds' business in the stables in Railway Approach, horses were stabled here for members of Whaddon Chase. In those days Hunt Specials used to run from London to Bletchley, often an engine and two coaches.

The hunting horses disappeared from these stables about the time of World War I and Sir Herbert Leon used the premises to house his steam ploughing engines. The Premier Press were its tenants for some years and the final occupant was a wholesaler for paint and wallpaper. The building was demolished in 1974 to make way for a new city office block, and did not see its 999 year lease out. Opposite was an entrance to Sir Herbert Leon's Park, where many Bank Holiday agricultural and sports events were held, justifiably described as the biggest and best in the County. At one of Sir Herbert's Liberal Party meetings, Sylvia Pankhurst chained herself to a tree, thus bringing the Suffragette Movement to the village.

The timetable for 1910 gives a good picture of passenger services at Bletchley prior to World War I. There were 29 down main line trains and 32 up trains stopping at the station. The first passenger train of the day was the Scotch Mail, due out of Carlisle at 8.42 pm and scheduled for five minutes' station time at Bletchley from 2.42 am. Within five minutes of its departure a 'perishable parcels' from Holyhead, travelling at the same speed as its predecessor, was due. An hour later, at 3.53 am a fast newspaper train hurtled through. The main lines were never really quiet for any length of time. Empty wagons went north, express and slow goods trains, loads of minerals, fish and meat passed through on their way north or south at regular intervals from midnight, to the constant flow of passenger trains.

In the whole 24 hour period perhaps the most striking scene was when the Postal ran through nightly about 9.25 pm, with not only the roof brilliantly illuminated but the footboards too. The fastest run through the station was probably the 4.5 pm from Euston, which, coming down 14 miles of favourable gradient, slipped a coach: with a further notch or two on the lever, the driver increased speed still further and left the coach to come gently to a stand in the platfom under the control of the Slip Coach Guard. Coaches were also slipped from trains leaving Birmingham at 7.30 and 10.5 am, providing convenient connections with Cambridge branch trains arriving at Cambridge at 10.41 am and 1.20 pm. Among the 14 daily departures from Bletchley towards Cambridge were 6 rail motor trains running between Bletchley and Bedford. These stopped at, in addition to the five stations in between, several low platformed stations or halts, which were opened when the new service commenced in 1905.

The carriage shed housed most of the local trains, and situated on the west side of the Oxford line, near Bletchley No 1 Signalbox, it was clearly visible from the station.

Horseboxes were an important rail traffic in those days. Racehorses to and from Newmarket; brood mares from the numerous local stud farms; hunters galore connected with the three packs of hounds which met, some not far distant along the branch lines and one on the doorstep at Bletchley; Shire horses on their way to the many seasonal shows.

At the north end of the station in the shunting yard, wagons crashed and banged night and day. Two shunting engines, a north and south of the yard shunter, knocked wagons towards each other and somehow trains departed in all directions. But this brief survey of the station area does not do justice to the many grades of worker involved in its precincts. The signalmen went far beyond the station boundaries; the permanent way men certainly did not see home every night, many lodging in some remote village for a week's work on a far-off stretch of line. Booking off away from home was also the lot of footplate men and freight train guards. The passenger guard was a man of importance. Before applying for the job he needed considerable years of railway experience, had to have a minimum height of 5 feet 10 inches, and a knowledge of First Aid. His uniform was a frock-tailed coat with leather bandolier, which had a watch pouch attached. He made an impressive sight as he stood on the platform, watch in left hand, lowered green flag in the other, until, on the dot of the advertised time, he raised his flag and, with dignity, stepped into his van and away.

By 1914 the Bletchley railwaymen were no doubt like those in most rural areas. Many had traditionally followed their fathers into railway service, and anyway there was an extremely narrow choice of jobs. The railway worker was low paid and subjected to harsh and arbitrary discipline, which he resented. However, railway service offered security, and the security and the very nature of his work made the railwayman proud of his calling and gave him a strong feeling of company loyalty.

The war came, the railways took the strain as never before and Bletchley and its branch lines were an important part of this great national asset.

Bletchley at this time was still described by the magazine writers as an important railway junction, but they all seemed to note the insignificance of Bletchley itself, despite its railway importance. It was invariably called a 'hamlet with the bulk of population at Fenny Stratford', and not until well after World War I as a 'small town'.

One of the first signs of war was the stabling of empty cattle wagons down the loco siding, where loco coal was normally stored. These awaited Army orders and were kept ready for immediate and urgent use.

On 2 September 1914, a special train left Wolverton with 441 Wolverton Works men, bound for Oxford to enlist in Kitchener's Army at Cowley Barracks. The driver of the little 0-6-0 DX tender engine hauling the train was Tommy Bazeley of Bletchley.

Before boarding the train, the 441 men marched to the station led by George Davies, Secretary of Wolverton Town Band, playing 'Colonel Bogey' as the crowd watched the heroes depart. Among them were a few Bletchley men from Wolverton Works. One was draughtsman Bill Sinfield, whose father was an engine driver at Bletchley and whose grandfather was a driver back in the days of the London & Birmingham Railway. Bill Sinfield survived the War, but paid the price with a leg. More than a hundred Wolverton Works men never returned from the mud of Flanders.

Fifty years after the journey to enlist in the war to end all wars, a reunion in the Crauford Arms at Wolverton saw nearly 50 survivors of that first train load of Wolverton Works men. Bill Sinfield was there to greet the guest of honour — Tommy Bazeley, train driver.

Railwaymen from Bletchley went off to war at various times throughout those years. Some could not be spared from essential jobs, but some went and the ladies took over. By 1917 not only men, but immature boys were called up. George Judge was a little white faced cleaner in the loco shed — 19 years old; with two other Bletchley railwaymen, Fred Elliott and Alec Battams, he reported to the Ministry of Labour in the Post Office in Bletchley Road, then went off to Cowley Barracks to enlist. As they walked into the recruiting centre, a woman outside said 'You won't have to go my dear, you're too young'. But she was wrong.

George asked to join the Railway Operating Divison, but was promptly told 'You can't all go in the ROD, we want some bloody infantry', and into the 3rd and 4th Bucks Infantry he went. Within three months, with his two railway companions, he was in a London 'bus going to the front line, into the wet, cold, mud-filled French trenches.

With a terrible cold, a box of Mills bombs on his back, a gas mask by his side and a rifle, the little soldier boy was exhausted and frightened, but ready to go over the top to meet the enemy four miles away. His two mates were also going over, but he did not even have the comfort of going with them

About 400 yards out, the journey ended with all the soldiers bogged down in the endless mud. Unknown to George, he had passed Fred Elliott, badly injured by the incessant shells. The cry of 'gas!' was given, but George was not strong enough to manipulate bombs, gas mask and rifle. He dropped his bombs, then his rifle, but before he could get his gas mask on, he inhaled, and after an agonising time in the mud, ended up in hospital. He came back to England for a spell, where he saw his friend Fred Elliott on crutches, but had to return to France, where on one occasion he saw Frank Gamble and Wally Goodman, two Bletchley loco colleagues, now soldier railwaymen on the French railways.

When it was all over, 30 railwaymen from Bletchley never came back; George Judge returned, became an engine driver and retired as one, but was never quite sure how he had survived. Fred Elliott had a light duty job oiling points around the station, but a glove on one hand covered the scars of a wound received in France.

Throughout the war, ambulance and troop trains passed through Bletchley and along the branches. A regular train from Liverpool to Oxford, with various pieces of military equipment, arrived at Bletchley in the afternoon and was stabled in the middle long siding for an early morning departure for Oxford. Bletchley men worked the train forward while the Crewe guard working it from Liverpool, lodged with Mrs Briggs of 49, Duncombe Street, until the return train arrived. The Crewe driver and fireman had the doubtful honour of residing under the tank in the Lodge.

Some of the traffic was of a secret nature; railwaymen can remember a train stopped for examination, when a peep underneath the tarpaulins covering the low special wagons revealed the first Army tanks of the War.

Mary Sinfield was a ticket collector during the war and acquired a reputation for being unbending with passengers. Right was right with Mary, and ticket dodgers had to look out. Mary seemed to glory in her new found power and doing a man's job. After the war Mary reluctantly gave way to Albert Perry, returning from military service. Fifty years later she would talk nostalgically of her ticket collecting days.

For that 50 years Albert Perry displayed his drawing talent to many thousands of admiring travellers. With a blackboard and a penny box of chalks, he advertised numerous excursion trains with displays of drawings that drew praise from many quarters.

Porter Jim Garner was remembered for other reasons. He was an emergency signalman for No 2 Box, which meant he was trained for the signalbox and received 2s 6d extra for that knowledge. Jim was also a trained weazeler. If there was a tip to be had, he knew how to get it. A story handed down through the years tells how he once assisted a passenger with cases, who near the waiting train gave Jim 2s 6d and asked for change. He had intended to give the recognised tip of 6d or 1s. As the passenger stepped inside the carriage he turned and said 'What about my change'. Jim quickly closed the door, said 'Change at Crewe' and departed: so did the train and the astounded passenger with it.

There were numerous characters in all departments in those early years. The main Permanent Way and Engineering Departments did not come to Bletchley as predicted by Richard Moon in 1887: there was a dispute about water supply and the plan was cancelled, all departments eventually going to Watford. Later, certain departments did come to Bletchley and the platelayers there and on the branch lines were the most rural types, the subjects of a wealth of tales, matched only by the almost legendary deeds of the old drivers and their engines.

Joe Fennell described Bletchley in the last quarter of the 19th century as a place 'made up of railwaymen and grooms'. It is these characters that made the history of the railway.

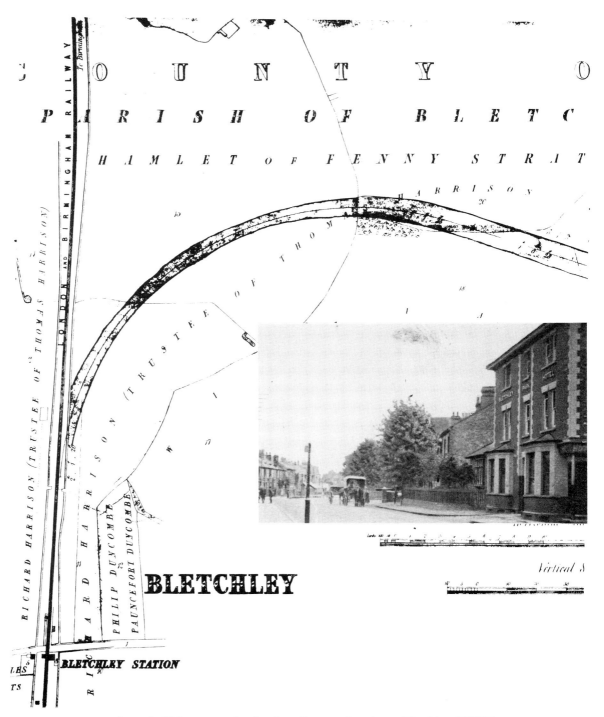

An early 19th century plan for the railway and station at Bletchley. INSET:
Parcel deliveries by Mr Richardson outside the Park Hotel at Bletchley,
early this century.

ABOVE: Bletchley Station Approach road. BELOW: 'Mad' Bill Brewer and a Jumbo, No 1677, *Badajos* on Bletchley turntable road, c1900.

47

ABOVE: The damaged engine in the March 1906 crash south of Bletchley Station and BELOW: the scene of the accident.

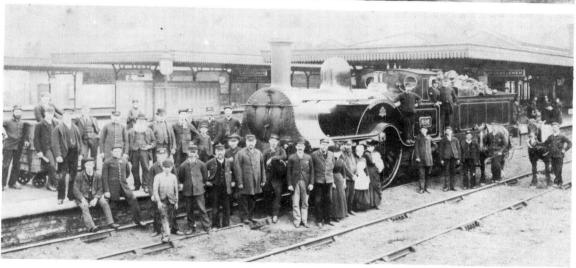

ABOVE: No 187 2-4-2 tank engine with Yard staff at Bletchley Yard c1900; CENTRE: Bletchley Station staff with *Waverley,* No 806 of the Lady of the Lake class, 1904; LEFT: after the crash, 13 October 1939 at Bletchley.

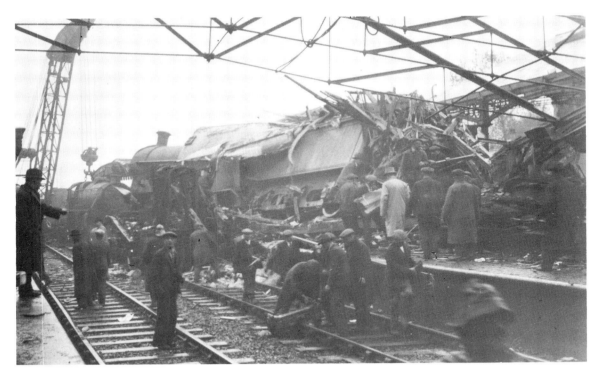

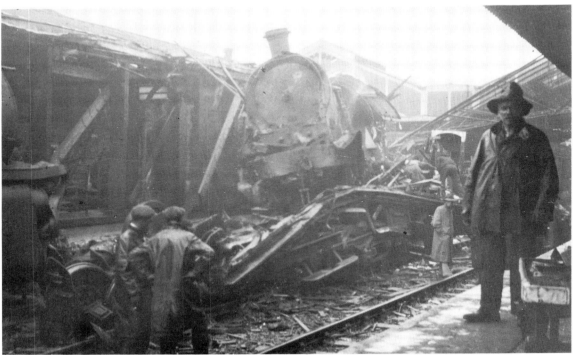

ABOVE: The 1939 crash and BELOW: driver Irving Butler lay dead under
the shunting engine for 19 hours; blacksmith Bill King stands on the right.

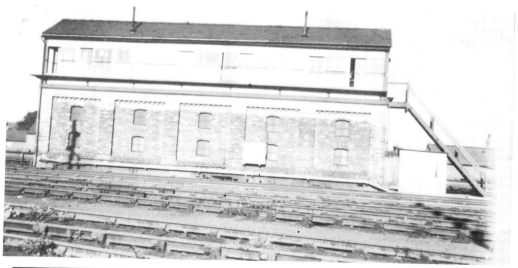

ABOVE: Bletchley No 1 Signalbox; CENTRE: inside the signalbox;
BELOW: Bletchley No 3 Signalbox looking north; RIGHT: Signalman
Harry Whitlock at the 96 lever frame in Bletchley No 1.

ABOVE: The loco shed about 9.30 am just after World War II. (Note the tall chimneys erected in 1925 to satisfy Sir Herbert Leon's complaints.)
INSET: Bletchley Station from the south in LNWR days.

ABOVE: Bletchley Station main entrance and booking office prior to 1952
and BELOW: Stanier Black Five No 45331 at the entrance to Bletchley
Carriage Shed post-1945; Railway Terrace in the background.

ABOVE: Bletchley Station up and down slow line platforms (left) and the Cambridge line platforms (right), BELOW: On the Bletchley Wheeldrop in 1965.

ABOVE: LMR 4-6-0 Jubilee class No 45613 leaving Bletchley for Euston, 9 June 1954 and BELOW: the Stanier Black Five No 44915 hauls the afternoon passenger train from Bletchley to Birmingham out of the north end of the Oxford Bay.

55

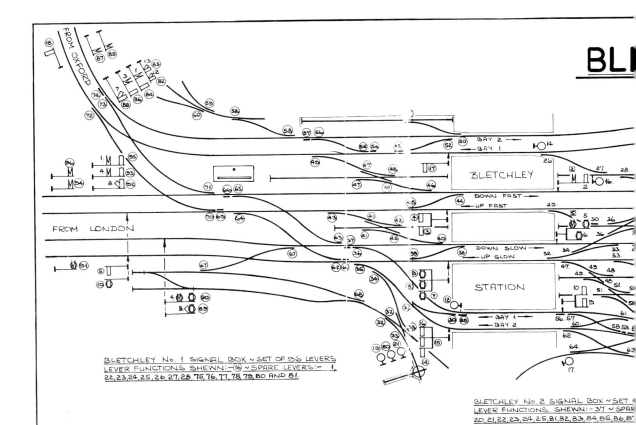

BL[

BLETCHLEY No. 1 SIGNAL BOX ~ SET OF 96 LEVERS
LEVER FUNCTIONS SHEWN :~ (16) ~ SPARE LEVERS :~ 1,
22,23,24,25,26,27,28,75,76,77,78,79,80 AND 81.

FROM OXFORD
FROM LONDON

BAY 2
BAY 1
BLETCHLEY
DOWN FAST
UP FAST
DOWN SLOW
UP SLOW
STATION
BAY 1
BAY 2

BLETCHLEY No. 2 SIGNAL BOX ~ SET
LEVER FUNCTIONS SHEWN :~ 37 ~ SPAR
20,21,22,23,24,25,81,82,83,84,85,86,8

NEW LAYOUT AND SIGNALLING 1881

ABOVE: New layout a
Station Approach, 19
Tavern behind the mail
with Cyril H-

LEY

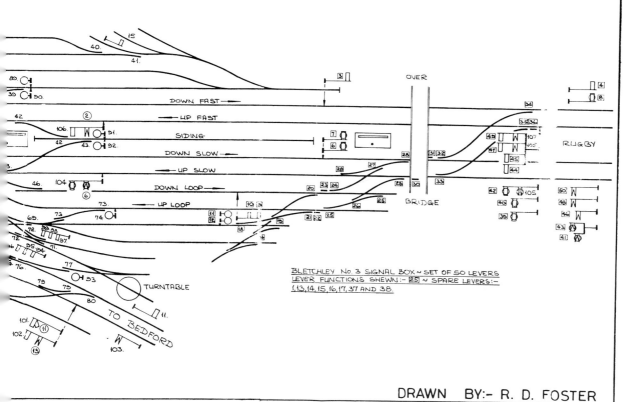

DOWN FAST ➝

← UP FAST

SIDING

DOWN SLOW ➝

← UP SLOW

DOWN LOOP ➝

← UP LOOP

OVER

BRIDGE

RUGBY

TURNTABLE

TO BEDFORD

BLETCHLEY No. 3 SIGNAL BOX ~ SET OF 50 LEVERS
LEVER FUNCTIONS SHEWN :- 25 ~ SPARE LEVERS :-
1,13,14,15,16,17,37 AND 38.

DRAWN BY:- R. D. FOSTER

Bletchley, 1881. LEFT: Bletchley
Bletchley station with the Coffee
RE: Railway Approach road, 1951
unting stables on left.

ABOVE: Swanbourne Station, early 1900s. CENTRE LEFT: Winslow
Station staff c1921; Station Master Brudenell fourth from left; BELOW
LEFT: Taking water at Winslow, an LNWR Class 7 freight engine (an old
'D') draws the Banburian on a nostalgic 1962 trip organised by the S Beds
Locomotive Club. CENTRE RIGHT: Cockley Brake Junction, where the
single line leads to Verney Junction. BELOW RIGHT: Verney Junction,
May 1936 — the end of Metro Land.

THE 'VARSITY LINK

Britain's two most famous Universities were joined by a direct rail link in 1862, with the insignificant little village of Bletchley at the main junction of the London and North Western Railway. As Bletchley gradually increased in importance as a railway junction, so, administratively it took over some of the working of the lines. The loco shed at Bletchley became the parent shed of the four others at Cambridge, Bedford, Oxford and Banbury. Permanent Way men from Bletchley lodged at villages along the lines to perform relaying work. Engineering staff lodged at various places while maintaining bridges, culverts and station buildings. Enginemen from Bletchley went to live and work at sub-depot sheds as part of their promotion. Signalmen relieved at signalboxes all along the lines and lodged nearby.

The Banbury to Verney Junction section of Bletchley's east and west branch lines boasted a wide variety of country scenery and station architecture. From Oxford or Banbury to Cambridge was 77 miles of changing scenery and the changing accents of the local railwaymen. In the 1930s a smattering of Scottish was not uncommon, as redundant railwaymen came south in the depression period. After a century of service, the lines were about to disappear or go into virtual decay, and so were the distinct lilting Oxfordshire and Cambridgeshire dialects that once made Bletchley men say — 'East is East and West is West and ne'er the twain shall meet'. They laughed and imitated the men at the extreme ends of their branch lines and could not hear themselves. It was left to the cockney to imitate the Bletchley men, calling them 'Bletchley Wills', the 'Swedenoras' and 'onion growers'.

The journey east from Oxford starts on former hallowed ground. The station occupies the site of Rewley Abbey, a Cistercian foundation dating from 1279. All that now remains is a boundary wall with a Norman gateway. The station was formally opened on 20 May 1851, built on the model of Paxton's 'Palace of Glass' at the Great Exhibition of that year. Its circular booking office, purchased from the Great Exhibition, was the most ambitious piece of carpentry in the whole building. In 1908 the station was rebuilt on the same site, to the same design, with identical accommodation.

The new station was first advertised as being on the Botley Road, but became officially known as Oxford (Rewley Road) and was separated from the Great Western Station by LNWR sidings. It had a V-shaped roof and two roads served by a single island platform 450 feet long. Though incoming trains always arrived at the right hand platform, it was not always customary for departing trains to leave from the left; by means of a trailing crossover just beyond the starting signal, both platforms could be used for departing trains.

As a train left the station, passing the goods and coal yards on either side, then the station signalbox, it immediately passed over a canal by a 73 feet swing bridge, hand operated and locked by the signalman in his box. The bridge contained about 85 tons of steel and worked on a central turntable or pivot. The arrangement for the protection of traffic during such periods as the bridge was open, was simply that the movement by the signalman to release the bridge also locked all points and signals in the station area. This arrangement appears to have been successful, but in 1853, when police and pointsmen were stationed at all points and signals, an engine managed to find its way into the canal while the bridge was opened for a boat to pass.

The loco shed was on the right, alongside the river. It was never a big shed, but possessed a turntable and a visible high water tank for the various locomotives that came onto the shed. The coaling of engines was by simply shovelling coal from wagon to tender.

It was on 2 February 1851 that the committee responsible for running this line approved the construction of the shed. On 14 October 1877 it was blown down. A Mr Webb, probably the Chief Mechanical Engineer of the LNWR, stated that the shed at Oxford was built on the same principle as the one at Bletchley (whatever that was) and he was instructed to deal with it. The shed was tinkered about with, but by May 1882 the Committee minutes stated 'that this shed was originally built of corrugated iron and has now got in such a state of decay that it is impossible to further repair it'. It was proposed to renew it with one of the standard sheds, holding six engines, at a cost of £1,817. The shed was built with two roads, each 150 feet in length and so it remained until it was closed in December 1950 and later pulled down.

On the opposite side of the main line was an exchange siding with the Great Western. Not until November 1940 was a direct junction made, at a signalbox called Oxford North on the Great Western. This was one of several wartime improvements to speed up heavy traffic that utilised this route. This junction made it an obvious economy to close Rewley Road station in 1951, diverting passenger trains from the Bletchley —Oxford line into the Great Western Station. The loco shed having just recently closed, the men and engines were operating from the GW Shed.

Less than a mile from Rewley Road is the site of Summertown Halt, opened on 20 August 1906 and renamed Port Meadow in January 1907. Apart from closing from 1 January 1917 until 5 May 1919, the Halt remained open until 25 October 1926, when the Rail Motor which served all the halts between Oxford and Bicester, closed down for ever. All the other Halts had been opened on 9 October 1905 when the service began.

Port Meadow stood unused for some years, then early in World War II, loop lines were put on either side of the main lines to accommodate the vast increase in traffic. A signalbox was erected, also called Port Meadow. The decline in traffic after the war made the loop lines and box redundant and they eventually disappeared.

It was on this stretch of line, running parallel with the GWR, that there occured, in 1853, what *Jackson's Oxford Journal* of 8 January 1853 describes as the most frightful accident since railways began. Seven were killed and 17 injured, some of whom may well have died later.

The 5.30 pm passenger train for London was standing in Oxford Station ready to leave. Driver John Tarry and Stoker Robert Bugden were on the engine, a Stephenson's Long Boiler, No 148, which appears to have been in a crash at Bicester in 1851, when six people lost their lives.

Wolvercote Tunnel, about two miles from the station, was under repair, due to a partial falling in, and all traffic was working over just one line. Orders were given that trains must not leave Oxford or Islip without telegraphic communication.

Mr Blott, Oxford Station Master, received a message from Islip enquiring if a coal train could be sent forward to Oxford. He was aware that it was nearly half an hour before the passenger train was due to depart, so he agreed. He informed most of his staff that the passenger could not depart until a coal train had arrived and was off the line in use for up and down traffic. He personally told Guard Kinch, but Driver Tarry was informed by Mr Hayes, Locomotive Shed Foreman at Oxford. All three of the train crew were Bletchley men. Sergeant Gwynn and another policeman on duty were told of the instruction and then went about their normal duties.

Driver Tarry and Guard Kinch were in conversation on the platform when a ballast train was seen approaching, which went into a siding about 100 yards away. Driver Tarry did not notice that the train was carrying a white headlight, otherwise he would not have mistaken it for a coal train, which carries a regulation green light. It had been working in Wolvercote Tunnel.

Guard Kinch had now taken his position on the train and the driver, without waiting for the authorised signal to start, opened the regulator and departed.

The hiss and rush of steam as the train moved away brought out Mr Hayes and Mr Blott, who instinctively ran along the line, shouting after the receding train. They succeeded in attracting the attention of the guard, who put down the brake handle, but, owing to the increasing speed of the train with its light load, this did not attract the attention of the driver.

About 200 yards from the station a policeman stood at an auxiliary signal. He was aware of the danger ahead and exhibited a red signal. The steam escaping from the front of the engine stopped the driver from seeing the signal until he was almost level with it; then he recognised it by blowing his whistle twice. But now the policeman unfortunately changed the signal to green, signifying only caution. This probably reassured Driver Tarry that everything was alright, for immediately he began to increase speed.

Soon after there was a terrific collision with the double headed coal train. The passenger train engine was turned completely round and, with wheels uppermost, fell into the water-filled ditch near the track. The leading coal train engine fell upon it, so that the wheels appeared transfixed and the engine underneath was shattered. The other coal train engine also fell into the ditch. The third and second class coaches were so smashed that scarcely two boards could be seen attached together. Passengers were scattered about the lines in all directions. Fire from the engines' fireboxes kindled the scattered wood and added to the hazard. Telegraph poles were torn down, stopping communication between Oxford and Islip. A messenger was later sent to Islip to telegraph Mr McConnell, Southern Division Locomotive Superintendent, at Wolverton.

Mr Hayes and Mr Blott had never ceased running and soon arrived at the scene of the accident. It was not long before hundreds of people had arrived and were giving assistance.

At one point there was a momentary panic when a GWR train approached on the adjoining lines and 30 or more people, thinking it was on LNWR lines, ran into the imagined safety of the watery ditch.

It was not until about midnight that Mr McConnell arrived with a large force described as mechanics. Mr Bedford, Chief of the Railway Police, accompanied him and early next morning one line was cleared.

At the inquest most of the facts emerged. Of the three drivers and three stokers, only Driver Lee, on the second coal train engine, survived. He saw the oncoming train only a few seconds after coming out of a curve, and called out to his mate to jump. Driver Lee jumped, but Stoker Wilcox hesitated, and next moment he was under the wreckage. The driver managed to pull his mate out of the wreckage, but he died next morning in Oxford Infirmary.

The badly shaken Guard Kinch was somehow taken by omnibus to the former temporary station, where the railway line crossed the Banbury Turnpike Road: it is quite likely that work was in progress at this place, laying a junction for a line to connect with the Worcester and Wolverhampton Railway. The 4.45 pm passenger from Bletchley had been stopped at Islip because of the accident. The train was allowed to proceed to Oxford Road, as the temporary station and junction was later known, and Guard Kinch was put into a first class carriage and taken home to Bletchley. The driver of this train was William Carrier, driver of the ill-fated Great Exhibition Excursion, which crashed at Bicester in 1851.

There were many terrible incidents related at the inquest. One unidentified male passenger was thrown under the wreck and before he could be extricated, the upper half of his body was burnt to a cinder. Julia Norman was thrown into the water and, by some means, became embedded under the passenger engine boiler. She was only discovered by her legs protruding above the water, and that not until 6.0 am next morning. Sara Smith of Steeple Claydon was discovered in a state of almost complete nudity on the buffer of one of the engines, a piece of iron firmly fixed across her throat. A horse dealer named Jones had £123 in notes and gold in his pocket when the accident occurred. He was badly injured, but what happened to his fortune is not mentioned.

While the inquest was going on, the bodies of the two drivers and two of the stokers lay in a public house in Horse and Jockey Lane, and Stoker Wilcox in the Radcliffe Infirmary. Two other bodies were not identified at the time and a week later one was buried, still unidentified.

Eventually poor departed Driver Tarry was blamed for an accident that has a great similarity to so many accidents in those early days of railways.

A few yards on from the scene of this terrible accident, still only 2¼ miles from Oxford, was Wolvercote Halt, served only by the Motor Train.

Through Wolvercote's 140 yard tunnel, on an easier gradient, was Oxford Road Halt, a junction signalbox with a level crossing and two nearby cottages for signalmen, until a bridge was built c1935. Although this Halt was served only by the Rail Motor and closed when that service terminated in 1926, it had the distinction of briefly being a station when the line ended there, while Wolvercote Tunnel was completed. Being on the Banbury Turnpike road made it a convenient stop.

Soon after the Oxford and Bletchley line was opened throughout, the LNWR were obtaining land from this Turnpike Road to Yarnton, to build a connecting line with the Oxford, Worcester and Wolverhampton Railway. By 1853 an Act had been obtained authorising the construction of a line one mile forty chains long; the two railways finally connected near the village of Yarnton, but a station was not built there until 1861.

At that time the Oxford, Worcester and Wolverhampton Railway commenced at Wolvercote, just over two miles north of the Great Western Station at Oxford, and ran via Chipping Norton Junction and Honeybourne to Worcester and Wolverhampton. A connecting line from Oxford Road junction to Yarnton was intended to give the LNWR a through passenger service from Euston to Worcester: the exchange station between the two companies would be at Handborough, about three miles beyond Yarnton. In the same period the curve at Bletchley was built, enabling trains to run direct from Euston to Worcester without engines changing to the other end of the train at Bletchley. So closely did these two companies work that the LNWR ran the section from Handborough to Worcester for a time until the OW & WR took over its own working. Another curve was put in off the Yarnton connecting line at Woodstock, about half a mile from the Oxford Road junction. This connected with the Oxford-Bletchley line south of Oxford Road and enabled the OW & WR to run their narrow gauge trains into and out of Rewley Road Station.

The Great Western acquired the West Midland Railway, which had already absorbed the Oxford, Worcester and Wolverhampton. This amalgamation had the effect of diverting OW & WR traffic from the LNWR to the Great Western. The diversion meant the Worcester Curve at Bletchley was so little used that it was abandoned. The curve at Woodstock on the Yarnton connecting line became obsolete and the rails were taken up; the Oxford Road to Yarnton connecting line became an exchange sidings, with Woodstock as the limit of LNWR freight traffic; and of course, it was the end of passenger trains to Worcester. So it remained until World War II, when the Great Western built a freight siding at Yarnton and the connecting line once again came into its own for through trains to Yarnton.

The end came for the Yarnton connecting line as traffic declined in the 1960s when the whole branch line was decaying. The lines were eventually lifted, but by this time the Great Western, as Western Region, had taken over the administration of the Oxford Branch from Bicester to Oxford.

It was 2¼ miles to Islip station, a little wooden building with a small siding. A few hundred yards before the station, a little-used road crossing was marked by the sturdy stone house of the crossing keeper. It was a unique crossing in that it had a distant signal in both directions, but not a home signal. One long-time resident shattered the peace of the crossing. Amos Walton had a lot of children and an annexe was built near the house to accommodate his large brood.

During World War II a petrol dump appeared on the up side with a siding connection.

It was six miles of level and almost perfectly straight railway to Bicester. With nothing but pasture land and a few farm crossings, many a driver had used this stretch to try out his engine, just to see what speed she could do.

Fairly evenly spaced along the six miles were three halts, Oddington, Charlton and Wendlebury, and then Bicester station, the end of the journey for the Rail Motor Service. When this was withdrawn in 1926, the halts reverted to insignificant farm crossings.

For one particular keeper in those years it was a hard life. An invalid wife to cope with did not help, but when she died life was even worse. The poor keeper, Fred, soldiered on in his lonely existence until he went for a holiday with his son at Bedford, and his life suddenly changed for the better. At Bedford he made friends with a tramp. As their friendship blossomed, so he offered to share his lineside cottage, and the tramp accepted.

Soon Fred was getting his early morning tea in bed, some housework was done and he had help with the gate. Life was really worth living now, and on his frequent evening visits to the village pub, he met a lady friend, and started courting. Local gossips talked of a wedding.

The tramp too had heard the gossip. One morning he brought his benefactor an early morning cup of tea then, without warning or goodbyes, disappeared for ever, leaving the crossing keeper once again on his own. Then Fred married his lady friend.

A ganger lived at Wendlebury crossing when the Rail Motor service commenced. Allen Wells was a fireman on the Rail Motor who married the ganger's daughter.

Bicester, like Winslow, was an important intermediate station, and it came into the news early in its history when less than a year after its opening, a fatal crash occurred. On the evening of Saturday 6 September 1851 a return excursion from the Great Exhibition left Euston for Oxford, made up of 14 carriages containing about 200 people.

The train arrived at Bletchley and Driver William Carrier went on to Oxford with a fresh engine, but for some reason kept the fireman off the engine from Euston. The engine was an LNWR (Southern Division) express engine No 148. Guard Benjamin Hood of Bletchley took his position on the train. It was a Mr Macfadzen, Foreman of Bletchley loco shed, who gave Driver Carrier his instructions to work the excursion between Bletchley and Oxford and, as it was not laid down in regulations or instructions to stop these excursions at Bicester, the driver set off with the intention of going rightaway to Oxford.

The line was single beyond the Banbury branch junction to Oxford, but at Bicester there were up and down platforms. Down trains to Oxford requiring to stop at Bicester would come off the single line approaching the station, and back again at the other end of the station when leaving. Trains not requiring to stop would not use this loop line.

Mr Bruen, Bicester Station Master, had received a message that the excursion was to be stopped at Bicester, and accordingly he informed Policeman Wilmott to pull the loop line points and exhibit a red flag. This he did, but the engine whistled and appeared to make no effort to slow down; as it hit the points it became derailed and the first three coaches overturned and were smashed to pieces. The engine was checked as it tore straight at the

Station Masters' house, by the torn up rails becoming twisted in the spokes of the wheels: this and a massive post helped to arrest its hurricane flight and prevented it from going right through the house. About two feet from the front door it came to a standstill.

Many people were soon on the spot. There were medical gentlemen on the train who gave assistance. It took up to three hours to extricate some passengers and timber had to be sawn to accomplish the task. Five people were killed immediately, and one, Joseph Luckett, a cheesemonger from London, was so seriously injured that he died on the next day.

Few of the train crew were injured. Those who were hurt were conveyed to adjacent inns. Among the dead was driver William Carrier's own 14 year old son, also called William, who had joined the train at Bletchley.

At the inquest in the King's Head Inn, Bicester, the bodies lay in the adjoining room, while the witnesses' evidence showed the risks involved in rail travel in 1851.

The jury's findings on Monday 15 September were: 'That a single line of railway necessarily involves more danger. The jury therefore earnestly urge upon directors of the Company ... that they will cause a second line of rails to be laid down without delay ...'

The Coroner added: 'I should wish that it might be laid down as a rule, that until a double line of rails is completed, every train may be ordered to stop at Bicester', and the jury found that comparatively little blame lay with the 'company's servants', and 'that in the monopoly which railways have achieved in travelling, the lives of passengers should not be jeopardised at the shrine of interest and dividends'.

Bicester remained a little country market town until World War II, when change really set in. A big Ordnance Depot was built with a large railway siding and its own railway running way back into the expansive area of the depot.

The old Worcester Curve leading from the main line just south of Bletchley to the Oxford line, was again relaid and brought into use. Regular trains of ashes came round the curve for Bicester until the sidings were built, and a new signalbox called Bicester No 2 came into use, controlling the entrance and exit of the depot.

Soon regular and special trains for Bicester were a daily feature of the line. Box vans with unseen contents, complete trains of heavy artillery guns, army motor vehicles and various implements of war went continually in and out of the sidings. Soldiers checked all trains and WD engines were waiting to take them deep into the depot's own network of sidings.

Soldiers going on leave became regular passengers and every Monday morning for years, soldiers could be seen waiting on Bletchley Station for the 5.20 am — the first passenger train to Bicester. Week-end trips from Bicester to Euston and back via the Worcester Curve, became expected special trains for Bletchley train crews.

As the depot progressed in size and importance, so its railway became more sophisticated with its own passenger trains from one end of the depot to the Bicester station end. Evenings out in Oxford for many of the army personnel lifted the passenger receipts for Bicester Station. This arrangement lasted for some years after the war, but gradually less staff were required in the depot and less traffic came until only the local goods called each day.

Before Launton, a now barely visible siding could be seen stretching way back as though going to nowhere in particular. The local goods would sometimes detach a few wagons and place them inside the gateway across the siding entrance and depart. Later a horse could be seen dragging the wagons away to Bicester Aerodrome well out of view of the railway passenger.

The station was quiet, peaceful and out of view of the village, with two wooden platforms and crossing gates over the road to the village. The up platform had a house for the Station Master who really did live on the job. What appeared to be the front room of the little house was the signalman's abode and booking office. A more independent railway house for a signalman or other employee stood near the down platform. On the east of the road crossing was the single siding that could only be used by up trains.

It was a little more than two miles to Marsh Gibbon and Poundon Station on a heavy up gradient all the way. It is doubtful if many railwaymen who worked along the line would have known where Poundon station was, or had even heard of it. It was mostly called Marsh. A road ran by the station under the railway to connect the two villages, with two railway cottages either side of the forecourt entrance to the station and siding. The signalman had the luxury of working in the booking office with his levers near a spacious bay window, overlooking the platforms and a wide expanse of fields. The station existed from 1880 until the official withdrawal of passenger services on 1 January 1968.

Before reaching Claydon Station about four miles away, the line passed under the former Great Central main line. This bridge would not have appeared until about 1897 when Britain's last main line was being built. Nestled in the bank nearby on the down side was a little signalbox displaying the name 'Itters Siding'. The name came from the former owner of the new large brickworks of the London Brick Company at Calvert on the Great Central line. Empty brick wagons were shunted into the brickworks via the Great Central and full loads dispatched via Itters Siding.

The brickworks of nearby Calvert, which came in 1900, probably saved the population from decreasing during the agricultural depression of the inter-war years.

In September 1940 a double connecting line was installed from the Oxford line, with facing point coming from Bletchley, to the former Great Central line near Calvert Station. The junction signalbox on the Oxford line was called Claydon (LNER) Junction. This connecting line was built in conjunction with a similar connecting line near Sandy between the LNER (former Great Northern) and the Bletchley to Cambridge branch, as a wartime diversionary route. The Claydon junction had the immediate effect of making Itters Siding redundant.

Charndon milk-landing stage had suffered redundancy by this time. This was a wooden stage in the vicinity of Itters Siding, but on the up side had as its only caller the daily milk train. It was situated at the foot of an embankment and a stout wooden trough from the top of the bank down to the stage allowed the farmers to slide the 17 gallon churns down with comparative ease.

Approaching Claydon station on the right one can see, between the distant trees, Claydon House and Middle Claydon Parish Church. Sir Harry Verney of Claydon House lived to be 93 and from his early years was the driving force in the building of railways in Buckinghamshire. He promoted the Aylesbury to Cheddington line which opened in 1839, the first branch line on the London & Birmingham Railway; he became a friend of George and Robert Stephenson and assisted them with railway legislation while he represented Buckingham in Parliament from 1832 for most of the next 52 years.

Of the Claydon villages (Middle, Botolph, East and Steeple) the nearest to the station was Steeple Claydon; it also had the choice of Padbury Station on the Banbury line about two miles away.

Claydon Station platforms commenced just inside the road crossing gates and the station house and buildings were attached on the up side. The signalman's frame was in the booking office — in fact the signalman was booking clerk, station master, goods clerk, porter and any other grade necessary. The station had the usual little sidings on the up side and a row of railway cottages nearby.

At Launton the Station Master was abolished, and a porter ran the station and opened the gates. He lived in the Station Master's house and his wife was responsible from 10.0 pm to 6.0 am for opening the gates if an owner of a road vehicle rang the bell to wake her up.

65

A porter signalman cycled daily from Marsh Gibbon on a company cycle to Launton to allow the porter, on a split turn of duty, to have his dinner while he opened the signal frame to allow the local goods from Oxford, called No 19, to attach and detach traffic. The porter signalman from Marsh Gibbon also had to find his way to Itters Siding when required.

The Station Master at Claydon was also abolished and two porter signalmen on two shifts ran the station.

The next station, less than two miles away, was the most important intermediate station on the Oxford or Banbury branch lines, as it was the junction to Buckingham and Banbury: but it could also be called the most insignificant. After the line and junction opened in 1850 until the last passenger train stopped in the last days of 1967, the group of houses that clustered around Verney Junction Station never exceeded 13, including a spacious pub called the Verney Arms Hotel. It was originally just a junction, and until the station came it was referred to as Claydon or Winslow Junction.

When the Aylesbury and Buckingham Railway Company opened its line from Aylesbury to this junction on the LNWR, a station was then opened and as Sir Harry owned the land on which the station was built, what could be more appropriate than the name of Verney Junction.

Despite its lack of population, it was the only intermediate station on the Oxford or Banbury lines to have more than two platforms or an overbridge from one platform to the other. In Edwardian times, when it perhaps saw the peak of its passenger travel, it could boast of a bookstall and a regular Thursday excursion to Euston. When the A & B railway was taken over by the Metropolitan Railway, for a few years before World War I, Pullman Cars *Galatea* and *Mayflower* came from Baker Street to this farthest point in Metro-Land.

Until a station was built at the junction, passengers travelling from the Banbury line to Oxford had to change at Winslow, then after a wait there, on to Islip where the line ended for some time until the completion right into Oxford on 20 May 1951. It was one hour's travel by omnibus from Islip to the centre of Oxford.

The Aylesbury & Buckingham Railway Company was established on 6 August 1860 by Act of Parliament to build a line from Aylesbury to Claydon, to form a junction with the Bletchley and Oxford line, where a junction already existed for Banbury. The Marquis of Chandos who became Duke of Buckingham in 1861, the Chairman of the LNWR, also became Chairman of the new company and subscribed £5,000 towards the capital, and his associate, Sir Harry Verney, became his deputy Chairman.

The contract to build the 12 mile railway was given to Francis Rummens, with Walter Brydone as engineer. Although work commenced from the Claydon end in February 1861, it was another 7½ years before the line opened. The enforced resignation of the Marquis of Chandos from the Board of the LNWR resulted in that company withdrawing from its agreement with the local company. This left the A & B with a line, but no rolling stock, or money to buy any as the new company was in financial difficulties. The cost of construction was £67,000, including the building of Verney Junction Station which, although built by the LNWR, was charged to the A & B.

The GWR enabled the little A & B railway to open to the public on 23 September 1868. Three trains ran daily in each direction with intermediate stations at Quainton Road, Granborough Road and Winslow Road. The little line was doomed and soon bankrupt.

For 23 years the GWR was responsible for running the line until the Metropolitan Railway Company purchased it from the A & B for £150,000 and took over on 1 July 1891. The Met immediately started doubling the line and rebuilding the stations. It was not until 1897 that they built one more station, called Waddesdon Manor for the benefit of Lord Rothschild. They immediately ran into another problem. They had no locomotives light enough to work over the line and were forced to seek the help of the LNWR, who loaned the necessary stock. By 1895 the Met had purchased some new side tank locomotives from Sharp Stewart and Company, two of which were destined for the Aylesbury to Verney line, but were not very successful and so were subsequently disposed of.

After a first failure in 1891 a Bill was passed in Parliament during 1893 to connect the Metropolitan with the Manchester, Sheffield & Lincolnshire Railway. On 15 March 1899 the Aylesbury to Quainton Road portion of this little line became part of the new main line from Marylebone to the Midlands and the North — the Great Central Railway.

On 2 April 1906 the Metropolitan and Great Central Joint Committee assumed responsibility for the new main line between Harrow South Junction and Quainton Road, including what was now the Verney Junction to Quainton Road branch line.

On 4 July 1936 passenger services were withdrawn from Quainton Road to Verney Junction, but the branch remained open for freight traffic. During 1939 work started on singling the line and on 28 January 1940, it was completed. The double line was actually left in from Verney to Winslow Road, the first station, but from a pair of stops near that station the second line was a long siding from Verney. The level crossing gates were then operated by the train crews and all signalling was removed to make the branch one section between the two junctions.

During World War II the little single line was quite busy with interchange traffic from the LMS. Coal for Baker Street and the return empties made heavy shunting in the small yard. When the War was over, interchange traffic was sent via the early wartime connection at Shepherd's Furze Farm near Claydon and on to the Great Central for remarshalling at Quainton Road and inevitably the Verney — Quainton line closed forever.

The double line from Verney to Winslow Road remained for the storage of condemned rolling stock, but the remainder of the line was lifted in 1957.

In the period immediately prior to World War II, the duties of the station and yard staff were more varied than the biggest London Terminus. Jack White was a number taker in 1939, and as it was a joint station, he had to make out Railway Clearing House sheets recording wagons from the LMS lines to the Met and Great Central.

The Station Master's house could not possibly be nearer the station, but it had a large garden with a veritable orchard of trees in it. A Mr Smith was the resident — a Yorkshireman with a love of gardening, and another love which fitted in even more admirably with the Verney community: cricket was a local speciality. The village team was more or less made up of the Newmans, Norths, Taylors and Cubbages, plus the Station Master.

The Banbury leg of the Buckinghamshire lines never did have the density of traffic of the Oxford line, which can be safely assumed as the reason why Verney to Banbury never progressed beyond a single line: although the bridges were built with the eventual aim of doubling, it somehow never quite made it.

The coming of the Buckinghamshire Railway to Banbury reduced the price of coal for inhabitants from 22s to 15s per ton and 150,000 tons were used annually. It was yet to become famous for its Cattle Market and the railway was to play a vital part in this.

There were four passenger trains to and from Bletchley each day when the line opened, but only one train in and out on Sunday. Freight traffic started a few weeks later and immediately the Gas Company increased its number of burners and erected another gasholder on the premises conveniently near the station, to receive coal by rail. The Gas Company's works could not have been more conveniently situated, as it was flanked by the Bucks line and the Great Western, which reached Banbury four months after the Bucks line. The station became an immediate gas consumer.

The little terminus station gradually developed in area and business, but with never more than one island wooden platform with a train able to arrive or depart on either side and the whole covered by a curved roof. The loco shed and yard was on the left hand side as one left the station, opposite the dominant gas holders. Buildings joined the far side of the shed to house the foreman, a clerk, a sand drying room, a toilet and the enginemen.

When engines passed through the shed towards the turntable, they passed the tank house. This place was the home of engine Driver Plackett until just after World War I: he was its last inhabitant. If Banbury loco ever had a foreman, he was gone by the early years of this century. Driver Plackett was in charge of the shed.

It was just after World War I that the Cattle Market moved alongside the LNWR station and was perhaps the largest cattle market in the country. There was an abundance of cattle trains in those days. Blisworth men worked trains off the SMJ Railway; their line came on to the Banbury branch at Cockley Brake. There were Great Western routed cattle trains and those to go via Bletchley. There were trains of 40 to 50 loads of cattle for Birmingham and Wolverhampton.

Cattle dealers used to come from the Birmingham area and stay overnight at Banbury to commence their cattle buying first thing on Market day. Bill Smith, District Traffic Inspector at Bletchley, would come down to supervise the cattle train marshalling and departures on that day.

Bletchley loco was the parent shed and had generally supplied the staff right back from the previous century. Drivers and firemen were sent from Bletchley as part of the compulsory system of promotion. They had to make their homes at Banbury until they could return to Bletchley, which could mean several years.

During World War I there were three sets of men — three drivers and three firemen — at the depot. One of their turns of duty was a night turn. Ammunition trains were worked into Bletchley from an ammunition depot about two fields away from the loco and they had a daily goods train out of the yard. After the War, Banbury men did not go beyond Buckingham, where they changed footplates with Bletchley men: taking an engine freshly coaled at Bletchley in turn saved coaling at Banbury which had no coaling facilities.

In 1925 Arthur Elson had to lodge at Banbury. He was a fireman who had to take his turn at outstanding duties for a few years. His driver was Jim King and they were now the only set of enginemen on the depot which was never again to increase its complement of enginemen.

There were duties at little depots like Banbury that were right out of bounds for enginemen at big depots. Driver Jim King was also responsible for checking the gas and water meters and advising Bill King the blacksmith at Bletchley if any turntable maintenance was required. Arthur Elson had to chop sufficient wood daily from the rough wood supplied from Bletchley Saw Mills to light up the engine.

Jim King was an old driver with the traditional ideas of how a fireman should behave. He would never allow the fireman to stand on his side of the footplate. He would personally acquire crushed bath stone for the fireman to clean the footplate brasses.

Arthur Elson, being on permanent afternoon shift had courting problems. He lodged at Banbury, had a girl at Buckingham and his home at Bletchley. He was passed to act as driver while at Banbury and his first driving turn of duty fell on a family wedding day. He was so proud, and so important was the occasion for him that he did not go to the wedding. He eventually came back to Bletchley.

There was no great variety of engines at Banbury at this time. It was generally a Cauliflower 0-6-0 LNWR Goods or a 5 feet 6 inch LNWR tank engine. About 1932 it closed as a functional depot and the men transferred to Bletchley. Bletchley men worked all trains from then onwards. The shed was demolished a year or so after the depot closed.

Bletchley loco had been upgraded and for the first time had a Superintendent in charge, a Mr Nelson, who took advantage of the good English oak from Banbury shed to make himelf some furniture. Harry Somerton, the signalman part-time farmer at Cockley Brake, went one better: he had the slates off the shed roof for the new house.

Banbury loco remained, although there was neither shed nor staff. The passenger and freight engines used the turntable and water column daily. Maintenance of the turntable was virtually forgotten, making the turning of an engine a sometimes worrying and very much manual performance.

Despite the dilapidated appearance of the depot, the water remained good. Numerous enginemen had brewed their tea from water straight out of the Banbury loco water tank, but one day Fireman Charlie Orchard took a cool, clear drink and in a few moments felt sick. Old Harry, the recently retired Cattle Dock Cleaner, had drowned himself in the tank, remained there undiscovered for some days, and had only very recently been dragged out.

Reuben was a signalman at Banbury LNWR before World War I until he retired in 1938. When he first came to Banbury as a porter near the end of the previous century, he attended religious services in the waiting room of the Great Western Station. Reuben and a GWR man became the leaders in this religious group. Soon they were able to build the Railwaymen's Mission Hall in the LNWR station forecourt.

The little chapel prospered. Reuben worked hard for his little Mission Hall and even let another struggling religious body share the hall for a while. The Mission was chiefly for railwaymen, and the large printed board over the altar denoted, 'A Saviour for Railwaymen and Railwaymen for Christ'.

On the departing train for Bletchley, once the signalmen had delivered the train staff into the possession of the driver, it was four miles along the single line to pass the little one platform wooden station of Farthinghoe. The GWR has run parallel for a short distance leaving Banbury and then turned southward. The Western's direct run to London via Bicester on a double track had made the Bucks line a link between villages.·

It could once boast a station master, but a porter was all it needed for a good portion of its 102 years' history. It was an isolated station, the ideal situation for old Jimmy Brown, the last resident in the house. He was a recluse in every way, except for meeting his few passengers. Jim did have a love of hard cash — and all his money was changed into coins and deposited in a large chest. The platelayers on the length were his only real contact with people and it seems he did not make any secret of his wealth. Jack Rawlings, one of the platelayers, tells the story of how Jim made an offer to let any of the platelayers have his wealth if he could pick it up and carry it away. Jack Rawlings knew his capabilities and refused. It seems no-one else could lift it.

The station closed to passengers on 3 November 1952; it was the first station on the line to close and was the only intermediate station on this line that was served by the S & MJ which connected with this line at Cockley Brake Junction, about two miles further along.

When the line from Cockley Brake to Blisworth closed in 1951, it could hardly be imagined that this quiet little line had, 90 years previously, been promoted by men who saw it as a profitable route, linking the Midlands with South Wales. The first step was taken by a company called the Northampton and Banbury Junction Railway (N & BJ), which secured powers in 1863 to build a line from Blisworth, on the LNWR main line near Northampton, to Farthinghoe, and join the same company's branch line from Bletchley. In 1865 two Acts were secured. One of these confirmed arrangements with the LNWR as to running powers from Cockley Brake Junction through Farthinghoe to Banbury, and the other empowered them to extend their railway beyond Banbury. Another Act authorised extensions and running powers on other companies' lines. This involved, among other things, a bridge over the River Severn with a clear span of 60 feet over the towpath and a 40 feet drawbridge opening.

The N & BJ grandiose concept evidently took the company far beyond the limitations implied by its name, and in 1866 an Act authorised the company to adopt a new title 'The Midland Counties & South Wales Railway', the whole project being 96½ miles in length.

The scheme did not materialise, and application was successfully made to Parliament for permission to revert to the original name and ambitions in the session of 1870, and thereafter the railway's affairs did not trouble the legislature further, except in 1910, when sanction was given to amalgamation with the newly formed Stratford upon Avon and Midland Junction Railway.

The line from Blisworth to Cockley Brake opened in 1872; even with the South Wales traffic this line was a risky speculation and it is astonishing how it managed to stay open for public traffic for so many years. It closed down for passenger traffic in 1951 and was soon closed for ever.

Cockley Brake Box issued the train staff for both single lines but was usually quiet.

Old Harry Somerton found it both profitable and practical to be signalman in the box and attend to his farm near Greatworth in his spare time, and he worked on this basis all his life. It was said that the railway work was his rest period. Brackley yard conveniently had the Northamptonshire Farmers' Depot in it so Harry was able to telephone Brackley signalman and get him to place all orders for cattle food and any other farm orders. The size of his farm grew and his sons became successful farmers in the area.

Jimmy Trotman was the last signalman. He was a reserved character, but not as unenterprising as he appeared. He was the line bookie and by use of the railway telephone could muster quite a number of clients.

His bookmaking career started simply in 1947 when lineman Harry Sheen on the S & MJ came into his box and moaned that he wanted to put eight shillings on a horse, but could not get near a bookmaker. Jimmy made a spontaneous offer to cover his money. He did not make any money out of this first venture, but it whet his appetite and soon he was bookmaker for the two branches. Signalman Arthur Marriott at Brackley became his runner, with the powers of a partner, and they had a friendly little business going until the line closed, although they never made the big time. Jimmy Trotman had a novel experience with bees. A swarm of bees settled on his signalbox door so that he could not get in or out in the orthodox manner. Each time he had to change the train staff, he had to climb in and out through the box window. This went on until Harry Somerton arrived for his shift. Harry was a beekeeper so he returned home for his equipment and all ended well.

Bletchley enginemen and guards did have some work during LMS days on the S & MJ line. There would have been special trains, but they had no booked daily workings; for no apparent reason they nicknamed it the Crab and Winkle line. When Northampton football team was playing at home on a Saturday, Bletchley would provide engine, stock and men for the Banbury to Northampton Excursion via Blisworth and the Crab and Winkle line.

It was three miles of open countryside to Brackley.

The ancient Municipal Borough of Brackley was near the home of the Deputy Chairman of the Buckinghamshire Railway Company. The Hon P. S. Pierrepoint lived at Evenly Hall and within a few days of the opening of the line he made his first public journey by rail to Brackley, which, although in Northamptonshire, is only just over the Bucks border. On alighting from the train he was received by 'tradesmen and other respectable inhabitants', who gave a hearty welcome, and he expressed his hopes for the prosperity of the town.

During the 1890s the railway was busy. A siding was installed alongside the single main line to accommodate material arriving to build the Great Central main line, which crossed this line by an overbridge barely a quarter of a mile east of the station. Much of the material was no doubt used for building the magnificent viaduct.

Brackley town could once boast of a thriving brewery which gave the railway considerable traffic. The brewery itself was well back from the railway sidings, a line was laid from it to the sidings and wagons were pushed down, arriving at right angles to the sidings; a turntable enabled them to be turned on to the siding rails, ready for the local goods engine to pick up and place for departure.

The Northamptonshire Farmers had a farm provenders' depot in the yard in later years.

The station had a water supply for engines, but it was a slow supply from a spring down the line. If too many engines stopped for water, the town supply could be switched on.

The Station Master's red and blue brick house was almost behind the iron tank and had a spacious garden backing onto an unattended graveyard.

The last Station Master, Mr Clare, lived in the house for several years after the station had closed. The last two signalmen were Arthur Marriott (the bookie's runner) and Sid Green.

In May 1950, a century after the station opened, Brackley had a Royal visit.

An all-Bletchley train crew brought the Royal train to Brackley. Two shiny Stanier Black Fives hauled the well polished Royal train from Euston with the King and Queen and Princess Margaret going to attend their first motor racing meeting at Silverstone.

The Royal train left the main line just south of Bletchley station via the Worcester Curve, now more appropriately called the chord line, and went onto the Oxford branch line.

Gradually the train gathered speed after passing Flettons Signalbox until it reached Verney Junction. A change of train staff at Buckingham, and it arrived punctually at Brackley. Timekeeping was spot on and with precision organisation all the dignitaries were waiting at the station. But it had been overlooked that Brackley's low platform would make too long a step down for the ailing King, and a humble box had to be hurriedly found.

Brackley Station settled down to ten more years of gradual decay, despite a brief return to youthfulness when the little olive green railcars breezed through to and from Banbury.

Fulwell & Westbury Station is just over two miles further on. The short single siding on the left and the station house at the rear are passed first. The road crossing gates stood between the house and the single platform, with a small ticket office and waiting room comprising the whole station. The station had a Station Master until 1930, but after that a solitary porter-cum-gatekeeper and ticket clerk were sufficient. The Buckinghamshire Railway Company did not see the need for a station here at first, and it did not open until August 1879 and made little difference to the working of the line; it was not a block post, just signals to protect the crossing gates. This was an advantage when the early turn porter overslept, for the train crew could let themselves through the gates and no one was the wiser. Only the village of Fulwell was visible from the station. In World War II Dolly became the porteress and lived in a row of cottages near the station. When Sid Green was on the station he had to cycle from Syresham, so a little late running was to be expected. Bert Kimble, during his spell as porter, kept chickens on waste ground near the station although he lived at Buckingham.

It is a four and a half mile journey to Buckingham, but within the first mile is Bacon House Crossing. The crossing gates are well back from the railway line and not protected by signals. The red brick railway house near the gates has been inhabited over the years by a permanent way man, with his wife generally having responsibility for the gates.

In 1848 Charles Whitehall of Gawcott in his poem *The Buckinghamshire Railway* gave a graphic description of the line's construction from Bacon's Wood to the junction with the Bletchley to Oxford line. Somewhere near Bacon House Siding grew the timber which helped to build the line.

'T'was Bacon's Wood, a place of note,
A favourite game preserve,
But the game was killed, the wood was felled
The Company for to serve'.

In the 1920s Farmer Treadwell had the farm at Bacon House Crossing and it was predominantly sheep that inhabited the fields. At least once a year Farmer Treadwell had a special train of 40 of 50 head of sheep from Hawick in Scotland. Because of the density of line traffic during weekdays, the sheep special was timed to arrive and be handled on a Sunday. This brought benefits to the signalmen at Buckingham and Brackley where Sunday was a split turn of duty. They normally booked on in the morning to deal with the first milk train then booked off, booking on again to deal with the last passenger.

In 1931 the sheep arrived as usual, but one load had a partition and some cattle for Farmer Treadwell too. This part load of cattle meant an extra charge, which Farmer Treadwell asked the Goods Agent at Northampton to overlook, as there was, after all, the same number of wagons. The Goods Agent insisted on the extra charge and the angry farmer threatened to have future consignments brought by road. The Goods Agent shrugged off this threat with confidence.

The next consignment of sheep from Scotland arrived in a large fleet of cattle lorries, and the Goods Agent's decision to overlook the part load of cattle came too late.

The local goods used to call at Bacon House siding to pick up or put off traffic, but gradually its need diminished. In 1958 Bacon House closed down as a public siding, just 50 years after its opening on 27 January 1908.

Before 1956 the next three miles or so to Buckingham would have been just fields of grass and grazing cattle as far as Buckingham Good Shed and sidings. In 1956 a diesel railcar experiment in single unit railcars between Buckingham and Banbury commenced. It was a valiant effort to save the line's passenger service and two single wooden platform stations were erected to serve the small villages nearby.

Water Stratford was near Bacon House siding and from the wooden platform, steps were made in the bank down to the road to the village. Radclive was nearer Buckingham, with the same type of platform near a little-used farm crossing and a platelayer's cottage. The farm crossing, or the grass field, was the passenger's route to the station. Ganger Jack Rawlings and his wife lived in the cottage.

The large black wooden goods shed and sidings were entered from the single line by a ground frame unlocked by the train staff. The brick station, nearly a quarter of a mile from its goods shed and siding, was pleasant, with neat flower beds.

There was a signalbox at the beginning of the down platform and a waiting shelter on the same side, matching the main building opposite. A second signalbox down near the goods shed and siding was dispensed with in the early years of this century and the station passing loop ran down as far as this signalbox, which was called Buckingham No 2.

The railway came in 1850 to Buckingham, a small market town, an ancient borough and once the county town, at a crossing near the source of the Great Ouse. This must have been an exciting time, but it did not inspire any large-scale expansion or prosperity. For 116 years it served the town. When the London and Birmingham Railway opened in 1838 through to Wolverton, 10 miles to the north east, a mail coach from Banbury ran daily through Buckingham to Wolverton, leaving Banbury at 7.0 am and returning from Wolverton at 2.15 pm.

At first Buckingham Station was just a small wooden station building on the Lenborough Road side of the line. Despite a Buckingham Borough Council minute in 1849 recording that the contract for Buckingham Station had been let to Mr Dunckley of Bletchley for £20,000, in 1854 the Council was still urging the railway company to build a 'new and sufficient station now that an excellent road has been formed at no expense to the company'. The station had a loop line for trains to pass, but at first only a solitary signal with an arm for each direction stood in the centre of the station. Soon after its opening, a poster on the platform encouraged emigration to New York via Liverpool.

The passenger fares were standard and there were many cheap excursions advertised in local newspapers. In 1851 an excursion train was run to the Great Exhibition in London and apparently many took advantage of the offer. A Buckingham baker sent 200 dozen Banbury Cakes by rail each week to the exhibition.

The first Station Master was Joseph Mayor. He was advertised in the 1850 directories along with the fact that omnibuses from the principal inns awaited all trains.

In 1869 E. F. Gravestock advertised his coal; and the price shows the advantage of rail transport, ranging from kitchen nuts at 12s per ton to Channel coal at 21s 6d. In the same year excursions to Euston cost 10s first class and 5s in a covered carriage; other excursions went to the Royal Show at Manchester and the Temperance Fête at the Crystal Palace. The excursion to Euston at Whitsuntide attracted 100 passengers. In 1879 a letter to the *Buckingham Express* complained of the mismanagement of the Banbury and Oxford lines; the reader demanded 'Is this arrangement likely to save the Company the loss (they state themselves) of £20,000 on the Banbury Branch?'

The line survived another 85 years; the Edwardian era saw the peak of passenger travel, when Buckingham Station could boast of a bookstall and a regular Thursday excursion to Euston allowed a late return, leaving Euston at 12.10 am and arriving at Buckingham at 1.50 am. One could also return from Euston by a through slip carriage detached at Bletchley and due at Buckingham at 5.39 pm. The White Hart Hotel looked to the railway for business and boasted that 'every train is met'.

The carriage of agricultural produce was of great importance to the town and surrounding villages; all the principal farmers had accounts for sending milk to Watford or London. The glories of Stowe had begun to fade before the railway reached Buckingham. The Marquis of Chandos, son of the second Duke of Buckingham, had as much enthusiasm for railways as his grandfather had hatred, and was Chairman of the LNWR from 1853 to 1861. According to J. K. Fowler in *Echoes of Old County Life,* the Marquis lost that position 'through the Liverpool and Manchester group thinking that he looked too much after minor details and failed to grasp more extended fields of operation afforded by the large manufacturing districts of the North of England'. Fowler had no doubts about the ability of the Marquis, and continues 'it redounds greatly to his credit that he forsaw the necessity of doubling the line of railway, and it was during his reign that the line of railway was laid down which has now culminated in four lines reaching Rugby. When the Duke first insisted upon laying down a third line, one of the leading engineers sneered at the idea "like the fifth wheel to a coach" he said it would be'.

The Marquis worked hard to restore the former prominence of Stowe. In 1861 he succeeded to the Dukedom, and had a railway built on his estate at Wootton: this later became a public railway, called the Brill Tramway.

From World War I the Buckingham goods depot had the traditional coal traffic and later two oil depots were situated in the yard. The Buckingham Agricultural Trading Association set up a sort of farmers' provender co-operative, which was later taken over by the Northampton Farmers. Goods were delivered in the surrounding villages and as small depots on other lines closed, so deliveries were made in a wide and sparsely populated area.

In 1921 the Stowe estate came up for sale and became a public school. Regular vacation specials ran between Buckingham and Euston, continuing until 1965, after the line was closed to ordinary passenger trains. The train usually had ten coaches and Buckingham Station platform was only of four coach length.

Signalman Harold Plant was chief gardener at Buckingham from World War II until the station closed, and took the station garden competition seriously.

In the four and a half miles to Verney Junction, Padbury is about half way. It took the people of Padbury nearly 28 years to convince the LNWR that a station was required. When it did open on 1 March 1878 there were scenes of rejoicing. The single platform and brick station had a small siding. In 1967 the rails were torn up.

Normal farming traffic for the siding was once quite heavy, but deteriorated in later years. The station was quiet throughout its existence, but once made brief national news in 1909.

Station Master Levi Ambler and his son, Porter Fred Ambler, were on duty, waiting for the local goods train. Fred Ambler's duty was to work the points while Guard Bates shunted wagons in the siding. About 12 low-sided wagons were being drawn out of the siding to place on the remainder of the train on the main line. Guard Bates decided to ride on the last wagon until it was over the points, then hand signal the driver back onto the train. When Driver Roberts came to a stand over the points, he jumped off to pick some violets on the bank. The driver and fireman were not on friendly terms and unknown to Roberts, fireman 'Cracker' Lines had already jumped off the opposite side because of an urgent call of nature. The regulator was probably not quite shut, or the waste water cocks badly blowing through, for the engine and wagons continued on their way with Guard Bates still in the rear wagon; Driver Roberts and his fireman ran panting behind, vainly trying to catch up with the runaway. Levi Ambler sent the alarm signal to Signalman Harry Harris at Buckingham. Guard Bates in the last wagon was not a young or active man, but he began the laborious task of climbing from wagon to wagon, reaching over the side to drop the long lever hand brakes, as he made his way towards the engine. When the train approached Buckingham, Harry Harris, concerned for the safety of the guard, laid the road straight through.

Old Tim, the checker, saw the train passing the goods shed and for a moment he wondered why the Brackley local goods was early, then realised there was neither driver or fireman, and saw the guard struggling from one wagon to the next.

The staff at Fulwell and Westbury were alerted, but the passenger had already left Brackley: to avoid a head-on collision the facing points to the siding were opened to the local goods train. But before the runaway reached Fulwell and inevitable disaster, it came gently to a halt. Bates knew the passenger was due so he quickly reversed the engine and set off back to Buckingham with all possible speed.

The evening newspaper placards in Euston Road informed the world of a 'Runaway Train in Buckinghamshire'. Guy Calthorpe, General Manager of the LNWR, saw the placards and was infuriated that this was his first knowledge of the incident. In the words of Jesse Ayres, signalman at Brackley in those days 'There was more bloody fuss about Guy Calthorpe not knowing about the matter before he saw the newspaper placards than there was about the runaway train itself'.

The newspapers proclaimed Guard Bates a hero but he modestly said 'I was only doing my duty'. His reward from grateful railway directors was a silver-mounted umbrella and a cheque for £20, with subsequent promotion to Station Master at Stonebridge Park. His colleagues commended him and inscribed their appreciation on a small plaque, accompanied by a walking stick. Both the driver and fireman were dismissed.

A station master was a luxury that branch line stations like Padbury had to forgo, but in 1942 it did have a Station Mistress. Mrs Bertha Allen, aged 38 and living with her husband and five children just across the road from the station, took on this temporary wartime job and remained until the station closed and she retired.

Platelayer Fred Aris walked this length of railway for many years. Each morning he caught the train at Padbury and with a large strap bag over one shoulder and a platelayer's long hammer on the other, alighted at Verney Junction and walked the track back to Fulwell and Westbury, a distance of nine miles. He had numerous snares laid and in his shoulder bag always carried a rabbit or two with his spare chair keys.

But it was when the line had completely closed down that Padbury station attained its crowning glory, when the Queen and the Duke of Edinburgh resided in the parish of Padbury for one night.

On 4 April 1966, some eighteen months after the passenger service was withdrawn, there was a Royal tour of North Bucks. The Queen and the Duke of Edinburgh visited Bletchley, Buckingham and Wolverton Stations. Out in the quiet Bucks countryside near Padbury, the Royal train stayed overnight, then punctually at 9.52 am next morning, quietly moved on to Buckingham to commence the Royal tour.

After the lines were lifted the stretch between Brackley and Cockley Brake was used by a local racehorse owner who let his horses stretch their legs on the straight course. Ganger Sammons reporting the fact, bringing in a small revenue for the Railway Board.

After passing Verney Junction Signalbox and giving up the single line train staff to the signalman as he leant out of his window, it was then two and a quarter miles on an up gradient to Winslow. There was little change in scenery as the line passed the clump of trees surrounding a lake at one entrance to Addington Park, a farm, then the large tarred goods shed and sidings on the down side before Winslow's pleasant brick station.

Winslow shared with Bicester the honour of being one of the main stations and centres of population between Bletchley and Oxford. It had a water column near the signalbox at the end of the down platform and another on the up platform. This was the only engine water column between Bletchley and Oxford and there since the railway apparently opened.

The local goods train would spend considerable time shunting at Winslow and it certainly would have had to shunt from the up main line to the down and vice versa, to let a passenger or through freight train go by. On the up side was a convenient long refuge siding, so when a freight train stopped for water and a passenger was close on its heels, it could be backed inside to let the more important train pass. During World War II many a train was backed into the refuge siding because Swanbourne Sidings or the main line was too congested.

Winslow Station had a good record of awards for a clean and tidy station and garden. Ernie Byford, the last porter on the station, managed to keep a little water mill turning near the up side platform.

The Station Master's house and garden, in the style of the station building, skirted the green forecourt, but undisguised and not far away was the familiar gas works. The station was lit by gas until the trains ceased to call.

The first Station Master, in 1850, was William Hazelgrove. The most enterprising Station Master, and perhaps the richest, was a Mr Horne, who was there for many years; in a New Year greetings message to all railway agents of the Railway Passengers Assurance Co (RPA) in 1922, he received congratulations for initiative in selling livestock insurance.

The best remembered and most colourful character among Winslow's Station Masters was George Brudenell. He was once SM at Swanbourne and lived in the station house, but in becoming the first SM to have Winslow and Swanbourne stations under his command, he moved to Winslow Station House. He wore a high fly collar that touched his ears and gave him the habit of a slight twitch of the neck. To add to his dignity, he wore a frock tailed coat and it was said that when Mr Brudenell discarded his bowler for his straw hat, it was official summer time in Winslow. If any of his few staff wanted to enter his office, he insisted on the due respect of a courteous knock on the door.

The coming of the railway in 1850 made considerable impact on the town, resulting in extension to the north, including the inevitable Railway Inn and Station Road.

The station's strangest building was a quarter of a mile along the line in the down side. The tank house was a gaunt, square, brick building at the bottom of the embankment, next to the necessary stream. The water tank was on top of the building and supplied water to the station water columns. The building housed not only the steam pumps but also the railwayman who attended them.

The tank house remained, redundant, until after the passenger service was withdrawn, then it disappeared unceremoniously into a pile of rubbish. It had an inhabitant until early in 1951, when the old lady who lived alone under spartan conditons appears to have fallen into the stream and drowned. Fanny Gayton, a widow of a platelayer, was 79 when she died, and had made the tank house her home for about 40 years. The only pathway to her home was alongside the line from the station. It was a quarter of a mile from the station, then 26 steps down the embankment, across a little wooden bridge over the stream and up 34 steps to her door. The old lady was well-known to the passing train crews whose only contact was a touch on the whistle and a waved exchange of greetings, but many a handy knob of coal rolled off the engine for her to pick up.

In the days when the tank and pumps were fully operational, Bletchley engine cleaners periodically used to have the task of scaling and cleaning silt out of the tank after it had been specially drained. Fanny Gayton would give the lads a glass of home-made wine, except for the occasion when cleaner Buddy Burdett hit the chimney which protruded from the side of the tank and soot fell on the old lady's washing.

During World War II, the outer edge of a wartime aerodrome on the opposite side of the line made her nearest neighbour a Wellington Bomber that often stood just off the main runway with its nose pointing to the sky.

The approach to Swanbourne is two miles of up gradient. The house and station are all one building with a good proportion of wood and red and blue bricks. Before the station closed, it had its own little siding with a goods shed the size of a garden shed, which is exactly what it eventually became.

The signalman had his block instruments in the booking office so he could fulfil the duties of booking clerk. The signal levers were out on the platform and, if the single siding or the crossover road between the up and down main line were being used, away he would go to unlock the points with an annett key.

On the north side of the station, well and truly obscured by a heavy belt of trees, is Horwood House. When the Buckinghamshire Railway Company was surveying the land to build the new railway, the Dauncy family occupied the house, which was then known as the Old Rectory. They had strong objections to the proposed line running near their house and had sufficient influence to get the plans altered. The railway was constructed a few yards further south, giving a curve to the line and moving the new station out of the parish of Horwood. It seems that the station buildings were in Swanbourne and the platforms and siding partly in the parishes of Mursley and Horwood. The station served all three villages, the nearest perhaps being Swanbourne, which was described in the 1854 Directory of Bucks as 'Having a neat station about 1½ miles from the village'.

According to the *Bedford Times* of 11 May 1850, Swanbourne was not a station when the line opened: it did not have to wait long, but when it did open it only dealt with passengers.

This particular shortcoming of the station was noted by Sir Harry Verney in a long letter, critical of the LNWR administration of the Bucks line, written in 1853 and intended for the Chairman of the LNWR, Lord Chandos. The station did handle milk and butter traffic and despite its isolation, was not a forgotten station without business.

The Dauncy's kept a herd of pedigree jersey cows before the end of the last century and used daily to send butter in special containers made of stone or slate to London by train for Queen Victoria and her household. The Dauncys left the house in 1911.

The little siding saw over 80 years of activity in the loading of hay and transport of horses. Rothschilds used to send horses by rail to Swanbourne for a day's hunting with Whaddon Chase. One or two horse boxes were detached from the down passenger in the morning. In the early inter-war years, as many as six different coal merchants used the yard. In those years many milk carts could be seen at that station unloading their milk churns for the fast milk train for London, which used to arrive at 8.50 am daily.

Considerable expertise was needed for the quick and easy handling of milk churns. Old railwaymen can remember how Ernie Dickens, before becoming a railwayman, was so expert in rolling the empty 17-gallon milk churns that he could get them at sufficient speed and balance to let them roll on their own. With perhaps over 40 17-gallon churns daily for Willesden and Watford alone, it is obvious they had to be marshalled in the vans for speedy unloading and to arrive at the correct destination. When Guard George Felce got into dispute with the farmers about the loading of the vans, they made sure he had a churn with a loose lid to lift from the low platform into the van. George just happened to have on a new uniform, to receive a milky christening.

The present resident of the station house, eight years after the last passenger alighted at the station, is as rural as many of his predecessors. Reg Waters, a permanent-way man, has the Bucks dialect that adds colour to his stories of incidents on the line. As late as 1959 he had a little horse and trap to make excursions to the shops at Winslow, and as his yard and siding together had a farm-like appearance, the pony was useful for other carting jobs. Now the station is closed and the siding lifted; the former goods shed is a garden shed. With many relics there, and in the house, Reg's collection would make many a railway enthusiast envious.

A fire put Swanbourne into the news in the early years of the Bucks Line. The story and consequences of the fire are told by J. Fowler in *Echoes of Old County Life*. Near to Swanbourne station, approaching from Winslow, can be seen a not unattractive pond which was dug out by the railway builders to form the embankment. Close by stands a farm that was once nearer to the line than it is today. Moco Farm, spelt in various ways over the years, was owned by Sir Thomas F. Freemantle, who later became Lord Cottesloe. When the farm caught fire and burnt to the ground, it was alleged that sparks from one particular engine passing by had caused the fire and Sir Thomas claimed damages against the LNWR. Apparently, for some years, farms throughout England had been damaged by fire caused by such sparks and considerable sums of money had been paid by the offending railway company without recourse to legal action. In this case the LNWR decided to make a test case to decide once and for all the legal question. The point should be settled as to whether a railway company was answerable for damages from its engines when working on the line if the company had taken every precaution that human skill could accomplish.

The jury gave a verdict for the plaintiff. It appears that the author of this little story was well acquainted with railway officials of those days and he records that some weeks after the case was heard, the Superintendent said, in conversation with the Locomotive Superintendent of the Line, that the evidence of the railway's own witnesses had been absolutely correct and it was quite impossible for that engine to have set fire to any place, 'But' he added 'the buildings were burnt by the sparks of another of our engines which had gone up the line a few minutes before the one in question, and this fact I knew perfectly, and so did the driver of the engines all through the trial'.

J. Fowler aptly sums up by saying, 'The jury's verdict, as so often is the case, though wrong on the actual strict facts of the case before them, was just in substance'. Perhaps a less kindly way of summing up would be to say 'Cheats never prosper'.

There were two dignified railwaymen connected with Swanbourne who were for many years, before and during World War II, characters destined to be remembered as the last of a breed. Fred Walters was a signalman at Swanbourne and lived in the station house until he retired. Always smartly dressed and wearing a high fly collar and bow tie, he performed his station duties, which also included booking office work and portering, with impeccable efficiency and dignity, until he retired and went to live in the village in an equally dignified retirement.

Very early in World War II, Swanbourne Sidings were opened. Why the sidings were called Swanbourne is not clear. They were a mile or more from the station and not only out of sight, but not even in the parish of Swanbourne. Nevertheless the name of Swanbourne was known to freight train crews all over the LMS system.

There were ten marshalling roads and three reception roads in Swanbourne sidings, built to relieve Bletchley of growing wartime traffic. Freight trains arrived and were remarshalled. Empty wagon trains departed for Toton or Overseal, coal went to Sandy where it was transferred to the LNER, coal to Corby Iron Works, and bricks came in from Newton Longville and Lambs Siding not far away and made up for a London or Oxford train. The local goods trains for Brackley, Banbury and Oxford, departed with their tariff van attached, while regular trip trains from Bletchley arrived throughout the day and night.

The sidings were situated on the up side, with a shunting neck and entrance near the ARP type signalbox. All shunting was done on a steep down gradient, with great financial reward for the breakdown gang over the nearly 25 years of its existence. When the sidings first opened, broken couplings were as common as the rabbits in the spinney across the line.

Shunter Rice Roberts saw some wagons he was shunting break loose and run down an empty road. He called to his under shunter to pin down the brakes, only to find that he was otherwise engaged. Rice jumped onto a 'cycle that was standing handy and tore hell-for-leather along the half-moon shaped path around the edge of the yard, only to stop, puffing and panting to watch the wagons hit the stops; the leading wagon was smashed to pieces, the stop block coming to rest in the field behind and several other wagons derailed. After the breakdown train had cleared up the mess, Ganger Ernie Dickens asked Rice if he could put half a dozen sleepers onto the verandah of a goods brake van that was standing handy, apparently already attached to the shunting engine, and take them down to the bottom end of the yard to renew some damaged sleepers at the scene of the mishap. The sleepers were loaded onto the verandahs at both ends of the brake van and away went the engine propelling the van. As the driver approached the required spot he braked, and it was then that he discovered the engine and brake van were not coupled together. The shunters ran after the runaway van and tried to climb on to apply the hand brake, only to find the sleepers were blocking both doors. The van careered away, the sand drag slightly checked its flight, but the stops had not yet been replaced from the last mishap and straight over the rail ends into the fields below went van and sleepers.

Shunting on a steep down gradient was the cause of numerous incidents such as these, but the real worry was if the exit points at the Bletchley end of the yard were open.

The sidings' only signalwoman, Mrs Murray, did on one occasion hear what she thought was a train gradually creeping away on a reception road. An engine was just departing and as soon as it was clear of the points, she closed them. Several bolster wagons loaded with steel rumbled their way up the sand drag and once again the sand slowed them down, but down went the stops and one loaded bolster wagon was partly in the field.

The stops at the end of the shunting neck were on an up gradient so they were as safe as houses, or so everyone thought. So apparently safe was it that a brick platelayer's cabin was built behind the stop block. At one period when extra permanent way men were required in the area, a coach fully equipped for them to live in was placed on these stops and there they lived quite unmolested for some time. Then early one dark morning, driver Sid Adams was waiting to leave with the Banbury goods. His engine was tender leading as it stood attached to the train in a reception road, which is proabably how the fireman came to look out the wrong side of the engine and say to his driver 'dummy off'. The dwarf signal was off alright, but it was not for going out main line. Straight up the shunting neck went the Banbury goods, but in the dark Sid Adams thought he was out on the main line. Too late the mistake was discovered, and braking was of no use. The coach and wagon behind it were concertinaed together, the stop block behind was pushed so far back that the platelayers' cabin became a pile of rubbish. The metal frame and sole bars of the coach and wagon were all that was fit to be taken away. Luckily the coach had no residents at the time and very little damage was done to the engine. Sid Adams and his mate were only shaken up.

It was a down gradient to Bletchley and, to continue the journey eastwards, over the junction across the four main line onto No 7 platform — the departure for Bedford and Cambridge.

The three miles approach to Bletchley was marred in scenery by the tall brick chimneys and the huge clay pit of the London Brick Company works at Newton Longville. A small signalbox on the opposite side of the line to the sidings was a block post when the local trip engine was placing empty wagons or drawing loads up the steep access from the kiln road. The signalbox was so near to a roadway that when it was not in use, the local kids took advantage to smash a window.

A row of cottages was built by Read and Andrews in the Newton Road, near the Works entrance, in 1910; marked in the brickwork are the words 'Model Workmen's Cottages'.

In the last few yards into Bletchley another brickworks with more high chimneys came in 1934. Fletton's Brickyard was on the same side of the line as the London Brick Company and also had a siding from the Oxford line. A part of this siding was on the site of the old 'Worcester Curve' which was built by the LNWR to make a direct facing connection from the main line from Euston to the Oxford branch and was used from 1854 to 1861 to run trains direct from Euston to Worcester.

With the construction of an Ordnance Depot at Bicester, the Worcester Curve, after 80 years of neglect, was rebuilt and opened for freight traffic on 31 August 1942. Bletchley No 1 controlled the points on the main line about half a mile south of the station and Flettons Signalbox controlled its connection with the Oxford line. When a loop line from Flettons Box to Bletchley No 1 branch line home signal was constructed, Flettons became an important little 24 hour a day box.

Signalwomen took command of the box during World War II and were still in charge when the bulldozers arrived to make the embankment for the coming flyover. In about 1960 the old Flettons Box disappeared to make way for the embankment, and a new ARP type signalbox took its place not far away on the opposite side of the line. The ladies continued in the new box, but when the power box took over the signalling in 1965, Flettons bit the dust forever. Housing estates were fast filling in the landscape where horses of the Grange had once grazed; the landscape now presents a vastly different view to the rail traveller, but after 1968 there were no travellers to note the change.

This particular journey continued by passing Bletchley No 1 branch line home signal, immediately prior to passing over the junction. The carriage shed on the up side and the reed and shrubbery-encircled water of the Newfoundout opposite, were the last lineside features before the journey across the Buckinghamshire lines was over.

ABOVE LEFT: Sid Sellers at Verney; RIGHT: Station Master and staff at Verney; BELOW LEFT: Mrs Bertha Allen at Padbury — Station Master, Booking Office Clerk, Porter, Ticket Collector, and here billposter, at Padbury. CENTRE: Buckingham Goods Yard staff before World War II, and BELOW: guard, porter, signalman and driver with the new railcar at Buckingham Station in 1956. (R. & H. Chapman)

ABOVE: Buckingham Station in the 19th century. LEFT: Dolly Chapman and Fred Kimble — Fulwell and Westbury Station staff during World War II. RIGHT: Banbury Merton Street Station in May 1951. BELOW: The Banbury Railcar gives up the staff at Verney Junction.

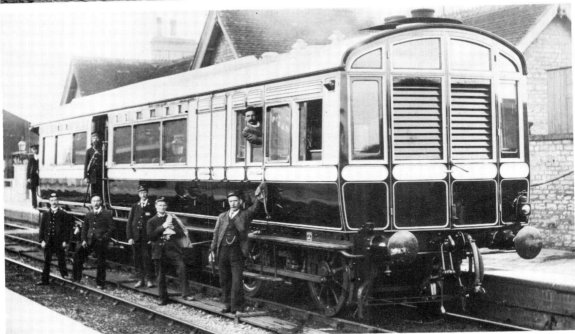

ABOVE LEFT: Claydon Station; RIGHT: Marsh Gibbon and Poundon
Station Master's House; CENTRE LEFT: Launton Station; RIGHT:
Alfred Paget, a small single wheeler of the Problem class on Oxford
Turntable, c1896; BELOW: The Steam Railcar No 3 in Bicester Station,
1905, Allen Wells in the driving compartment.

EAST FOR CAMBRIDGE

The Cambridge train in the platform faced north, but gradually turned east on departure to stop at Fenny Stratford, just one mile distant. There were sidings on either side after Bletchley, then double track until Bedford. Before entering the two staggered platforms, Watling Street passed overhead, then a view of the Tudor style half-timbered station house. Opposite, a small siding was sheltered by trees. The signalbox was on one side of the road crossing gates before the platforms and a company house opposite at the entrance to the goods sidings. One road in the siding ran alongside Messrs Rowlands Timber Yard.

The Watling Street overbridge at Fenny Station has vastly altered since 1846 when the road had to be raised 6 feet 8 inches to allow the new railway to go underneath. It became known locally as Stag Bridge when a stag, chased by Lord Southampton's staghounds, jumped off it onto the railway line where, lying with a broken back, its throat was cut by John Higgs.

A tragedy occurred at the road crossing gates on 7 December 1925 when six residents of the nearby village of Woburn Sands were killed, seven seriously injured, three dying later.

Approaching closed crossing gates and signalled train, was a Ford converted one-tonner bus filled with people returning from a rally at the Freeman Memorial Chapel. The approaching train was the 6.15 pm passenger from Cambridge, headed by a 2-4-0 Jumbo class ex-LNWR engine No 170 named *General*. Driver Tommy Bazeley and fireman George Atkins were on the engine on this dark wintry evening and all signals were in the clear position.

The 'bus made no attempt to stop (it was later suggested the brakes had failed) and crashed right through the gates. Signalman W. Souster could only watch helplessly as the train hit the 'bus squarely on its side. Police, railway workers and the breakdown train were immediately called. An ambulance class at Bletchley Railway Coffee Tavern rushed to assist.

The early arrivals found an overturned 'bus, terribly mutilated bodies and others badly injured. Rev Nightingale's head was reported to have been lying just outside the signalbox. The bonnet of the 'bus, which belonged to Mr Rice, a garage proprietor of Woburn Sands, lay some 50 or 60 yards along the line. One coach of the train had been derailed.

A special train took the injured to Bedford Hospital and the dead were taken into the goods yard to await identification.

A Ministry of Transport enquiry was held, conducted by Major Hall. His report found that the accident was more likely an error of judgement than a mechanical failure of the 'bus, the driver of which was well aware of the crossing position and the closed gates. The accident attracted considerable attention as an early example of a fatal road-rail collision.

Near the level crossing gates were the Grand Union Canal and then the River Ouzel and nearer still once stood an old pump house, with a lengthy front garden stretching down to the crossing. Many years ago it was the home of Harry Barden. He maintained the pump beneath the house, which pumped water from the canal to the loco shed tank at Bletchley.

Harry was a scouts drummer until he was quite old, and a quiet, mysterious man. He would often disappear, always dressed in black. There was speculation about his comings and goings, but it was not until he died that it emerged that he was the official cross carrier at executions.

The canal bridge gave passengers a good view of the Fenny Stratford Canal lock and lock house. The canal enjoyed some 45 years of uninterrupted trade in Fenny Stratford before the Bedford - Bletchley line was opened, and so the Grand Junction Canal Company, as it then was, did not make life easy for its new and successful competitor.

Before building the bridge over the canal, penalties were laid on the Railway Company to 'make and maintain and keep in perfect repair a good and substantial bridge over the said canal ....and the soffit of such bridge shall be at least ten feet above top water level and the arch over the towing path shall be at least eight feet above the said top water level'.

Also laid down was a further penalty that if work on the bridge caused any obstruction impeding the passage of boats or other vessels on the canal, the Railway Company should pay the Canal Company £10 for every hour of such obstruction. If this continued beyond 72 consecutive hours or was occasioned by any wilful act on the part of servants or persons employed by the Railway Company, the Company would have to pay £30 an hour; in default of payment, the Canal Company could sue for recovery of money plus costs.

A mile from Fenny was Bow Brickhill Halt, the first of seven halts all opened in 1905 between Bletchley and Bedford. Also in 1905 a daily steam rail motor service started which stopped at the existing stations, while the railcar's revolutionary design enabled the halt platforms to be at rail level. The single vehicle was provided with steps at the central vestibule entrance. These were swung to the side when in motion and were so arranged that when in use, a valve in the main vacuum brake pipe was held open; thus the driver could not create the required vacuum until the steps were folded back and locked in position.

The service lasted until 1926, apart from World War I when it was briefly suspended. When this odd little vehicle stopped running, it also ceased between Oxford and Bicester. The latter service never restarted, but between Bletchley and Bedford it resumed in the form of a Push and Pull service. The little steam engine remained at one end of a vestibule coach with vacuum controlled steps and the driver, being able to drive from either end, was able to sally up and down the line. Not all the halts have survived; Kempston and Elstow, Wootton Broadmead and Husborne Crawley were all temporarily closed in 1941, but never again proved necessary and were finally officially closed in 1949.

It was not until Diesel Railcars without vacuum controlled steps came that the platforms were raised to normal level.

Woburn Sands, two miles distant, was the stop for Woburn and Woburn Abbey, seat of the Duke of Bedford. A small brickyard on the right just before the station, was closed some years before World War II and is now overgrown, the clay pit filled with water. But this does not spoil the entry into a station described in 1885 simply as 'picturesque' by Williams in *Our Iron Roads*. This cannot be said of the gasometer on the opposite side of the line. When the station was built, it was really in the unfortunately named hamlet of Hogsty End. It is said that the Duke did not like the undignified name and was instrumental in having it re-named Woburn Sands.

The various Dukes and Duchesses were important passengers and had their own saloon which was attached to an up train from Cambridge; at Bletchley it was placed on the rear of an express, whatever their destination, which often seems to have been Scotland. During World War I, the Duchess was frequently seen at Bletchley station, supervising the transfer of wounded officers from arriving ambulance trains onto her own road motors which took them to her hospital at Woburn. The same Duchess preferred flying. The Duke would arrive in a Rolls Royce at Bletchley Station and he and his servants would go by train to Scotland; the Duchess would take to the air. She learned to fly at the age of 61.

There were level crossing gates at the end of the platforms and a signalbox near the gates. In the mid 1930s a wheel in the box made it easier to operate these busy gates. Sidings on either side of the main line were visited daily by the local goods train. One side held coal for the gasworks and local merchants.

On Tuesday 30 August 1910 signalman Steele stopped a runaway engine from Bletchley. This was no dramatic feat for the little DX class engine was already slowing down through loss of steam pressure. It was probably more exciting for the signalmen and a crossing keeper inbetween.

Driver Joe Marshall and Fireman Frank Pacey arrived in No 4 platform (later renumbered No 7) with the local goods train from the Oxford Branch. Frank Pacey jumped off the engine to uncouple it from the train, as usual. Seeing the guard walking towards him, Frank went to meet him to get the train work sheet. Quite unknown to him, Joe Marshall decided to walk along the other side of the train to pick up the same work sheet.

Whether the regulator had been left slightly open or it was blowing through, is not known. The engine gently but with gathering speed moved away and was soon merrily puffing its way towards Bedford. The signalmen and the gatekeeper at Bow Brickhill were all alerted that the rebellious little DX was on its way, and the gates at Fenny, Bow Brickhill and Woburn Sands were opened.

When the engine left Bletchley, its fire was getting low because it was due to go on the shed and be disposed. By the time it passed Bow Brickhill the steam pressure was getting low too, and was on the point of giving up when Signalman Steele climbed on the footplate at Woburn Sands. Another engine came from Bletchley to drag home the exhausted truant. Joe Marshall was suspended for two weeks and reduced to shed labourer, while Frank was put back on cleaning for six months. Both men were eventually reinstated.

Two halts intervened in the two and threequarter miles to Ridgmont station. Within a mile at Aspley Guise, the crossing keeper's house has an exceptionally attractive design.

Just before the Halt an avenue of trees and overgrown bushes can be seen stretching away from the upside line towards the denser trees of the Duke's estates, outlining the route of a former siding laid and used during World War I. Canadian Sidings, as it was called, transported timber used mainly for pit props and felled by prisoners of war who were supervised by Canadian soldiers.

Husborne Crawley, a mile or so along the line, can hardly be traced as a former Halt. Once there were crossing gates, signals, a house for the crossing keeper and the low level platform. A small petrol dump with rail access was built nearby during World War II, and remnants of this can still be seen, plus a roadside petrol station to mark the spot. The rest has completely disappeared and the quiet road over the line became a concrete bridge carrying traffic from the M1 motorway, which crosses the line nearer to Ridgmont Station.

Ridgmont Station has long lost any claim to beauty, although once, with its Tudor style house, it must have been picturesque. The signalman's instruments were in the booking office, but the signal levers were out in the open, as, of course, were the manually operated gates. A signalbox was demolished in the early 1930s and the new arrangement in the booking office saved one porter. Near to the gates was the unmistakable entrance to Ridgmont Brickworks.

For over a century the Bedford Arms has faced the station, across the road. One Duke of Bedford thought an inn was needed, and there was no problem, since he owned nearly all local land.

None can have been as reluctant a landlord as Mr Francis, who kept the pub purely because he needed its stables. His main business was as a coal merchant and the wagon loads of coal in the station yard were conveniently near his horses and carts.

There were drawbacks to his commercial venture. He was not in the best of health and every time a customer called for a pint it was a journey down the steps below the taproom to draw the pint, then back up the steps again. If one of the station staff went across for a midday pint, Mr Francis would reluctantly descend to get it; if he asked for a second pint, his host would most likely reply 'Ain't one enough, a lot of beer wont do you any good?'

One railwayman went across for a quick pint and the landlord took the order without enthusiasm, then disappeared. When he returned he was carrying a basin of bread and milk which he placed in front of the waiting railwayman. 'Here you are,' he said, 'that'll do you more good than beer.'

Ridgmont was once a quiet little station, well away from the village centre; the station staff received a small extra remuneration for daily emptying the GPO letter box in the station street side wall and forwarding the contents to Bletchley.

There was a daily service into the brickworks with empty wagons for setting in the kiln roads and for withdrawing the loads. A shunter was attached to the station for shunting the brickyard with the assistance of the train guard.

Guard Ron Webb was shunting the kiln roads on one occasion when he failed to notice a lorry back into one of the gaps along the long kiln road. Fortunately the driver was not in the cab, but Ron had to explain how a large brick lorry looked like the proverbial pancake.

Nearly two miles through Brogborough Cutting, after a steep down gradient, was Lidlington Station. The cutting caused problems for the contractors in 1845.

The first of the big clay pits lie well back from the downside line and then, passing through the level crossing gates at Lidlington, it is a quarter of a mile or so before Marston crossing, now an automatic barrier. After more chimneys and an ugly, disused claypit, came Millbrook Station and crossing gates.

Lidlington Station is near the village. A crossing keeper is now the only staff, with an outside frame for his signal levers that only protect the gates. Until the turn of the century, Lidlington was a block post with a station master and signalman among the staff. There was a crossover road between the two lines, but it was the only station on the Oxford, Banbury and Cambridge branch lines (apart from halts) without a siding.

The heavy gradient from Millbrook to Ridgmont was the cause of anxious moments for many train crews; it led to the death of at least one man and was costly in derailments and smashed wagons, but it probably put some money in the pockets of the breakdown gang. On this steep bank there were many incidents of heavily loaded trains almost reaching Ridgmont and over the summit, only to find that the load was just too heavy for the engine, or that the damp rail made the engine slip when the top was in sight; it was then that help was needed at the rear or front of the train. Assistance was not always quickly available; more often than not it was a case of splitting the train, going forward with the first half, backing it into Ridgmont sidings and then returning for the rear half.

A tragedy in 1929 did produce some positive action to eliminate at least some of the dangers of this steep gradient. On a Monday night in October, Driver Sam Cutler was coaxing his old 'D' class engine up the bank with a heavy brick train. The top was almost in sight. Guard Bert Coley was in the brake van at the rear and with him was Guard Frank Burridge, travelling home after shunting duties in Forders Brick Sidings. Both were aware because of the slow speed that the engine was having difficulty with the heavy load on the 1 in 129 gradient, when a slight reverse movement was felt. Soon they discovered they were moving backwards and the train was divided, the rear portion running away down the bank. Frank Burridge jumped out and with a brake stick tried to pin down as many wagon brakes as possible. As Bert Coley screwed on the hand brake in desperation he could hear the wheels skidding, but the wagons gradually gathered speed.

The porter at Lidlington saw the skidding wheels and realised what was happening. The gates were placed against road traffic and he telephoned Millbrook to suggest the train be diverted over the crossover road or into a siding. But it was too late.

The gates at Marston were open to rail traffic, as it was then a small byroad, the brickyard not being there at that time. Approaching Millbrook was the up goods from Cambridge and Driver Arthur Hankins and Fireman John Scott on the engine were quite oblivious of the danger. Then Arthur saw the three red tail lights coming towards him and tried to reverse his engine, but in vain.

Arthur Hankins was thrown out of the cab, over a hedge and into a field. John Scott was not so fortunate; he was pinned down by the heavy tender doors and died almost immediately. Guard Coley hung on desperately, tugging vainly at the handbrake until he saw the engine, then he jumped. Debris and bricks were piled high over the crippled engine. Rugby breakdown train had to be called, as Bletchley breakdown with its hand crane could not handle a mishap of this size.

At the inquest in the Morteyne Arms the Coroner said no one was to blame; in fact, he said, everyone did their job well. The jury gave a verdict of accidental death, with a rider that the train was overloaded and should have been reduced, which was obvious.

In a belated but wise move, the railway management fitted trap points on the up line at various intervals between Millbrook and Ridgmont, so that any future runaways would be derailed. The heavy brick trains would also have a Bank engine at the rear from the starting point at Forders Sidings to Ridgmont.

Many hair-raising incidents still occurred, but the trap points did no doubt prevent another tragic accident. In the first year of World War II a brick train was chugging slowly but surely up the bank and had almost made it. The old 'D' itself had just reached the summit, when the draw bar pin between engine and tender is said to have broken. Whatever it was that did break, the train and the tender only went careering back down the bank. Jack Jones, the guard in the rear, screwed on his handbrake in desperation, but down it continued until the trap points checked its runaway flight and off the line went the train; out in the field the brake van came to rest, mangled under tons of bricks and scattered broken wagons. Jack Jones hung on to his handbrake until the last moment and somehow crawled out of it all alive.

This was during blackout hours and the driver and fireman suddenly found themselves with only a narrow footplate to stand upon, a blackout sheet around their necks and a tender disappearing down the bank. How they fared in throwing out the fire under the circumstances can only be imagined.

Millbrook has had three names since it opened in 1846, but does not seem to be near the centre of any of the three. It was first named 'Marston,' then renamed 'Ampthill (Marston)' about 1850. It was not until 1877 that it was altered to 'Millbrook for Ampthill' and finally became 'Millbrook' in 1910. The Morteyne Arms is the station's nearest neighbour and had no doubt been reasonably prosperous in the days when horsedrawn vehicles were in common use. It did not maintain appeal in the motor car age. It was large, with little to commend it architecturally and now looks even less attractive as an ice cream storage depot.

The signalman is now the only station staff. He pulls his signal levers in the open signal frame and manually operates the gates, then disappears into his little brick cabin.

But Millbrook has not always had this dejected look. The 1930s was the peak of brick traffic along the branch line and the clerical work involved in the movement of bricks by rail from Marston, the London Brick Company and Eastwood yards, was performed at Millbrook Station. Station Master John Harris had five clerks and used to say that his ambition was to transport 500 wagon loads of bricks daily. He never quite achieved it

Millbrook also had its own siding on both sides of the station for coal merchants, horse dock and goods shed. There was always work for the local goods train.

It is just over a mile to Stewartby Halt. Over the years vast clay pits have developed on either side of the line. In Stewartby, the works of the London Brick Company, the largest in the country, hem in the railway as it passes through the centre.

Stewartby Halt was named Wootton Pillinge when it opened in 1905. When the brickyard enlarged and the old Forders Company disappeared, a Brick Company village sprang up. The village took the name of Stewartby, after Malcolm Stewart, Chairman of the LBC. In 1928 it was decided to add the word 'change for Stewartby' below the name of Wootton Pillinge; in about 1935 it became Stewartby.

The kiln roads on either side of the line have seen busy times. They were regularly drawn and set, the yard itself was utilised to make up the trains for various places and shunting went on for most of the day and night. With the increase in the road motor vehicle fleet of the LBC, activity in the yard decreased and many of the kiln roads disappeared. The post-war railway service left much to be desired. Many railwaymen believed that the supposed shortage of wagons and the damage to bricks during shunting hastened the decline in the carriage of bricks by rail. In 1974 a mini-freightliner depot opened in the yard and raised hopes for brick traffic.

The yard was busy during World War II, although less bricks were produced. Part of the works became an Army tank repair depot, utilising rail transport.

The all-timber signalbox controlling the sidings and main line has always carried the name of Forders Sidings, despite the change in works ownership. Jack Dilley was a wartime signalman in Forders Box and, quite unofficially, kept a gun in the box; this was not for spies or any such unlikely event, but purely to poke out of the door for a pot shot at a pheasant, should one come within range of his box, and no one of consequence was around.

Wootton Broadmead crossing gates and the site of the halt are near the Forders sidings exit points for Bedford and Cambridge. The halt was temporarily closed in 1941 and got the final seal for closure in 1949. The lone crossing house of two-tone bricks lasted for about another 20 years before it was pulled down, leaving the keeper a little wooden hut.

Kempston Hardwicke is less than a mile farther on and still retains its house for the crossing keeper. The halt has signals to protect the gates and the status of being the last stop before Bedford. Eastwoods Brickyard is near this crossing, but has long lost its siding and signalbox.

There is a two mile stretch of straight railway to Cow Bridge, which carries the Midland main line over this branch, and then a gentle curve into Bedford. Along this seemingly level stretch it seems odd to see trap points on the up road. There is no history of derailing runaway trains. In fact it seems that many train crews have forgotten their existence. But many years ago one driver did get a sharp reminder of their existence and was derailed.

What was once the last halt before reaching Bedford is now only identified by the house near Cow Bridge. Kempston and Elstow closed in 1941, officially and finally closing in 1949.

The last mile into Bedford is now a built-up lineside with factories and houses until within a few hundred yards of the station. In these last few yards the branch line from the Bedford Midland Station to Hitchin passes directly across and on the level of this line, one of the few junctions of this type in the country, which came in 1857 when the Leicester-Hitchin line opened and became part of the Midland main line into London.

The line opened on Thursday 7 May 1857. Regular passenger traffic started on the following day and until February 1859 all trains used the LNWR station. This was a time-consuming operation, for the Hitchin line trains reversing movements had to be made to get into the station. On that date the Leicester-Hitchin line opened its own new station near Cox Pit Lane, (as the western end of Midland Road was then known).

At this time the Bedford LNWR station was on the site of the later St John's Goods Depot. It was not until 1862 that the LNWR had a new station, enabling the line to be extended through to Cambridge.

That brief period of using one station was, in the view of influential people, sound economics, and they continued to urge only one station. In May 1861, when construction of the extension to Cambridge commenced, the Mayor of Bedford headed a petition urging the two railway companies again to consider a joint station.

Over 100 years later, the Cambridge extension track ripped up and gone forever, there is still controversy about the need and the economics of one station for Bedford.

Only the Bedford to Bletchley line served the town when a Mr S. Sidney took a trip down the line and mentioned it in his book *Ride on Railways* in 1851. Of Bedford, he wrote rather contemptuously that it had been 'pauperised by the number and wealth of its charities'.

There is no evidence that its charities pauperised the town, which certainly had some enterprising inhabitants. Their enterprise caused the Bedford-Bletchley line to be built, with considerable advantages to the town. The extension of the line through to Cambridge by 1862 was again due to the persistence of its wealthier men.

When the extension to Cambridge was opened in 1862, there were many doubts as to its ability to yield a fair return to its shareholders. There was certainly very little population between Bedford and Cambridge.

The *Bedford Times* appears to have had little doubt, about the future prosperity, and saw great potential in the fact that the line ran through the heart of country famed for its agricultural and garden produce: here top quality crops were raised in abundant quantity and their most profitable markets would be in the populous and wealthy coal and iron districts of Birmingham and South Staffordshire. There would also be the transit of cheap coal and manure which would increase the productivity of the soil.

The agricultural traffic did flourish with benefits to the country as a whole. In two World Wars the line was a national asset. Passenger traffic was mainly east to west, travellers and village people going shopping in the larger towns of Bedford or Cambridge. There was no denying that the Bedford-Bletchley section was always better patronised by passengers.

Bedford Station handled a lot of them, but when the new Midland main line opened to passengers in 1868, London travellers from Bedford took the quicker route.

This new route crossed over the LNWR at Cow Bridge and the Hitchin line was reduced in status from main route to branch.

The sidings developed with a brewery alongside and all the usual coal traders' private patches. An exchange siding with the Midland became well utilised. The loco shed closed down soon after the amalgamation of the railways on 1 January 1923, but the coal stage continued in use for coaling the small tank engine that worked the Bletchley-Bedford Push and Pull passenger train. This service came into operation when the Steam Rail Motor was withdrawn in 1926. From then until 1959, when the Diesel Railcars took over, the Bedford Motor, as it was called, ran up and down with regular Bedford depot crews. The guards knew the passengers, collected the fares of those who embarked at the Halts and made it a friendly, happy-go-lucky line.

A great asset of the station was, and still is, the angle formed by the two up and down direction leads into the sidings and towards the connecting road into the Bedford Midland Yard. The area now looks like waste ground, apart from the signalbox in one corner, but the loco shed, pump house and coal stage were once here. Traces of the water supply hole can still be seen and where the Hitchin line also passed through near the signalbox.

The angle was useful for turning tender engines working into Forders Sidings and requiring to turn for return working. When the angle was taken out on the former Wolverton-Newport Pagnell line, the Bedford angle was found to be handy for turning coaches of the Royal Train.

The only serious collision at Bedford took place in 1875 where the Hitchin line crosses the

LNWR. Enquiries into collisions by the Board of Trade brought to light defects in equipment, breaches of regulations or lapses in human judgement. In this case the dilatory signalling at Bedford left much to be desired, but it was the engine driver's moment of forgetfulness that landed him in court, charged with manslaughter.

On 12 March Driver John Perkins and his Fireman, Edwin Leadbeater, booked on at 6.30 am and prepared their engine No 1886 for the 7.15 am passenger from Bedford to Bletchley. The engine went and stood, attached to its five carriage train, including two brake carriages, in the platform awaiting the guard's whistle to start.

The starting signal was on the Bletchley side of the Hitchin line, opposite the signalman's cabin, so if a train moved up to and stopped in obedience to the signal, it would foul the Hitchin line. It became a custom, therefore, for drivers not to depart from the station if the signal was at danger. This was obviously an unsatisfactory arrangement, but it seems to have worked without mishap for 18 years. However, it does seem that some drivers, having received the guard's signal to start, would draw up towards the crossing if the signal was on, and stop short.

On this particular Friday morning, Signalman Bishop accepted the 6.45 am Midland train from Hitchin, lowering the signals for that train and leaving the LNWR signal on. Within a few seconds of the Hitchin train being accepted, Bedford Station Master, Mr Warren, rang his bell to indicate the Bletchley train could depart. Guard Henry Clarke blew his whistle at exactly 7.15 am and Driver John Perkins, perhaps absent mindedly, set off towards his signal. The fireman was immediately engaged in shovelling coal into the firebox, while the driver was peering through the smoke and steam as it beat down and around the engine's front end. He was having difficulty in seeing the signal, which was invariably off because the LNWR train usually went before the Midland train, which was due at a similar time. Upon hearing the LNWR engine approaching the crossing, Signalman Bishop ran out with a red flag but was unable to attract the attention of the driver or guard.

Driver Perkins saw the Midland train. He made a quick decision to open the regulator wide in an all-out effort to clear the Midland train. He managed to get his engine and three carriages clear, but the fourth carriage was caught squarely by the Midland engine. The carriage was crushed to a heap of firewood, covering a pile of bricks that was once the signalman's cabin. The Midland engine left the rails and buried its wheels deep into the ground.

The three injured occupants of the demolished carriage were Rev William Sprott, a United Presbyterian Minister from Glasgow, Charles Wilkins and Mrs Stimson, both of Bedford. The unfortunate Rev Sprott died of his injuries.

The inquest was held in the Bedford Infirmary before Dr Prior, the Borough Coroner. A Capt Tyler came to Bedford to conduct an enquiry into the accident on behalf of the Board of Trade at the LNWR station, and offered advice.

The jury returned a verdict of manslaughter against John Perkins. They were of the opinion that the signal arrangements at the North Western station were defective and antiquated and that alterations should be made as suggested by Capt Tyler, to be approved by the Board of Trade.

In July 1875 John Perkins stood trial at the Bedford Summer Assizes. Again railwaymen gave evidence and rules and regulations were quoted. The signalling left much to be desired. Richard Bishop had eight signals to attend to, none were locked and all were in different places and not worked from his cabin. He too had once suggested the starting signal should be near the water tank at the end of the platform.

The Judge in his summing up said that the arrangements of the two companies could be faulty. If they were very faulty, and the jury might think this, it could tell against the prisoner. The more danger there was owing to faulty arrangements, the more necessity for greater caution. It was absolutely certain that he should have stopped short of the crossing until the Midland train had passed and his signal lowered. There was no doubt that Mr Sprott came to his death from the collision and if the prisoner was responsible for that, in point of law the jury must find him guilty. He said one could not help thinking that great credit was due to the prisoner for what he did, and there could be no doubt that if the clocks at the two stations from which the trains started had been correct, the accident would not have happened, but he (Perkins) would have been about a minute ahead of the Midland train. He concluded that to be short of perfectionist is not criminal, but there may be that amount of difference and recklessness which makes a man a proper subject for punishment.

The Jury found John Perkins guilty of negligence, but recommended mercy.

The Judge said he was sorry for the prisoner, but he could not see how the jury could possibly return any other verdict; as the jury recommended mercy he had the power to impose a fine of £20 instead of sending John Perkins to prison. A coincidence about the mishap was that the drivers of both trains had the name of John Perkins.

The LNWR dismissed John Perkins from the service, but they lost no time in resiting the starting signal.

A century later the Hitchin line was no longer to be seen, but those who dared to use this route and change trains for the former Midland main line, faced a mile walk across town.

During World War II it was a familiar sight to see servicemen and women alight at Bedford St Johns and, with a kit bag on the shoulder, set off across town for the Midland station. For many years RAF men used this route for their establishment at Cardington. The Air Raid Defence Balloon attached to the high mast was a familiar sight to all trains.

This high mast and the large hangar nearby was once the home of the ill-fated R101 Airship. It was down the Bletchley-Bedford line that the wreath-covered engine on the funeral train travelled, carrying to a common grave at Cardington the bodies of those who perished in the crash at Beauvais Forest, France, on 5 October 1930.

It is eight and a half miles of single line to Sandy. The double track from Bedford station merges into a single line immediately before crossing the Ouse. Here at Bedford No 2 Signalbox the signalman leans over a veranda holding the Train Staff — the key to the trains's safe passage to Willington. Bedford to Sandy remained single line from 1862 until the line ceased to exist: the Electric Train Staff was brought in on this section of line, and for the first time on the LNWR, in 1888 and was safely worked throughout its lifetime.

Within a mile or so, the wartime signalbox and passing loop of Goldington once stood. It served its purpose on the heavily congested line during World Wars I and II. Only flat grasslands surrounded the box, with the Ouse not far away until Willington was reached. One inconspicuous and seldom used single siding did intervene. It bore the inappropriate name of Summer House Siding, and it had a few trees, some slimy water and a smell which gave it away as a sewage outlet.

Willington Station was alongside the River Ouse, and was the only station to be erected after the Bedford to Cambridge line opened in 1862. The small sidings were opened for goods traffic in 1896, but it was not until 1903 that a passenger station was erected, and then, probably because of its late arrival, it never progressed beyond wooden up and down platforms and wooden station buildings. There was no sturdy brick-built house for the Station Master as at other stations. Halfway along the down platform the signalbox stood all alone with its back near to the river and facing the station buildings opposite.

Part time market gardening was a recognised sideline for most of the railwaymen who worked along this stretch of line. One of these was Signalman Bert Watt, who had a considerable amount of ground, including a handy patch alongside the railway line. During

World War II, when the big professional growers were unable lawfully to grow flowers, Bert specialised in growing Statice, an everlasting flower, in large quantities. He sold it in an organised fashion through an agent at Manchester and his much-demanded product travelled by rail, so he was able personally to see to its safe departure. There were also many good, if small, customers amongst railwaymen, especially as in these cases transport was free.

It was a steady up gradient, partly through a cutting, before the line reached Blunham, passing through the sidings on the north side of the line before reaching the station on the down line. From the far side of the station, at some elevation above the village, the interested traveller could see and appreciate the once tranquil Blunham. In those few yards from the station, the line crossed the River Ivel on a lattice girder bridge which could better be appreciated from below. From this spot in 1862 the *Bedford Times* reporting on the first passenger train, described the bridge as 'a lattice girder of 60 feet span with three spans of brick arches at an elevation of 20 feet from the road. The scene from the bridge is the most charming bit upon the line'. One hundred years later this decription is still accurate.

The trim brick station buildings with the Station Master's house and his tidy garden, faced the white Railway Tavern on the opposite side of the wide forecourt entrance to the station and goods sidings. A road passed by and under the railway and across that road, still looking in the same direction, was Blunham Park. Immediately below the traveller, the River Ivel ran with quickening speed around the old bone meal manufacturing mill on the other side of the railway. A single siding on an extraordinarily steep gradient led into the Mill.

The main station sidings dealt with the local coal merchants' wagons and vegetables were its main traffic.

The stretch to Sandy was a little more than four miles, with Girtford sidings in the first mile. A small sidings for goods traffic only was opened on 6 July 1863 and became a busy vegetable traffic yard. By the end of World War II, yard traffic had lessened and the yard was closed down on 1 November 1950. A short wooden platform alongside the main line had a short life as a halt for a few passenger trains. It opened on 1 January 1938 and a few Bletchley to Bedford passenger trains were extended through to Sandy, stopping at Girtford Halt. This does not seem to have been a successful experiment and it closed on 17 November 1940.

A few hundred yards further was the World War II connecting curve on to the LNER main line from Kings Cross. It was a double line and generally referred to as the Tempsford to Blunham connecting line when it was opened on 13 September 1940. A signalbox with single line instruments was near the south junction and was called Sandy LNER Junction. It was built in conjunction with the connecting curve at Shepherds Furze Farm near Claydon on the Oxford branch as a wartime diversionary route. The connection gave good service during the war, but thereafter the curve was left to virtually decay.

It was a steady up gradient from this point until the LNER main line was crossed obliquely by an overbridge, then the train glided gently down into Sandy Station.

In 1862 this overbridge was described in the *Bedford Times* as a 'lattice bridge of three spans and a girder of 240 feet and covering all the spans'. The LNWR station was described by the same newspaper as a 'handsome station eclipsing its neighbour and on a level with it'. The stations are best described as being joined together. The LNWR down platform held the Station Master's house and waiting rooms. The up side was an island platform with the former Great Northern up line on the other side, going in the opposite direction to the LNWR up line. The Great Northern had a Station Master's house and other station buildings on the extreme side platform to the LNWR.

The station ceased to have two station masters in 1917. The Great Northern SM took over, but there were separate signalmen and signalboxes. The LNWR No 1 Signalbox was situated at the east end of the island platform, ideal for handing out the Train Staff to the driver of a train from Cambridge. There was also a Sandy No 2 Box for working the points and signals at the eastern end of the yard; this was generally switched in as required. There was an exchange siding between the two railways, but they also had their separate goods sheds and yards for local coal traders.

From 1862 Sandy was ideally situated for speedy rail transport of its market gardening produce to the industrial Midlands, but somehow it never became renowned for passenger train connections.

Potton is almost four miles on and the new double line makes a sweeping curve away from the brief parallel run with the former Great Northern main line. On this curving up gradient can be seen the high ground on the left where once the gallant Sir William Peel had his home between long adventurous periods in other parts of the world. His restless temperament found vent at home in the construction of a Lilliputian railway here for his tenants and the people of Potton.

When the Bedford and Cambridge Railway purchased the Lilliput line for £20,000, considerable alterations were made to it; the line was relaid, the embankment raised and the cuttings lowered, but a steep curved gradient remained until the end of its day. The little engine shed for the line lasted much longer. Prior to entering Potton Station on the right, the tiny brick engine shed looking as if it is in the middle of a field, still looks down on the vastly changed scene.

While *Shannon,* which once had its home in the shed, is having a long retirement with VIP treatment, the little shed is still used, doing the everyday job of storing sacks of fertilizer and market gardening implements.

So steep is the gradient between Sandy and Potton that trap points are fitted and on the opposite line — the up road — there is a long check on the curve and a permanent speed restriction.

A World War II petrol storage sidings on the down side near this curve was hardly in the ideal position. Sandy Heath, as it was named, had a small signalbox which was a block post, although built purely for these sidings.

The Germans made attempts at bombing Sandy Heath during the war. There was one near miss when a bomb damaged the foundations of the signalbox and the signal rodding.

It was a continual up gradient and curve until just before Potton, then a seemingly compact little station immediately passing under a road bridge. The up side platform was certainly well filled with buildings. The Station Master's house had a wide bay window right on the platform, there were a waiting room and offices adjoining the house and part of this platform had a glass canopy over it. Potton No 1 Signalbox was on the platform and a passengers' overbridge to the down platform was the only one of its kind from Bletchley to Cambridge. The station shared with Bedford the distinction of having the only two engine water columns on this line. The column bag ran straight from a tank at the west end of the up platform, and underneath the tank the steam pumping engine was once housed.

The maintenance of this pump was the responsibility of the loco foreman at Bletchley and the pump house keeper was also a loco department employee. The well where water was pumped into the tank was situated in the Station Master's garden, right next to his cherry tree. When maintenance work was performed in the pump house or well, it was the job of the Bletchley boilersmith, Fred Pratt. Fred recalls often going to Potton in cherry time, when the bearded Station Master would never leave the side of his cherry tree. At that time the pump house was less well guarded and was an attractive place in which to work. The keeper, Bill Chamberlain, always kept the inside walls decorated with pots of growing flowers. The only trouble was that it looked rather depressing in winter time because the pots were reclaimed old chamber pots that the people of Potton had dumped in the disused sand pit not far from the station.

Before the railway came Potton enjoyed some importance when the wheat and barley of Cambridgeshire and Essex paused here en route for the malt kilns of Hertfordshire. This endowed Potton with many large granaries and warehouses.

The railway brought further and lasting prosperity. It became a busy yard with a large goods shed and a further signalbox — Potton No 2 — which controlled the exit and entrance to the yard on the east side of the station. A photograph of the yard in 1905 shows horses and carts congesting the yard like a busy London market. Apart from sending train-loads of vegetables to London, for many years it received two train-loads of London manure, much from Regents Park Zoo.

An early reference to traffic at Potton and Sandy stations said that in the year 1900 no fewer than 200 tons of potatoes were forwarded from these two stations in one day during the week ending 11 July. This appears to have been a record for that year.

In the two and a half miles of near level railway to Gamlingay, a small signalbox and siding called Belle Vue once intervened. During World War II this was a prisoner of war camp. It is not certain what the wagons that were placed in the sidings contained. It had once been called Denis's Sidings, with pigs and fowl giving an untidy look to an area where a lake edged with grass and reeds provided a charming local fishing spot. The lake was a legacy of a small brick or tile works of long ago.

Gamlingay Station is built at the southern end of the village and the Station Master's house and signalbox are all on the station platforms. The character of the station was enhanced by the tidy Station Master's garden and the pub in the wide forecourt entrance to the station and goods yard. The goods shed and sidings approaching the station on the down side handled mainly market gardening produce.

Railway timetables have always been a favourite target for the critic. The following letter appeared in the *Cambridge Chronicle and University Journal* only a month after the station opened in 1862:-

'Gamlingay — The New Station

The station at this place opened on Friday, 1 August for merchandise and coal. We wish the passenger trains had been so timed as to cause less delay at Sandy to travellers to and from stations on the Great Northern Railway, especially by the Parliamentary trains on the GNR entailing a loss of two hours. As it is many persons are obliged to proceed to Sandy as if there was no railway here, which is a great inconvenience to the inhabitants and a loss to the Bedford and Cambridge Railway Company.'

The electric telegraph was still in working order in Gamligay Box during World War II, but only the old signalmen could use it efficiently, because the telephone had long since taken over. When first installed at Gamlingay the telephone was one of the wonders of the world, and one old signalman gave it credit for powers it did not possess. He had the regular habit of taking a quick drink in the pub just outside the station at the same quiet time each day. Signalmen's Inspector Lambourne knew about this, so he used the new-fangled telephone at Sandy to call Gamlingay, just as the old signalman returned from the pub. 'You are back from the pub early today', said Inspector Lambourne, making a noise as if he could smell foul breath. 'I have only had one sir, I have only had one Sir', retorted the surprised signalman, convinced that this weird instrument had enabled the Inspector to watch him and smell his breath.

Looking towards Old North Road there was a straight long upward climb of 1 in 110 to the summit; on the down side was a platelayer's house and a large spinney opposite marked the beginning of a down-hill run and an opportunity to make up lost time.

Open fertile-looking land stretched all the way to Old North Road Station, nearly five miles away. It was known as Haley Wood Bank to footplate men.

The house on the bank summit was visible a long way back and often thankfully reached when the train was heavy and steam pressure low. This was a lonely, isolated place with a farm crossing gate nearby. Usually a platelayer lived in the house and his wife would be responsible for the crossing gate.

It did have various tenants in its time, but always had poor amenities and no drinking water. The local goods train used to make a daily delivery of water in cans.

One driver used to have the water cans on the engine and personally carry them right into the house. He was the essence of helpfulness but the time taken to deliver the cans safely lengthened remarkably. When the lady's husband came home unexpectedly with a gun and angrily threatened the driver, the water cans henceforth became the responsibility of the guard. It was not the same lady in residence when driver Ern Orchard made a regular delivery of a woman's magazine called *The Sunday Circle*.

On this bank during World War II a German Messershmidt 109 attacked a freight engine, bullets raking along the railway fence. At the 33 mile post the engine stopped and Driver Ernie Church and Fireman Jimmy Woodward hid underneath; then they realised a bullet had penetrated about ¾ of an inch into the right leading tender horn plate. The train eventually arrived at Cambridge all in one piece.

From here the track went down into the Old North Road. The bridge carries the Great North Road over the railway and the station took its name from the road. In 1862 it was described as situated between the villages of Caxton and Wimpole. In coaching days Caxton was a prosperous little posting town and when the railway came it was a mere three mile walk to the station.

The Station Master's house was in the station buildings on the platform, as was the signalbox. A siding and quite spacious goods shed were all on the down side of the station, while the up side possessed a little shelter on the platform and plenty of open fields behind.

There were three platelayer's cottages near the station and before World War I, when they were thatched, the platelayers used to take it in turn to stand outside the cottages and watch the 10.55 pm goods from Cambridge get well by the station. This was always a well loaded train and the non-superheated Cauliflower on the front was generally hammered to get over the top of Haley Wood bank so that sparks as big as walnuts would come from the chimney.

It was a little more than five miles of continual down gradient to Lords Bridge and there was a marked absence of houses or other buildings all the way. A public siding connecting with the up road by trailing points was the only intervention on this rural stretch of line. Only the goods attached or detached at Toft Siding. It was opened as a public siding for goods traffic on 24 July 1911. On 1 August 1912 it was renamed Toft and Kingston, but railwaymen called it just Toft Siding.

There was seldom any sign of life as trains for Cambridge passed, but it did have its prosperous period. The sidings held only a dozen wagons and once sugar beet and hay loading was its main traffic.

After World War II, timber was stored in the siding. Driver Bob Hancock looked out as his train passed the siding and saw the timber beginning to burn. He stopped at Lords Bridge and informed the signalman, who in turn called out the Fire Brigade. On his way back to Cambridge he saw the firemen working their hoses. What Bob did not see was that the hose pipe was across the rails from a ditch on the opposite side of the line. As the engine and train passed over the hose pipe he looked back to see the triumphal water arch turn into an ignominious trickle.

Lords Bridge was a station without a village, Barton being the nearest, but it did have passengers and it certainly had a bridge, although this was an ordinary bridge over the Cambridge line. Driver Jimmy Harding remembered Lords Bridge throughout his career. He never failed to get a laugh when he told the story of the man who stood on the parapet of this bridge, intending to make the final severance with this world by jumping under Jimmy's train as it tore down the bank to Cambridge. No doubt as he balanced on the edge he closed his eyes and contemplated eternity. As the engine rushed under the bridge he jumped, but he picked the wrong line and instead of meeting his maker, he got two broken legs.

The Station Master's house and signalbox graced the down platform and a large goods shed and sidings were all on the same side of the station and did quite a lot of business. During World War II a large ammunition dump with several sidings was built on the opposite side of the main line, and Lords Bridge became important.

Porter Signalman George Rayner found the soldiers stationed just across the line useful and no doubt they were also obliged to George. He had four fruit farms and, because of the wartime labour shortage, employed soldiers to pick his fruit. George had long found it sound economics to work for the railway and employ others to work on his fruit farms.

George was once asked how many trees he actually possessed. 'I don't know' he said, 'but the last farm I bought has 1,495 trees.'

Despite the odd bomb coming out of the end of a wagon through rough shunting, there was no recorded catastrophe at Lords Bridge. Perhaps the nearest thing to serious accident was when the Cambridge Mails crashed into the platform during World War II, without serious injuries. The war was long over before ammunition ceased to arrive and depart.

It was 5¼ miles to Cambridge and an easy almost level run to the end of this cross-country jaunt. Passing over the river Cam, the line took a bold sweep to run in a northerly direction and gradually converge with the LNER main line from Liverpool Street, London.

In 1862 this journey was described as passing over the Cam by a bridge of nine 28 ft spans and passing the fine woods of Trumpington before the towers and spires of Cambridge come into view, then around that same bold sweep into the station of the Eastern Counties Railway. In the same year the Eastern Counties amalgamated with four smaller companies and became the Great Eastern.

While it was the Great Eastern, running powers were exercised by the LNWR with trains from Oxford and Bletchley, the Great Northern regularly used it for trains from Kings Cross via Hitchin, and the Midland drove a single line into it from Kettering by way of Huntingdon.

The long platform had a scissor crossing at about the centre of the platform line to let up trains into the south end and the down trains into the north end. The platform line was long enough, at 1,254 feet, to accommodate two full length trains standing tail to tail. Even if the trains were going in the same direction, the scissors enabled the rear one to move away, passing the train in front.

When the platform was built it was the longest railway platform in existence, but Perth took over that distinction. In Great Eastern days, Cambridge was the key to the eastern counties from the north and west of England and also from a good deal of the south. From Wales and the west of England the eastern counties were conveniently reached by way of the Oxford to Cambridge branch lines.

In the period just before World War I, only at Carlisle could so many of the old companies' engines and trains be seen together at one station. The chocolate and white coaches of the LNWR were gradually changed to red after 1923, when it became the LMS. The only company colour of the main trunk routes to the north not to be found at Cambridge was the Great Central's.

In those days all trains stopped at Cambridge except for race specials, which consisted of first class coaches. There were no fewer than eight race meetings in the season, and the handling of horse boxes was an important part of Cambridge traffic. During the time of the 'classic' races at Newmarket, valuable horses passed through Cambridge and over on to the LNWR branch lines.

The long single platform had great advantages, making subways, overbridges and level crossings unnecessary. There were bay lines at the south end of the station for the LNWR and the Great Northern, while a bay at the north end was for the Midland and the Great Eastern's own requirements.

Each Company had its own goods yard. Before converging with the Great Eastern, the LNWR had its yard with a loco shed, turntable and other small servicing amenities alongside its own down line. One signalbox controlled the entrance to the yard and loco and the branch line from Lords Bridge.

The loco shed was now used for timber storage, having been officially closed since 2 October 1935, although it continued to function as normal and engines were stabled in the shed for some time after this, until they were eventually integrated into the working of the Eastern loco shed. But Bletchley men still took their engines on to their loco yard to turn and fill the tender or tank with water, or perhaps clean the fire and throw coal forward into the tender before returning to Bletchley. If coal was required, they went on to the eastern shed and quickly coaled up under the giant coal hopper. This move always pleased the loco shift foreman at Bletchley. A large tender filled to capacity with coal would enable the engine to by-pass the hand coaling stage at Bletchley, and perhaps be re-diagrammed to Cambridge next day to repeat the process.

During the war the shed suited the Home Guard for a rifle range, but the turntable deteriorated through lack of maintenance. Engines had to be exactly balanced and many enginemen strained themselves until they were blue in the face pushing the table and wondering if they would ever make it. Many a driver got half way round and stuck, then in desperation he would move the engine one inch to try and balance it. Trying to move an engine one inch with only two inches to rail end, is courting trouble. More than once the inch was exceeded and a driver was stuck with an engine 'on the bloody floor'. It was then that the breakdown had to be called and a 'please explain' answered.

Being a small shed with a capacity of about four engines and enginemen, it did not warrant a foreman. Bletchley loco was its parent shed and a driver was just designated Driver in Charge. He was paid a few extra shillings, but just performed his normal duties. Driver 'Jammy' Tarbox held this position for a number of years before the shed closed.

For many years it had been the practice to send young engine cleaners from Bletchley to Cambridge as well as Oxford and Banbury: there they lodged for a week or more and not only cleaned engines, but more often did general labouring work in the shed.

LIST OF LEVEL CROSSINGS.

At the following level crossings provided with gates, but not block posts, drivers must give one whistle when one mile from crossing, or, if there is a station within a mile from the crossing, the whistle must be given when starting.

*—These are block posts during certain hours. When the signal box is switched out, the crossing is operated as a non-block post.

Crossing.	Situated between	Whether there are indicators.	Whether there are signals.	Whether gates are interlocked with the signals.	Remarks.
Potton	Potton and Sandy	D No	No	No	D— Bell only.
Sandy	Sandy and Blunham	Yes	Yes	No	
Girtford	„ „	Yes	Yes	Yes	
Goldington	Willington and Bedford	No	No	No	
Kempston Hardwick	Bedford and Millbrook	Yes	Yes	Yes	
Wootton Broadmead	„ „	Yes	No	No	
Green Lane	„ „	Yes	Yes	Yes	
*Millbrook	At station	Yes	Yes	No	
Marston	Millbrook and Lidlington	Yes	Yes	Yes	
Lidlington	At station	Yes	Yes	No	
Husborne Crawley	Ridgmont and Woburn Sands	Yes	No	No	
Berry Lane	„ „	Yes	No	No	
Aspley Guise	„ „	Yes	No	No	
Bow Brickhill	Woburn Sands and Fenny Stratf'd	Yes	Yes	No	
Watereaton	Oxford and Islip	No	No	No	
Islip	„ „	Yes	E Yes	Yes	
Oddington	Islip and Bicester	No	No	No	
Langford Lane	„ „	No	No	No	
Tubbs Lane	Bicester and Launton	No	No	No	
Launton Crossing	„ „	No	No	No	
*Launton	Launton Station	Yes	Yes	No	
*Claydon	Claydon Station	Yes	Yes	No	
Woodstock Road	Yarnton Junction and Oxford Rd.	No	Yes	No	Down home signal only
Warkworth	Banbury and Farthinghoe	No	No	No	
Fulwell and Westbury	Fulwell and Buckingham	Yes	Yes	Yes	
Bacon's House	„ „	Yes	No	No	
Radclive	„ „	No	No	No	

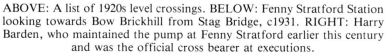

ABOVE: A list of 1920s level crossings. BELOW: Fenny Stratford Station looking towards Bow Brickhill from Stag Bridge, c1931. RIGHT: Harry Barden, who maintained the pump at Fenny Stratford earlier this century and was the official cross bearer at executions.

LEFT: Bow Brickhill Crossing with its keeper, Wally Oxford in the 1950s; RIGHT: Aspley Guise Halt, 1905, and BELOW: Woburn Sands Station, c1880.

ABOVE: Lidlington Station, c1860. BELOW: The *Bedford Times* coach
passed away in 1846:

There is an innate feeling clings
Around this mortal clay;
A fondness for immortal things,
That will not wear away.

INSET: Wootton Underwood Broadmead Crossing, 1960s.

ABOVE: Bedford St John's Station, c1873 with an Allan 2-2-2: CENTRE: a Prince of Wales class locomotive hauls a freight train from Sandy on the single line to Blunham in 1935; BELOW: a two cylinder Stanier tank No 2600 leaves Sandy in 1937.

ABOVE: A Special Passenger Guaranteed Excursion passes Sandy No 2
Signalbox bound for Cambridge in the 1950s; CENTRE: chaos at Berry
Lane Crossing, c1962; BELOW: an ex-LNWR Cauliflower 0-6-0 Class 2F
No 8439 passing Trumpington in 1932.

BRANCH LINES

When the Bedford to Bletchley line opened, the branch line passenger service provided rail communication for the county town of Bedfordshire to London and the north. But even then it was visualised that it would eventually be a cross-country route. In 1862 when the line was extended to Cambridge, Bedford had an alternative rail route into London. The branch lines from Oxford and Banbury to Cambridge were a cross-country service with intermediate stations catering for village people.

In 1846 the Bedford line commenced with five trains each way daily and two on Sundays: a similar service to that put in on the Oxford and Banbury branches when they opened in 1850-1851. In those early years the Bedford line must have had its ups and downs with calls for economy, for the timetable for 1851 shows four trains each way and only one train each way on Sunday morning. In 1859-60 there were nine passenger trains between Bletchley and Oxford, four of which ran to and from Handborough, branching off at the new junction near the Banbury turnpike road about two miles from Oxford. Of these four trains, two up and two down, the fastest trains were the up trains from Handborough which took 55 minutes for the 32 miles 49 chains to Bletchley, while the non-stop run between Bletchley and Euston took 70 minutes, making a total running time of two hours five minutes.

An 1867 timetable of the Oxford and Banbury branches shows seven trains departing from Bletchley. Of these, four appeared to divide at Winslow with one portion going to Banbury and the other to Oxford. Return trains from Oxford were six, with similiar arrangements for connecting the trains together at Winslow. On Sundays two trains departed from Bletchley, one for Banbury and one for Oxford, with the same number returning. There was no station at Verney Junction until the following year, which accounts for the dividing at Winslow. Marsh Gibbon, Padbury and Fulwell and Westbury did not yet have stations. At its opening in 1862 the Bedford-Cambridge line was jubilantly advertised at Cambridge as giving a service by 'Direct Route to and from the West and North of England via the London and North Western'. There were five trains each way between Bedford and Cambridge, with a Sunday service, although there was only one train between Bedford and Bletchley each way on Sunday and six daily. The Bedford-Cambridge Railway Company's timetables showed not only the miles between their own stations, but between other stations where connections could be made at Bletchley: Liverpool, Manchester and Birmingham were shown, but not the very long distance stations such as Aberdeen, Perth and Dublin, presumably because they were not on the LNWR system. The timetables also gave the class of travel on trains advertised between Cambridge and Bedford, the fare between stations, including the Parliamentary train fares, but not the fares beyond Liverpool and Manchester. Tourists' tickets were also advertised over the same routes, to such places as Windermere, and Aberystwith. To ensure that passengers had no doubts about departure times, it was clearly advertised that London Time was kept at all stations.

In 1883 there were five trains each way between Bletchley and Oxford, with one train each way on a Sunday and average running time of 1 hour and 15 minutes. Between Bletchley and Banbury there were six trains daily with five returning from Banbury. On Sunday there was only one train to Banbury and back, but there was a further one to Buckingham and return. The first three daily trains to Oxford were also the Banbury trains. They divided at Verney Junction which had been opened 15 years earlier.

The Bletchley-Cambridge line supplied a daily five trains each way, but two extra trains between Bletchley and Bedford gave that section of line a better service than the rest of the branch lines, something which it always maintained. First and second class travel were advertised. A Sunday service gave one train to Bletchley in the morning and return in the evening.

Students of the two Universities were respected travellers who descended upon the railway stations at vacation times. According to the Railway Travel Monthly the busiest time at Oxford's two stations in the pre-war period were the days preceding 15 January, 10 April, 25 May, and 10 October, and the days after 30 March, 24 May, 6 July and 17 December, at which time over 30,000 students arrived and departed by rail. This routine lasted well into the mid-war years, with special trains. The *Railway Travel Monthly* thought the most distinguishing feature of these busy days at Oxford was the marked absence of fond relatives.

The 19th century trains on the branch lines had gradually improved in comfort during their 50-odd years of life. Open carriages were replaced by ones that at least kept out the wind and rain. Carriages heated by iron hot water bottles distributed by station staff were luxury, compared to the open carriages and Parliamentary trains of the railway's early days.

The locomotives had changed in size and ability, but on these cross-country lines it was the top express engines of earlier years, now superseded by bigger and more powerful engines on the main line, that came to spend their declining years.

In 1905 came the first real change in passenger service with the introduction of two independent passenger services between Bletchley and Bedford and between Oxford and Bicester with steam Rail Motor Cars. A number of ground level platforms were placed at the nearest accessible place to villages along the line, and a conductor on the train issued tickets at these halts.

This was luxury travel as well as bringing the train much nearer to the smaller villages and farms. The passenger compartments were heated by a steam storage system of long heaters fixed under grids, which ran alongside the compartments. The seats for 48 passengers were double and reversible, covered in closely woven rattan and with sufficient space to make them comfortable and roomy.

There were drawbacks to these little craft, although they were welcomed by the passengers. Fitters detested lack of accessibility to parts. Should a car have to be turned on a turntable, several men had to stand on one end of the table to even out the weight. They were also restricted to draw only one vehicle on the rear if a horsebox was needed to be taken to the main stations on their route. An additonal passenger vehicle could not be attached without the authority of the Superintendent of the Line.

The obvious development from the Rail Motor Car was the motor train — an engine adapted to push or pull a vestibule coach with vacuum controlled steps, which did not have the same maintenance problems, and was capable of taking four vehicles such as horse boxes or cattle vans on the rear.

The General Instruction for working these trains gave a description of the Rail Motor Car, as a vehicle with a self-contained non-detachable engine capable of being driven from either end. The motor train was a small train consisting of a detachable engine and one or more coaches capable of being driven from the coach end.

These two independent services continued until 1926, except for a spell during the war when they ceased for economic reasons; then the Rail Motor Cars were withdrawn. This was the end of the Oxford-Bicester service and the halts just gradually disappeared. The Bedford-Bletchley service continued with a motor train worked by Bedford Midland men, the engine being serviced and stabled on the Midland Loco Depot. The LNWR loco shed had now been closed for a few years, but the ashpit and coal stage were used during the day by the Bedford Motor engine.

During the life of the steam motor cars and the Bedford Motor, the normal through passenger services across the branch lines were giving quite a good regular service, but of course, not stopping at the halts.

In 1910 there were 29 daily departures in the direction of Oxford. These included the Banbury trains, and a Steam Motor Car departed for Buckingham at 1.20 am on Fridays only, for people living in the villages between Bletchley and Buckingham, who had taken advantage of the cheap late night return from Euston. Of the passenger trains from Oxford, three went through to Cambridge without the need for passengers to change at Bletchley and with limited stops from Oxford, and took only 45 minutes to reach Bletchley. Departures in the Cambridge direction were 14 with 14 arrivals, but this included the six steam motor cars to Bedford and return.

There was no great change in the passenger services during the inter-war years. In 1931 the 10.45 am and the 3.15 pm departures from Oxford were regarded as expresses to Cambridge, stopping at principal stations only. The 10.45 am was allowed 42 minutes to Bletchley with one stop at Bicester, while the 3.15 pm was allowed 50 minutes, making two stops, Bicester and Winslow. There were nine departures from Bletchley to Oxford and eight from Oxford. Of these seventeen, nine were all stations and the remainder stopped only at the principal stations. The slow trains were allowed 63 to 66 minutes to stop at nine stations. The 4.20 pm from Bletchley was allowed 48 minutes to stop at two stations from Oxford.

In 1932 an unusual experiment with a pneumatic-tyred petrol driven railcar between Bletchley and Oxford was certainly the first non-steam unit to run on the branch lines.

The railcar travelled under its own power from the Michelin Works at Chateau-Terrand to Dunkirk where it was shipped to Tilbury and then taken on a special machinery wagon to the LMS Works at Derby for inspection; it afterwards ran to Bletchley for tests. Tommy Hankins was its pilot driver for the tests. It was always accompanied by a French engineer/driver and given acceleration, timekeeping and braking tests. Its timetable demonstrations were compared with steam train timetables and came out favourably.

It was the first vehicle in this country to run on the railways with pneumatic tyres. It had a light metal-framed body and was of the same pattern as several supplied to the Eastern Railway of France for use on branch lines.

From the front it had the appearance of a road motor bus, but its overall length was 44 feet 9 inches with a seating capacity of 24 in a passenger compartment 21 feet long and 8 feet wide. The vehicle had ten wheels carried in two bogies of six and four wheels respectively. It was fitted with a 27 hp Panhard and Levassor sleeve-valve engine, driving through a clutch and four speed unit-mounted gear box. A separate reverse gear allowed four speeds to be used in either direction. The engine was water-cooled by means of aeroplane-type radiators attached to the sides of the roof. Control was similar to road motor car practice with the exception of steering, which was not necessary. Braking was also similar to road vehicles, with Lockheed hydraulic control of the shoes on the drums of all wheels. There was electric starting and lighting, and the heating of the passenger compartment was effected by air passing over the exhaust. The car weighed five tons when empty and did 12 miles to a gallon of petrol.

The wheels were removeable from the hub; on each wheel a pressure gauge recorded the normally 85 lbs psi. Should this pressure drop more than 14 lbs, an audible warning signal was given; this obviated the risk of running with a deflated tyre. In the event of sudden deflation there was a wooden hoop inside the tyre which took the load so that there was no loss of stability. Behind the metal guiding flanges of the wheels were rubber inserts which effectively deadened noise due to lateral motion. The life of these tyres was 20,000 miles and the permissible load per wheel, 12½ cwt.

There was the all important problem of exploding detonators and actuating track circuits, but the car's most noticeable characteristic was its silence. It gave no sound of approach and was therefore a danger to those working on the line, although the driver could sound a horn.

The experiment at Bletchley was only for a short period, but attracted considerable attention: the public was informed that it was being tested, but it never ran in public service.

An exciting advance in branch line rail travel came in 1938. A streamlined articulated three car Leyland oil engined train came to Bletchley and was put into service between Oxford and Cambridge on 12 September 1938. The service never figured in the public timetable and only remained a few months, but it was an elegant train giving real luxury and speed to branch line travel.

The timber-framed bodies, with outer panels of steel welded together, provided 24 first class, and 138 third class seats. Air operated Apex sliding doors gave access to the interior and were controlled by the guard. They were also interlocked with the engine control so that the driver could not start the train while any sliding doors were open. Passenger control switches were fitted to the doors so that they could also be opened by passengers, provided the guard had previously set the controls. The interior was panelled in veneer three ply and all partitions were hollow for the sake of lightness. Three lavatories were provided, with green painted walls and aluminium mouldings. Hot and cold water was available, the hot water provided by a Westinghouse heater. The seats were reversible, except against the partitions, and trimmed in uncut moquettes.

The streamlined cars were painted aluminium colour above a line a little below the side windows, and Post Office red below this line.

The train was designed by (Sir) William Stanier and built at Derby Works. The object was to investigate the possibilities of a light oil engined train in developing traffic on certain lines, and the economies to be obtained from self-contained passenger units of this kind.

Fred Healey, Hollis Wheeler, Joe Keen and Harry Cook were the Bletchley drivers during its experimental period on the Oxford-Cambridge branches. The three double trips daily between the two University Cities made a total daily mileage of 462 miles. The overall time allowance for the 77 mile trip, including stops at Sandy, Bedford and Bletchley, was about 1¾ hours: the fastest start to stop schedules were 53.3 mph between Bletchley and Bedford and 52.1 mph between Oxford and Bletchley.

Before the train came to Bletchley, test runs on the main line between Euston and Tring had attained a maximum of 82 mph. When the branch line tests were over, its next testing ground was to be on the Midland main line from St Pancras and so to the Bedford Midland shed the train went for stabling. Fitter John Gibbons went to Bedford to continue maintaining the train as he had at Bletchley. Unfortunately he was not used to the limited clearance between the train and the shed wall and leaned out when the train was in motion and was killed.

This was the last railcar development before such experiments were halted by World War II. The train was then stored at Bedford and not used during the war. It was after nationalisation that the two end units were converted into a self-propelled articulated unit for the installation and maintenance of overhead equipment on electrified lines.

There were excursions right from the beginning. The Great Exhibition of 1851 created the demand for many special trains from Oxford and Banbury. The cheap day or evening excursion to London was advertised way back in the previous century. The great advertising campaigns of the inter-war years made Blackpool, situated on the LNWR/LMS, a virtual Mecca for working class families and various works and club outings. Works Staff Outings, from Morrell's Brewery, Oxford, Wolverton Works and Meltis Chocolate from Bedford, would advertise themselves with a round board the same size as the smokebox door, fixed over that door in the front of the engine. Their glorious day out ended with a late night return, complete with paper hats and well-fed with whelks, cockles and shrimps.

Mail trains took their routine runs over the branches and were always known as either the Oxford, Cambridge or Banbury Mails. For many years before World War I, until slight timing alterations during World War II, a mail train departed for each of the three branch line terminus stations at 4.15 am. The Oxford and Banbury was a combined departure as far as Verney Junction where it divided. One old guard, Charlie Hood, was on the Oxford Mails for years. He booked on at 3.45 am daily and worked the 4.15 am Oxford Mails, returning with the first passenger, to then take a local freight trip to Fenny Stratford and shunt out the yard. When he retired, the job went into the normal link working for Goods Guards.

Milk from farms, especially along the Oxford and Banbury lines, was a vital traffic to every village along the railway. Every day cart loads of milk churns made their way to the station for the early morning milk trains. There would always be the late arrivals galloping down the road as the train could already be seen approaching the station. Sir Harry Verney expressed his concern in 1853 about the need to save farmers long bumpy road journeys to the station. There was milk from most of the village stations and a milk landing stage was erected at Charndon, although there was no station. Some stations had their own daily train which was brought into Bletchley and marshalled into the regular milk trains to London.

There was a daily train from Verney Junction called the Tutbury Milk. An engine departed from Bletchley each morning to Verney to bring in vanloads of milk off the Metropolitan line; a regular milk van also came in from Castlethorpe.

The transport of race horses and hunters was perhaps the most glamorous service on the line. Trainloads of perhaps 25 horseboxes carried costly horses to famous race meetings. Horseboxes with the owner's name or crest emblazoned on the side added a further air of importance to the traffic. There were not only special trains of horses, but also the odd loaded horsebox on the rear of the ordinary passenger service train.

Over the years, many railwaymen have thought the rider accompanying a race horse to a race must have first hand knowledge of the horse's capabilities or any potential winner. Invariably these escorting riders would offer a tip and more often than not the tip was hopelessly wrong. There is the story of the honest stable boy or escorting rider who replied when a tip was requested 'Do you think I would be sitting here if I knew the bloody winners?'

When the lines first opened, the carriage of coal into the district by rail probably had a more profound effect on the lives of the poorer classes than the passenger services. The immediate substantial drop in price was one good reason to offer thanks for the new railway. The improved standard of living through wider markets for gardening produce and quick journey to that market, were more important to them than being able to spend a day around the venerable halls of Cambridge.

Most of the coal was delivered to various sidings for the small coal merchants by the local goods trains, but there were through coal trains from the Great Western via Oxford Road exchange sidings, going out on the main line at Bletchley. For many years there was one going on to the LNER at Sandy and others from the north to Verney Junction making their way to Baker Street on the Metropolitan.

Most market gardening produce was brought into Bletchley by the various local goods trains and attached to main line freight trains to the north and south. In the season, special trains of produce were despatched to the London markets.

Brick trains were running on the branch lines way back in the previous century, but it was not until after World War I that a modern brick industry developed; clumps of tall chimneys appeared on the horizon and bricks became a really heavy and lucrative rail traffic. It was about 1934 that the brick traffic was at its peak.

Forders Sidings was the largest brickyard. In 1934 trainloads of bricks of 50 or 60 wagons were departing from Forders at 3.30 pm for Willesden, where they were remarshalled for destinations in the south of England; at 5.10 pm for Verney Junction and the Metropolitan and Great Central line; at 6.5 pm for Willesden and the south and a further train for Willesden at 8.30 pm: at 10.45 pm a train for Oxford and on to the Great Western; at 11.30 pm a train for Bletchley was remarshalled there for various train departures. Marston Valley brickyard had a train departure at 2.30 am and Ridgmont traffic came into Forders for marshalling onto the previously mentioned trains. There was, of course, a corresponding amount of empty wagon trains into the brickyards, to be set at the kilns for loading.

World War II was now just around the corner and the Oxford and Cambridge branches were about to move from the moderately busy to the positively congested.

On 1 September 1939, 28 trains loaded with evacuees from London passed through Bletchley, causing some dislocation. On that same day 800 children and the adults in charge were evacuated from London and arrived in Bletchley to become the town's first Cockney invasion. The official declaration of war was then only two days away.

On 13 October a terrible crash in Bletchley station brought home to railwaymen and the public the dangers of wartime travel during the blackout hours.

It was dark and wet when the *Royal Highlander* stopped at Bletchley. The shunting engine, a LNWR 0-8-0 freight engine, attached a van to this Inverness train. Station Inspector Walter Nursaw first saw the signs of impending disaster as he noticed the headlights of an express coming towards the shunting engine. He frantically called out to all those working around the van and shunt engine to get out, and this saved many lives.

The express was the *Stranraer,* with two engines on the front, a class 5 No 5025 leading, and a Royal Scot class behind. The West Yorkshire Regiment No 6130 had run by its signals and it was a mighty crash when No 5025 and the heavy freight engine met smoke box to smoke box.

Four people were killed, including Driver Irving Butler on the shunt engine, and 40 injured. But for the shunt engine absorbing some of the force of impact, and Walter Nursaw's mighty yell, the death toll would have been much higher.

The station buffet on platforms 2 and 3 was wrecked, but two young ladies working inside escaped with slight injuries when an engine came through the wall to join them. The adjoining waiting room did not fare so well, but collapsed, killing a young RAF man waiting to go to Bicester.

The rescue services that came from far and near coped with speed and efficiency and it was a long spell of duty for the 50 men of the Bletchley and Rugby breakdown gangs. It was 44 hours after the crash before the lines were once again opened for traffic.

For driver Cyril Haynes on the leading engine of the *Stranraer* it was to be a long and terrible ordeal. The young cleaner who had transferred to Liverpool about 18 years before and was a driver there, had run by the signals at his own home town and caused a terrible crash and loss of life: now he was to stand trial on a charge of manslaughter.

On 12 January 1940, trial at the Bucks Assizes opened and in the same afternoon closed. The jury dismissed the charge without hearing the defence. Cyril Haynes was never again to drive express trains and after a spell as shunting engine driver at Liverpool he came to Wolverton and was employed in the Railway Works.

At the enquiry, inquest and trial, it became increasingly clear that the strain of working in the blackout was an important factor in the accident.

The branch line passenger service of World War II suffered from wartime conditions. The late running of main line passenger trains through various causes from bombing, air raid warnings, shortage of staff, engines or stock, made a late departure for a branch line connection. There was no question of putting on extra trains.

Departures two hours late were not uncommon. The last train to Oxford at 10.10 pm was guaranteed to be a later runner, often departing at midnight.

Servicemen and women going home on leave or returning, or perhaps going to a posting somewhere, were a sizeable portion of the regular travellers. Exhortation by advertising posters and downright physical suffering, especially in the winter, deterred other long distance travellers. A YMCA hut erected at the north end of No 2 and 3 platform at Bletchley was a welcome warm shelter and resting place for many thousands in the services.

A regular wartime scene on Platform One was the long row of cycles which seemed always to be there, day and night. Those who worked on the station and surveyed them daily could see that some were regularly used, but many were deteriorating with lack of use. A new one might appear and a careful watch reveal it was still in the same position months later, but others would disappear and it was not necessarily their owners who took them. Soldiers often borrowed cycles without the owners' consent and dumped them at the station.

Early Monday morning saw the young soldiers waiting to catch the first passenger train to Bicester at 5.20 am. Many arrived on the Sunday evening and found various warm places to pass the long night hours. An express from Glasgow, called the *Limited*, stopped at Bletchley about 4.0 am and out would roll many sleepy-eyed soldiers, complete with kit bag or cases, looking for the Bicester train.

The wartime passenger service may have been unreliable in time keeping, but at least always ran, and arrival was usually guaranteed. But there were problems that would not even occur to the passengers. War traffic such as troop and ambulance trains was given priority; inferior coal on the engine made it difficult to keep steam pressure; the shortage of staff resulted in young, inexperienced firemen on the footplate. All were hidden factors unseen by those impatiently waiting on the platform.

There were no seaside specials on the lines, but there were specials of a sort, which had absolute priority and were run at short notice. Troop trains were so regular that a number of LNWR 0-8-0 freight engines were specially fitted with heaters and kept for these alone. This did not mean there was no problem in producing the motive power at a moment's notice. On Bletchley's packed little shed an engine invariably had to be 'dug out' of the congestion and serviced. It was often quicker to use an engine already in service and delay the less important train that it was attached to or booked to work.

Where some notice was given, an engine would be despatched from Bletchley shed to perhaps Oxford to attach to an ambulance train or a troop train coming off the Western. The Western engine would detach and depart for the Oxford loco shed. The Bletchley engine, probably an 0-8-0 LNWR freight engine, would attach to the train and then go off to Cambridge where the LNER would take over. Before this departure a ritual had to be performed at Oxford that must have puzzled many onlookers. The Great Western created 25 inches of vacuum in the train's braking system while the LMS had only 21 inches. The cord on the brake cylinder of each coach had to be pulled to reduce the vacuum on the reservoir side of the cylinder before the train was able to depart. This was the guard's immediate duty on taking over and failure to reduce on one coach would mean a dragging brake throughout the journey. Vacuum-fitted stock going from the LMS to the GWR did not need this ritual.

Often an ambulance train would request a reduction in speed or even a stop while an operation was performed. Train loads of Army tanks, petrol or ammunition travelled from east to west or off the main and on to one of the branch lines, with comparative secrecy.

A VIP train came across the branches from time to time in absolute secrecy. There would be an order through the control office for an engine of a certain class to meet the train at perhaps Oxford and go on to Cambridge. The composition and tonnage of the train would be known, but the secrecy of the instruction and the type of stock gave it away as a VIP train. Driver Ernie Perkins drove Mr Churchill's train from Oxford through to Cambridge, arriving at 6.00 am. The LMS engine was uncoupled for an LNER engine to work forward. As Ernie returned with his engine down the running round loop at Cambridge, he ran alongside the train; the only sign of life at that time of the morning was a lady, presumably a secretary.

The most macabre traffic on the branches were certain trains that ran near or shortly after the end of the war. Ordinary metal wagons covered by a tarpaulin sheet carried dead American servicemen from east to west on their way home for reburial. There was no advertising of their contents, and the trains were unrecognisable from any other sheeted goods wagons that passed in the night.

A passenger train ran daily, including Sunday, between Bletchley and Bedford; it was strictly a wartime train and was appropriately nicknamed *The Whitehall*. Although it was in the Working Time Table it was mainly for the staff at Bletchley Park, Sir Herbert Leon's former mansion, now taken over by the Foreign Office, who lived at Bedford.

Each weekday morning a Bletchley driver and fireman travelled down to Bedford in the brake van of the Cambridge Mails; they made their way to the Bedford Midland shed to prepare a Midland class 2 engine to work the *Whitehall* from Bedford St Johns station to Bletchley, departing at about 8.0 am. Engine No 551 was diagrammed for the train throughout the war. During maintenance or examination periods another class 2, No 515, would invariably take over.

The engine did not waste its time only on that train. On arrival at Bletchley it would take up its diagram working on the 9.30 daily passenger to Oxford, where it would shunt all day, until returning with a 5.0 pm passenger from Oxford, and then continue through to Bedford for the return home of the *Whitehall* staff. The engine was then stabled at the Bedford Midland loco for the repeat performance next day.

They were a mixed bag of passengers on the Whitehall. There was the city gent in his uniform of brolly and bowler and the more humble brigade in the third class compartments.

When Charlie Cope was guard, the brolly and bowler cut no ice with him. He believed in maintaining the dignity of the passenger guard. At the precise moment of departure from Bedford, he blew his whistle and waved his flag. Late stragglers running across the barrow crossing got no sympathy from Charlie. If a first class passenger managed to scrape into the third class at the last moment, Charlie would not let him change compartments at the next station, and as for anyone riding in his guard's van, that was completely out of the question.

At this time the Bedford Motor was pulling or pushing its way between Bletchley and Bedford without recourse to strong discipline.

A regular guard for many years was George Horne, tall and red haired, always sporting a flower in his buttonhole. George was also a good story teller and a friend of his passengers. His hobby of collecting and swapping cigarette cards made him a favourite with the kids.

When a lady was appointed as a Motor Guard during the war, despite her hefty appearance and rather masculine looks, she carried on the tradition of friendliness on the Bedford Motor. She had a voice to match her appearance, which effectively intimidated the sometimes unruly school children.

The well-proportioned Gerry, as she was called, was affable and quite popular. The Motor Coach was always stabled overnight and at week-ends in the middle siding at Bedford St Johns Station: during the war, servicemen who had changed trains at Bedford Midland would walk over to St Johns and find there was no train for Bletchley or Oxford for many hours, so into the Motor Coach they went to sleep away the night hours. Some would invariably get well soaked in drink so by morning the coach would smell like a brewery or worse. One morning Gerry could stand the smell no longer and at Woburn Sands she made the porter disinfect the coach interior.

For railwaymen who worked during the dark hours, the blackout was their greatest irritation. For the footplate men the blackout sheet on the engines was a positive torment.

Good timekeeping did not return immediately the war was over. Bletchley had a staff shortage: locomotive maintenance and cleanliness were never to return to their pre-war standard, the conditon of the track left much to be desired and Permanent Way men were no longer in abundant supply. As the track deteriorated so speed limits came, and some sections were never to return to their normal limit.

Nevertheless, it was still a busy, if rural line, that seemed to be struggling to get back into its old routine. In all the years of war and peace, the little local branch line goods trains never ceased to run. These trains, until the end of the steam engine, served the little station with the single wagon load and the even smaller consignments carried in the tariff van. During the last 40 years they altered very little. Before World War II they started from Bletchley Yard and when Swanbourne was built some commenced from that yard.

The 97 odd miles of branch lines could not possibly be covered by one local train, with sidings at nearly every station and a few public sidings not near a station. There was the Bedford local goods, the Gamlingay's, the Banbury's, the Brackley's, the local starting from Cambridge, and one starting from Oxford and worked by men from those depots. The Oxford local was once given the number 19 and continued to be unofficially known by that number until the last steam engine had gone. The Gamlingay's did so much shunting with vegetable and other traffic on its way out, that the train crew was relieved for the return trip.

The Banbury branch was transversed by two local goods daily, one going through to Banbury and the other terminating at Brackley. The engines on either train would have been a little ex-L&YR engine 0-6-0 freight engine, known locally as a Gracie Fields. Their lifting type injectors and constant over-heating of the injector delivery pipes made them unpopular with the Bletchley enginemen. The other likely engine was the LNWR 'Cauliflower', an 0-6-0, possibly with wooden brake blocks on the tender. Both engines shared the same design in cab roof — it was narrow and the crew were exposed to wind and wet weather. By this time the Midland Freight Four did occasionally come on the scene, and the consequent improvement in comfort was luxury.

The engine for the Banbury's came off the loco at 5.45 am, possibly coupled to the Sandy Coal engine, and after picking up the guards on No 1 platform, went right away to Swanbourne Sidings to attach to their respective trains. Then it was off with the local goods, stopping to shunt out and deliver to Buckingham, Brackley and Banbury.

Later in the morning the Brackley Goods engine came off the loco shed, so leaving Swanbourne Sidings at about 9.30 am to deliver and pick up at all the stations and sidings to Brackley, except Verney Junction, which received its deliveries on the various freight trains taking traffic for the Metropolitan line.

The Brackley Goods' first call after departure from Swanbourne Sidings was Swanbourne Station, where Signalman Fred Walters was waiting on the platform complete with his immaculate bow tie, and after securely locking the booking office, would greet the guard on the platform with 'Hello Bill, two empties to pick up'. Guard Billy Norman would exchange the greeting and give the information that there were three loads of coal for him.

Upon departure for Winslow an onlooker may have noticed a two finger sign from the guard to a platelayer. It was no victory sign or rude gesture, but an order for two rabbits.

At Winslow, the tariff van would be backed into the shed for sorting and then shunting out empty wagons and placing the loads was the task for the next 40 minutes or more. It is understandable when, after an hours shunting, an exasperated driver would lean over the side of his cab and say impatiently 'Are you getting these bloody wagons in number order?'

It was Padbury next stop. The single line train staff was taken from Charlie Batsford at Verney Junction. He stood on the adjoining track with the staff held just above head level, to be grasped by the fireman as the train slowly passed.

An exchange of staff at Buckingham station and, if there was not work to be done in the station, it was way down to the Goods Yard. It is hardly likely that the brief stand in the station was without some conversation with signalman Harold Plant.

Arrival in the yard and the expertise and confidence of the experienced goods guards of Billy Norman's generation were evident.

Passing ganger Jack Rawlings' cottage at Radclive Farm Crossing, a few lumps of coal would quite likely fall off the engine almost at the front gate, as Mrs Rawlings acknowledged the 'accident' with a hurried wave at the window.

Bacon House public siding seldom had any traffic now, but Bill could remember when a few wagons in or out were regular traffic and a glass of wine from the lady at the crossing house was just as regular. No doubt she appreciated a few lumps of coal.

Rabbits abounded along the line and several drivers and firemen would cheaply purchase them, perhaps for office workers at Bletchley who never saw the line. There were some who kept an eagle eye open for a platelayer's snare and if one was seen, stop and pocket the rabbit. The platelayers knew this happened and on one occasion Jack Rawlings put a note on one of his snares, saying in effect 'Keep your bloody thieving hands off, the rabbit is ours'. The rabbits still disappeared and an attached reply was found, 'Thanks, we had it'.

Signalman Arthur Marriott would be waiting to take the staff and confer with Billy Norman about the shunting required. Arthur would have the kettle on the stove in his box so that when shunting was over, the train crew adjourned to the box for tea. Billy Norman would be seen to pass a small piece of doubled white paper to the signalman; its thickness made it obvious that a coin of some decription was inside. It was accepted quietly and without surprise by the signalman. The secretive transaction was Bill's bet.

Arthur was a Bookies' Runner, and in his own pleasant manner he collected bets from railwaymen and others. He was in telephone communication with Jimmy Trotman at the next box at Cockley Brake, his partner in 'crime'.

If tea in Brackley Signalbox commenced with speculation about the winner of the 2.30 it would quite likely turn to rules and regulations. Billy was hard to catch out.

Whilst shunting was in operation at Brackley, the men on the Banbury local goods were probably cooking their egg and bacon in the shovel. The little Cauliflower did not give dining comfort. A half moon seat on either side of the cab would be utilised as a table to accommodate the egg and bacon, while standing with knife and fork was not a hardship under the circumstances. It had advantages over an L&Y engine that was without seats. The tea can and two cups on the drip plate above the fire hole door were convenient and ensured constant hot tea.

The arrival of an engine from Bletchley for the regular Thursday-only cattle train meant the invitation to the arriving train crew to join them for a cup of tea. A brief conversation, ranged from a dirty joke to complaining about the link roster or Sunday work; it was time to whistle up for the signal to leave the dilapidated little depot and to couple up to the train, now ready for departure.

Passing Farthinghoe's little wooden station nestled peacefully in the cutting, old Jim the porter might just put his head out of the door, but quickly take it in again.

A change of train staff at Cockley Brake while still moving did not allow lengthy conversation, and the same procedure at Brackley would be accompanied by a whistle to the train crew having tea in the signalbox, who in turn would hold up the tea can and a cup.

The passing of the down passenger denoted the time for departure of the Brackley goods. As the train crew descended the signalbox steps the argument about rules and regulations could still be in full swing, but one of the crew still remembered to pick up a bundle of cabbage plants, that Arthur had grown in his allotment behind the signalbox.

The train comprised mainly empty wagons on the return home. The empties placed on the front road in Buckingham Yard were now picked up on the way back. It could be that the up passenger from Oxford was hard on their heels at Winslow, and the signalman would keep his starting signal on and, coming to the open window, would hold his crossed arms high in the air to denote they were backing inside the refuge siding, or across the road to let the passenger go by.

It was of necessity a slow journey approaching Swanbourne Station. If Ernie Dickens was not working on the length, Billy Norman's two rabbits would be suitably hung on a stick, firmly stuck into the ground to enable Bill to reach out and catch them as he passed.

Swanbourne Sidings was the end of the train journey. The trains securely left in the reception sidings for the shunt engine to deal with, unless a trip train was required at Bletchley, it was right away Bletchley with all the train crew on the footplate. Bill Norman, probably putting the finishing touches to his time sheet on the way in, alighted on the platform at Bletchley and the little Cauliflower came to rest on the ashpit to await disposal and servicing. The driver had only to do his last duty — make out a repair card and sign off.

Soon after World War II there was a change of mood about steam traction. Steam standardisation programmes were revealed and standard locomotives were soon to replace the Cauliflowers, Lanky and York and little tank engines of similar antiquity. The LMS and the LNER disclosed that they also proposed to venture into diesel traction for main line work. The LMS produced two prototypes, the 1,600 hp 'twins' 10,000 and 10,001, and the 827 hp branch line type 10,800.

In 1947 the Diesel Electric No 10,000 stopped at Bletchley and gave rise to speculation on what a railwayman's life would be in the near future, and the part this beautiful looking machine would play.

Within a few months the LMS ceased to exist and BR became the new initials. Nos 10,000 and 10,001 did eventually come back to Bletchley, after a year or two, for main line local passenger trials.

It was No 10,800, the branch line type, which came for trials in 1951 and stayed for about a year. Earlier passenger trials had been made between Euston and Watford, where a maximum of 70 mph had been reached. As a general mixed traffic loco, it came to Bletchley for freight working. No 10,800 was a Bo-Bo (a double motor bogie) 16 cylinder diesel by Davey Paxman with electrical equipment by British Thompson Houston. Unlike the 'twins' with a cab either end, it had a single cab with a design that had some similarity to the steam engine.

No 1 road in the loco shed was its stabling road, although its subsequent diagram was for it to be in the shed only at weekends for maintenance. Paxton's own engineering staff had a workshop erected in the shed at the bottom of No 1 road and worked on the diesel loco, not only at weekends, but while it was actually out on the road. Like the 'twins', some Bletchley drivers were trained to instruct their colleagues who were in the links where the local freight trains were rostered.

On Monday morning at 5.45 am 10,800 departed light engine for Swanbourne Sidings and at 6.25 it departed with the local goods for Banbury. It returned from Banbury with a daily iron stone train to Swanbourne Sidings, then light engine to Bletchley loco where it generally arrived at about 2.0 pm. Within the hour another set of men were off the shed with the engine to work a 3.0 pm empty brick wagon train to Ridgmont Brickyard. After setting the empties and drawing the loads, they were worked into Forders Sidings and marshalled into various trains. At 10 pm the engine was once again on its way with a brick train across the Oxford line to Hinksey on the Great Western. At about 2.0 am it was due to depart from Hinksey with a freight train for Swanbourne Sidings, where it was again placed on the 6.5 am local goods to Banbury. Another set of men and guard were taken by the Hostel 'Bus to Swanbourne and 10,800 was once again off on another day's diagram working. Not until it returned from Banbury on Saturday, was it given a rest

At times it did fail and if Paxton's engineers were not riding on it, they were sent for and travelled to wherever it was. The drivers overcame many minor failures.

The loco shed at this time had a Superintendent with an office at the shed. Northampton loco shed being annexed to Bletchley as the parent shed, had given it this rise in status.

When the branch line tests were over, 10,800 went to Rugby and later to other testing grounds, undergoing various technical changes. It appears to have been withdrawn from service by 1959, but it helped to pioneer future diesel designs.

The Sunday seaside excursions started again after the War, but the bigger engines were making for easier work for the footplate crews. Excursions from the London area were routed via the Cambridge branch to Yarmouth or Clacton. Facilities were given for some branch line stations to join evening excursions to Wembley Ice Hockey or a day excursion.

Somehow the pre-war effeciency was lacking and nationalisation did not bring an end to inter-company rivalry. Despite this, there was no delay when the Royal train passed over the branch line onto other regions.

The Royal Train travelled the branch lines several times over the years, but it was nearly always from many miles away. In July 1956 it arrived from Scotland; at Bletchley the magnificently polished *City of Hereford* was too heavy for the Oxford line, so Bletchley men with two well-polished class 5 mixed traffic engines worked forward to Oxford.

At this time iron stone trains from Irthlingboro were regularly crossing the Oxford line, bound for South Wales via the Western Region exchange sidings at Yarnton. The same engines could be seen returning with perhaps smudge coal for Corby or the empty iron stone wagons. There was also a noticeable deterioration in branch freight traffic. The vegetable trains were fewer and by the late 1950s the local goods was daily missing some of the small sidings. Even coal could be seen arriving at Flettons Brickyard in lorries with high side boards and the horse box was now an oddity. The Railway Modernisation Plan of 1955 was inevitable.

ABOVE: Bill King shoeing a drayman's horse in the Loco Shed yard in 1935; CENTRE LEFT: Driver George Betts and Cleaner Jimmy Walker on the Bletchley shunting engine, a L&YR saddle tank, c1938; RIGHT: the French driver of the *Micheline* at Bletchley in 1932. BELOW LEFT: Bletchley Loco Shed Shop grades c1954 and RIGHT: the *Micheline* in Bletchley Loco Shed.

ABOVE: A Jumbo No 2186 *Lowther* at Bletchley; LEFT: a Lanky passes the south end of Bletchley Station — these were often called Gracie Fields; RIGHT: George VI's Royal train crew at Bletchley from Brackley (the author on the left; Tommy Hawkins, Wally Goodman and Inspector Powell). BELOW: *Tishy,* the only Prince of Wales built in LMS days, at Bletchley in 1938.

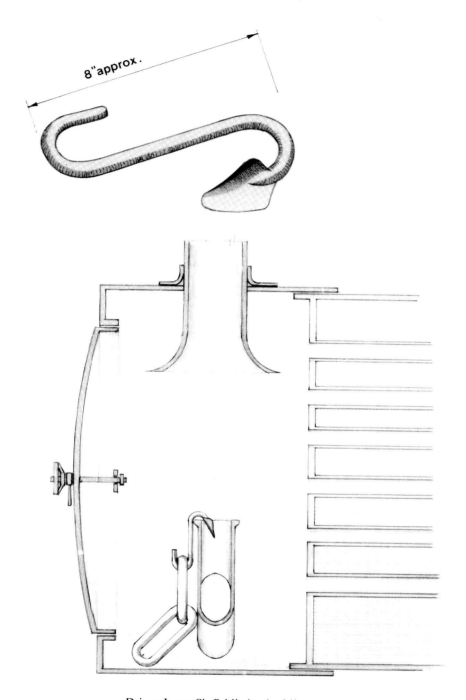

Driver Jonas Sinfield's ivy leaf jimmy.

Driver Jonas Sinfield retired around 1921 and into retirement also went his Ivy Leaf Jimmy. This unauthorised and home-made instrument was carried by most drivers in Jonas Sinfield's day. However, with the coming of superheated engines drivers gradually ceased to carry them and by the end of World War II they were rarely seen.

When a saturated steam engine was shy in steaming the driver would place the ivy leaf end of the Jimmy in the blast pipe orifice and obtain an old link coupling to hang onto the oppsite bent end of the Jimmy to hold it in position.

This resulted in 'splitting' the exhaust blast as it proceeded up the chimney, thus 'lifting' the fire. If the driver also worked the engine heavily by using the reversing gear to lengthen the valve cut-off, sparks, in the form of large, white-hot lumps of fire, would issue from the chimney.

The steaming qualities would improve whilst the Jimmy was in use, but the coal consumption, along with the fireman's workload, would also increase.

117

Other instructions (cont'd)

Setting Back movements are prohibited from Cambridge Bay lines towards No. 1. except to Water Eaton Siding & the latter movements must only be made when points are set for Siding & the disc (No.) is off.

Before Signalman at No. 5 Box allows an Up Passenger train to run to Down Cambridge the special signal 3-4-3 will be sent to this box. This signal must be repeated & needle placed T.O.L. & maintained there until T.O.S. is rec'd from 5 or if line cleared at No. 1 latter will give special signal 5-2-2 & needle placed to line closed, unless section otherwise occupied when disc will be turned back one number.

All movements from Oxford Bay lines to Main lines, Cambridge Bays, or Goods Yd must be made from the Up Oxford line, except vehicles from down Oxford which requires to be attached to down fast line trains & these may be worked over the crossing leading through the short siding between the down Oxford line & down fast line.

When a train, engine, or vehicle is standing over 72 points on down Oxford line waiting to set back into Oxford Bays, the signals for the Up Fast line must not be taken off unless No. 72 points are set for Oxford Bay lines.

Working over Oxford Bay lines. - treated as incoming lines.
When necessary for trains not conveying passengers to be set back from No. 2 to No. 1. through either of the Oxford Bay lines during the times the Bay line is already occupied by a train not conveying pass'rs. the Signalman at No. 2 Box is authorised to send the 2-3-3 to No. 1. & this signal is ack'd by the special bell signal 4-2 & disc of block inst. will be moved forward one num for each train so admitted.
Should a train be cleared from No. 1. the Signalman there, must give 5-2 to No. 2 & Signalman at No. 2 will move disc back one number. When whole of trains have been removed + Section again clear, the indicator of block will be placed to Normal.

Duties of Signalmen. :   No. 1. Signalmen take charge of levers 49. to 96 (inc), all Main line Block Ints & all fog machines from the signal box.
  No. 2. Sig take charge of levers 1. to 48 inc working into & out of Oxford & Cambridge Bays. Newton Longville Block Ints & the two mechanical indicators, the one working in connection with Oxford Bays Starting signals & the other working in connection with Up Slow lines starting signals.

V.o.L. indicators :-   Up & down fast, Slow, & Cambridge Bay lines.

Rule 79 & 80. & B.T. Reg. 4E - fog object.   No. 1 Oxford Bay starting signal.

Bell Codes :-   Rings

From No. 5. Box   Take of Cambridge Bay Starting signal for train to draw up   1 - 2. 3.
                     Replace   "   "   "   "   " train has set back.   3 - 2. 4

From No. 2 Box.   Take of Up Fast or Up Slow Home signal for train to draw up. 1 - 2. 3
                     Replace   "   "   "   "   "   " train has set back   3. 2 4

To. Tip Siding :-   Cease shunt'g for Pass'r train to pass on down slow line.
                     To be given a ack before T.L.C. for a Down Slow Pass'r train :-

A page from a Signalman's Inspector's note book in 1935 — it shows layout and notes for teaching signalmen the operation of each signalbox in the Bletchley area.

MEN AND MACHINES

Before modernisation or the drastic changes that came with dieselisation, electrification and 'rationalisation', the steam engines and the men who worked and serviced them — the signalmen, permanent way men and other related grades — added colour to the service. Unlike the steam engine, such men cannot be preserved by museum or preservation society.

The first named engine to work the branch lines appears to have been the *Trio*. Later a little tank engine called *Shannon* puffed its way along the Cambridge branch between Potton and Sandy, until that line was completed and opened to traffic in 1862.

There is little doubt that every class of engine built by or for the LNWR, had a period of allocation to Bletchley.

Probably the best engines in the 1860s were those designed by J. E. McConnell of Wolverton. His Bloomer class engine worked on the Southern Division. The large Bloomers were so popular that 40 were built, not all at Wolverton. A small Bloomer named *Bela* was located at Bletchley in 1879.

By 1877 John Ramsbottom, locomotive engineer of the Northern Division, was in charge of locomotive design for the whole LNWR: a period notable for the introduction of the 'Problem' class, better known as 'Lady of the Lake' class, the 'Samson', 'Newton' and 'DX Goods' classes.

In 1903, among the engines stationed at Bletchley were four of these dainty little Lady of the Lakes: No 33 *Erebus*, 675 *Ivanhoe*, 1432 *Panopea* and *Egeria*. At Oxford was No 1429 *Alfred Paget* and 1433 *Daphne*. In about 1904 a famous engine of this class was at Bletchley, running on the branch lines. No 806 *Waverley* hauled a train of four coaches weighing about 80 tons behind the tender in the Race to the North during August 1888. It shared with another of this class, No 667 *Marmion* on the south of Crewe section, working turn and turn about during the month of the race. The last of these left Bletchley in 1906.

From about 1912 until the end of the War in 1918 there were probably more named engines located at Bletchley than at any time in the loco shed's history.

There were at various times engines of the Samson class with the names of *Bee, Croxteth, John o'Gaunt, Sutherland, Woodlark, North Star, Saddleback* and *St Patrick;* Precedent class, better known as Jumbos, *Miranda, Princess Louise, Robert Benson, Sir Alexander Cockburn, Perseverance, Minotaur, Pitt, Princess Helena, Countess, Fairburn, Prince Leopold, Mabel, Booth, Precedent* and *Dagmar;* Experiment class, *Staffordshire, Atlanta, Greystoke, Saracen, City of Paris, Worcestershire, President,* and *Glendower;* Precursor class, *Servia, Daphne, Bucephalus, Brougham, Viscount, Greyhound, Rowland Hill, Alecto* and *Pandora;* George V class, *Woodcock* and *Racehorse*.

In 1917 there were 46 engines at Bletchley and 14 at the outstation depots. Among these were the big passenger tender engines of George V, Precursors and Jumbo classes and also two Precursor 4-4-2 tank engines to work branch line passenger trains.

The majority of engines were still freight engines, and at this time there were three Webb compounds and other eight wheel coupled freight engines, probably G1s, the nonsuperheated D, which with the Cauliflowers, also at the shed, dominated the branch line freight traffic trains until after World War II.

There was a famous Jumbo class located at Bletchley in the early post World War I years. *Hardwicke* was built in 1892 and hauled a train on the Northern section of the 1895 Race to

119

the North on 22 August. *Hardwicke* averaged more than 67 mph between Crewe and Carlisle on the race and was now relegated to branch line work. In 1932 the engine was withdrawn from service and is now preserved.

There were engines that had no name and were hated and detested by drivers, firemen and even fitters. These were the 0-6-0 saddle tank shunting engine.

In the latter half of the mid-war years, the George Vs and Prince of Wales class were the biggest passenger engines at Bletchley, working the main line local trains and sometimes on the branches. The top link drivers on these trains would all have been men who started their railway career in about 1890 or even before, and they were true descendants of the Victorian drivers who stood pilot with the little Lady of the Lakes.

In the 1930s a Midland Compound passenger engine came onto the branch lines, and a Midland Freight Four was an occasional sight. A little engine that also came about this time was a former Lancashire & Yorkshire Railway 0-6-0 goods engine. Two or three of these stayed until after World War II. They were soon named 'Lankies' or 'Gracie Fields', but without affection.

All the Georges had gone before World War II; only a few Princes remained right until 1947 and then they, the last of the Precursor family, disappeared. Among the last to leave was *Lusitania* and an unnamed Prince No 5845 that was the most famous of them all. There were 245 Prince of Wales class built between 1911 and 1921, all with Joys valve gear.

After many years of main line express work, the Royal Scot and Jubilee classes eased the Princes from main line supremacy and 5845, without a name, a number altered to 25845 and a nickname of *Tishy*, came to Bletchley to work the main line local passengers to Euston and between Oxford and Cambridge.

As the George disappeared, so LMS 2-6-4 tank engines came to mingle with the Princes and later, during World War II, a few Stanier 2-6-0 mixed traffic tender engines came: then some Stanier class 8 freight engines mingled with the old 'D'.

From 1947 the branch line passengers were run with a medley of engines. There was an occasional Midland 4-4-0 class 2P and a Midland Compound. These mixed with the 2-6-4 LMS tanks and then the first batch of Ivatt class 4 tender engines, Nos 3000 to 3005. Later came BR tender and tank engines.

For several years Cambridge loco supplied a LNE 'Claude Hamilton' on the first early morning passenger from Cambridge, going through to Oxford and back in the afternoon. After the demise of the Claudes a B 12/3 took over, only to be displaced by a B1 and eventually a Brush Type 2 diesel.

On the Bedford Motor a Midland 0-4-4 pushed and pulled until 1952, then an Ivatt 2-6-2 tank and later a BR No 84005. All these gave way to the Diesel Railcars in 1959.

On the freight side, the old 'D' was seen less and less, the class 8 freight and the class 5 mixed traffic gradually easing it right out. The Eastern region supplied a B1 and a GE 0-6-0 for their small amount of freight work on the branch lines.

Gradually diesels took over the decreasing freight work until 5 July 1965 when engine No 48610, a class 8 freight, left Bletchley shed, and steam on the branch lines was gone forever.

Some of the greatest characters were among the engine drivers. It was World War II that put the final seal on the old style driver, who was a despot on his engine, and thought the fireman a boy if he was under 40 years of age. With the shortage of staff, the youngest were without experience, training or discipline.

There are no good records of Bletchley's earliest drivers. It is certain that some would have come from Wolverton where there was a locomotive department from the beginning of the railway. Over the years, it was to a large extent, a father and son or nephew job, and up to World War II, a relative on the railway was an advantage when applying for a job.

When driver Len Foolkes retired in 1969 he was the last locoman in his family. His father and grandfather were drivers; if they arrived and there was no work they were sent home without pay. His grandfather wore corduroy trousers and most drivers had long beards to keep their chests warm in the days of cabless open-top engines.

Many Bletchley men who retired just prior to the end of steam had driver grandfathers. Bill Sinfield retired as a draughtsman at Wolverton Works after commencing his career in the loco shed at Bletchley before World War I. His father was a driver in the previous century and his grandfather was a driver in London & Birmingham Railway days at Wolverton. There was a driver in the Howe family going back to L&BR days until Stan Howe died and left a son in the Control Office. Many drivers who retired after World War II had fathers who started as cleaners in the loco shed in the 1880s.

By the time the steam engines had gone, there were few drivers from Bletchley or the surrounding district. The grandsons and great-grandsons of the old drivers who made the little Ladies of the Lake show a clean pair of heels on the way to Crewe, were now working in a factory on the new industrial estate.

Some early stories of the drivers of the 1870s and afterwards were supplied by Joe Fennell in 1949 to the *Bletchley Gazette* whe he was nearing 90 years of age. Joe joined the Railway Telegraph department in the 1870s and retired as Chief Clerk on 31 December 1920.

Joe Fennell recalled the names of some of the drivers when he started his railway carreer: Dan Purcell, Dan Collier, Dan Garner, W. Green, W. Sedgwick, J. Lane, C. Cundell, G. Bowler, J. Bowler, and J. Selby. Born and bred Bletchley railwaymen with similar names continue to appear over the next 70 or more years.

Selby was something of a humourist. If he saw a workman passenger with a nose as large or larger than his own, he would offer him a penny with the remark 'I see you belong to our club'. He was called Duke. He also owned a dog called 'Snatch' which he frequently took with him on his engine. It was said that Snatch was so experienced he would bark when the signal was against them.

One night Coddy Foster left his engine warming up in the hands of his fireman, who ran it through some trap points in the Newfoundout bank and down into the water. Foster was dismissed and went to South America where he became a driver on the Argentine railways.

Coddy told the tale of the day in South America when a railway officer said to him 'Driver give me a lift back to the depot on your engine'. 'Certainly, Mr Trevithick'. He looked at Coddy and then asked 'Where do you come from that you know me?' When told, he said 'What? Coddy Foster, whose engine went into the Newfoundout?'

Mr Trevithick was the loco shed chief during Coddy's days at Bletchley, but if he played any part in Coddy's dismissal, Joe Fennell never said: but he did say that the famous Francis Trevithick, who built the 'Treavy engine', as Joe called it, was the father of this Trevithick.

As late as 1938 there were still 32 of the 100 drivers who started their railway career in the previous century.

Lodging away from home was quite common before World War I and drivers had to be self-sufficient. The rural nature of Bletchley drivers necessitated a large wicker basket. To fry a pound of onions and put a whole cauliflower in the saucepan was their normal way of life. Few drivers would have had less than 20 poles of garden or allotment. The wicker basket lasted until after World War II, and as lodging turns decreased, disappeared in 1949.

Even the familiar overalls changed with fashion. Until about 1925 sensible flop-fronted trouser overalls were worn, then the flop was replaced by a vertical row of buttons.

A stone bottle of cold tea to stand on the warm engine drip plate, directly above the firehold door was a vital piece of equipment: this gave way to the blue enamel tea can in the post-World War I era.

Reports of the railwaymen's Trade Union meetings show that in 1895 Bletchley men were sufficiently pious to abhor Sunday meetings, and Bible classes were at that time regularly held in the Temperance Rooms above the Coffee Tavern. Many were church sidesmen or bell ringers, while others played an equal role in the various chapels. They were respectable God-fearing family men who, by thrift and virtuous living, had bought their own homes.

There were those who gained respect for another reason — being able to hold their beer. In pre-World War I days, there were no licensing hours and pubs were open from morning until night — a fact taken advantage of by many of the renowned drinkers. It was not unusual for one particular driver to visit the Park Hotel when leaving work in the morning and still be there in the evening.

In the mid-war years the drivers may have been a little less formidable, the long beards and sideboards had been gradually disappearing from the beginning of the century, but otherwise their characteristics were much the same. The new licensing hours had curbed the marathon drinkers and no doubt the number of church sidesmen had not increased. There were still some good drinkers, enough to keep the Workingmen's Club flourishing. The Railway Institute was just across the road to the Club, but that was strictly Temperance.

These two places and the pubs were the main places of entertainment in Bletchley and Fenny Stratford. Only the King George Cinema, converted from a former Chapel, offered an alternative.

The job of engine cleaner was the first step to becoming an engine driver. Generally when leaving school, or within a year or two, they started on the long road which was seldom smooth and never clean.

Cleaners were often used for labouring work when labourers were sick or there was a staff shortage; they were ideal call boys and useful to send to the sub depots at Oxford or Cambridge when coalmen, firedroppers, or any other shed grades were in short supply.

The number of cleaners in the shed varied throughout the years as did the time they remained cleaners and the number of years before becoming firemen. Being passed to act as fireman could still mean several more years of cleaning with odd days of firing turns of duty.

There was little change in the utilisation and deeds of engine cleaners, nor did the method of recruitment vary much. To be given a job on the iron road in Bletchley was an honour, especially if there was a possibility of becoming a driver or top class signalman. Three references were required, including the inevitable minister of religion.

The references were not merely a matter of form. Soon after the Great War, a railwayman asked for a job for his young son, who was at that time working in his first job for a local baker. The local railway boss accepted him, he passed the medical examination and started work, while references were awaited. Two extolled the boy's virtues, but the third, from the baker, although saying he was a good worker, mentioned that he was once 4½d short in his change. His railway employment ceased.

Sympathy was shown by many railwaymen who pleaded on his behalf through their Trade Union. His parents intervened and the local boss had a change of heart: but by now so had the boy, and he bitterly refused to follow in his father's footsteps.

In the cleaning gangs there were black-faced boys of varying ages, easily led into mischief. Among them there was always one who would display his daring or strength. Joe Turney, a cleaner in the early years of this century, would jump from the boiler top to the shed floor, especially if he was dared, and to prove his toughness, carry a bucket of sand in his teeth.

At that time the Shed Foreman was a Mr Tabener, who liked to lecture the lads in the mess room. It was the time of the incandescent gas lights and often one boy would manage to creep out and blow down a gas pipe in a nearby room, probably the fitter's shop, and out would go the lights. Mr Tabener, a northerner, used to fume and say 'I'll sack the scump'.

Cleaners worked round the clock before World War II. On the day shift they lined up when booking on and Freddy Butterfield, the chargehand cleaner, would allocate and supervise the work. He was a 'Company's man'; waste of time or materials was like taking money out of his pocket, so he kept an eagle eye open.

The two senior cleaners would often be put on shed sweeping, which meant a higher rate of pay and was therefore accepted with pleasure. The remainder would be put in gangs of four and given certain engines · clean. There would generally be a toss-up to see who cleaned the dirtiest parts.

Freddy Butterfield or the foreman on duty could not watch cleaners for 24 hours a day. At night it was a hurried clean of the night's allocation of engines and then some would be away to the warmth of the 'Sand Hole' — a place where sand was heated dry for the engine sand boxes — some into a warm firebox which had recently had the fire thrown out, and others to various dark recesses of the loco shed. If the foreman came snooping to see what the cleaners were doing, there was generally someone to raise the alarm and then there was a rush to positions, if not their proper ones, while they looked as innocent as possible. The late returners, who probably had to squeeze through a firehole door, would try to walk on top of the engines, high in the black soot-encrusted smoke troughs where it was hard to be seen, and then descend as black as crows pretending to have been cleaning the boiler.

The standard of engine cleanliness deteriorated between the wars, and with the outbreak of World War II it fell lower. The few cleaners in the depot were required to be passed out for firing as soon as they started in the department. The minimum age was lowered.

From this time onwards the three references were no longer required. When the war was over the position did not improve. In 1965 the engine cleaner was no longer a practical grade: when the last steam engine departed, the traditonal line of promotion disappeared. When the loco shed disappeared, so did the black-faced cleaner boy.

Call boys to awaken drivers, firemen and guards during the night hours, existed for so long that their origin is obscure. They were never used for benevolent reasons; purely to make sure the man called was alive and well and would be at work on time. The call boys to call locomen were recruited from engine cleaners and one from a junior porter to call the guards. The loco call boys took over all calling up in later years.

Before 1919, when there was no guaranteed day's work, a call boy would often call a man, perhaps at 3.0 am, but before he had arrived at work the boy would be told to go and stop him as the train had now been cancelled. The driver or foreman would quite likely be met half way to work.

There was consolation in the guaranteed six days exclusive of Sundays, and the last turn of duty must commence by 11.59 pm on the Saturday. If a man got behind in his turns of duty, and booked off after midday on Saturday for his fifth turn, thereby not having twelve hours rest before 11.59 pm he was laughing. It was a day's pay without coming to work.

This did happen, but the foreman watched out and made sure they were given jobs so that they returned to the depot before 11.59 am on Saturday. It was considered fair game, to scheme to get a Saturday night off.

Men were often called out for a lodging turn of duty. Men were permitted at least nine hours of rest when lodging at another depot, which would therefore perhaps bring a man from a late turn of duty on to a morning turn.

If a man was first in the book for Monday, his special paper showed a call as from midnight and he could expect to hear the call boy knock at the door any time about midnight, giving him one hour's notice to book on for a single or perhaps double trip turn. He would probably have gone to bed early to be ready for this early call.

Throughout its existence, the special link was generally the bottom link for drivers and firemen; it was accepted as an evil that had to be endured in the line of promotion. But it was an unsocial system of working that could not possibly last in the post-World War II era. A system of having a booking-in time that could, if necessary, be moved two hours either way, was substituted, which of course still kept a daytime call boy in existence.

The call boys were invariably the youngest cleaners, about 14 years of age. During World War II and a short period afterwards, adult 'caller ups' — the official term — were used, and a 'lady call boy' was utilised in the daytime. Other than this short period the call boy was Bletchley's night owl for several generations.

The call boys in the early years of this century would have walked the district to call enginemen and guards. Men lived within a radius of about a mile and a half of the depot, and as this was required of special link men, they were all on call. If their home was outside this distance, they had to move home or find lodgings.

When the bicycle came in after World War I, the call boys would often use their own cycles, without recompense, but no doubt saving in footwear. Later official call boys' cycles were supplied by the Company, complete with an LMS number and a 'penny stinker' oil lamp to light the way.

The call boys generally worked so that one called the Fenny end of the town and one Bletchley end, giving each man to be summoned a one hour call prior to his booking on time. Some of the dragons wanted one hour exactly. If he was called a few minutes before or after that hour, there was trouble. He would tell the shift foreman and it would mean a ticking off. A call boy would often stand shivering in some doorway, waiting to give an exact one hour call.

Often the two call boys doing either end of the town would accompany each other when one had a spell without a call. It was so on a particular occasion when two call boys pedalled down Brooklands Road to call driver Charlie Blane. Reggie Bowler and 'Baggy' Healey were heard by Charlie as he lay in bed wide awake. They appeared to be uncertain of his exact address as one said 'He lives here' then the other one said 'No, he lives here'. After a short bandy back and forth with a disagreement in words as to the right house, a final agreed decision was made when one said 'Let the old bugger lay' and away they went.

In the late years of World War II, adult caller ups took over. The first were redundant brickyard workers, some of whom stayed to see calling up abolished in the early 1950s.

Bar boys were generally young boys who had either just commenced as cleaners or were employed as a bar boy pending being made up to cleaner. The smaller the boy the greater the advantage in quick and easy access or exit through the firehole door. He was easily distinguishable from others moving about the shed doing various dirty jobs; he was the little dusty urchin carrying a firebar on his shoulder.

The bar boy came under the supervision of the boilersmith, who also had under his command the tubers and washerouts.

It was never really light in the shed, even in the daytime, and there were always men moving around doing various jobs. The washer-out with leggings and perhaps an old mackintosh with string, would be walking around an engine as water surged out of its side. As water drained out of the boiler of the lifeless engine, so more water flowed in and the washerout continually puggled away with a long wire into the water spaces through the mud hole joints and washout plugs, to loosen and dislodge scale.

The tubers replacing the boiler tubes and rolling the ends, were either in the firebox working at the tube plate or in the dark gaping smokebox working at that end of the tubes. Both ends were dirty, with smokebox ash and semi-darkness.

During World War II, women turned their hand to this most unladylike job. It was hardly expected they would attack the tubes as conscientiously as 'Knocker' Chamberlain, who for years cheerfully haunted the shed with a perpetually black face.

The brickarch man was one more to attend to the need of the boiler and firebox. A wheelbarrow loaded with large curved firebricks and a bucket of fire clay was wheeled to the engine, now cold and lifeless, for him to place inside the firebox to repair or build a new brick arch.

The bar boy's job was to crawl inside the fireboxes when the fire was out and the box cooled down, to clean the firebox roof and sides. If new firebars were needed, he put them in. If a small amount of fire was in the box, he would use tongs to change the bars, a heavy task for a small boy. It was not unknown for a small boy to slide quickly into a firebox and rapidly change a bar although a small fire was still in the box.

A steam-raiser cared for the engines in steam in the shed for 24 hours a day, every day of the year. He kept sufficient fire and steam in stabled engines until they were taken over by enginemen for train working. He fired the dead engines and raised steam after repairs or examinations, but it was on Sunday evening and Monday morning that he was busiest.

Fitters and their mates in greasy overalls moved about the shed doing their various tasks. There were shift fitters who attended to the small daily repairs booked by the drivers on repair cards; a wheeldrop fitter who specialised in the repair of axleboxes after overheating, which needed the wheels dropping for attention; a mileage fitter who performed the work on such parts as piston cross-heads at high mileage examinations. A vacuum fitter was a specialisation that was dropped some years before World War II.

The shift fitter studied repair cards throughout his shift and, if the engine was on the shed, attended to the smaller immediate repairs. His most common tools were the hammer and the ⅞th spanner, which were used for most repairs.

The fitter's mate was seldom without an outsize spanner to adjust the brakes of a LNWR engine, a repair that occupied a good part of his day.

The wheeldrop fitter was the only one that could be said to be static. His position at the wheeldrop had the advantage of regular day work, but brought him into contact with elements far more deadly than rain, snow or sunshine, without means of escape. George Caldwell was the wheeldrop fitter for the last 25 years of the shed's existence.

In the cold wintry weather, fires were often lit on the shed floor at intervals down each road and burned day and night to prevent frozen injector feed bags. In the abnormal winters of 1947 and 1963, huge fires were lit between the roads and only 20 or 30 yards apart in the pits, some as big as half a ton of coal. Fires were also made outside the shed near the water tank and at all water columns, but still engines froze up. The fitters' routine of repairs was chaotic in the three months of severe weather in 1947. They went from engine to engine with a paraffin-soaked lighted cloth on the end of a metal rod and held them under frozen injectors.

The blacksmith and his striker pursued their engine repair tasks at the forge next door to the fitter's shop. Bill King became the blacksmith in 1906 and took on the additional task of shoeing all the railway horses, which had formerly been the job of Webster and Keyte, the local blacksmith's in Duncombe Street. Draymen's horses and shunt horses came into the loco shed and Bill shod them just outside the blacksmith's shop.

Bill did not worry about demarcation of duties. If iron work of any description needed repair it was always 'Let Bill King have a look at it.' Among his unofficial jobs was the making of screw bar or ivy leaf jimmies for drivers. The jimmy was a thin piece of metal made into an ivy leaf shape, to place across the blast pipe aperture in the smoke box with a heavy coupling link to hold it in position. This reduced the blast pipe orifice and sharpened or cut the blast, with the added effect of improving the engine's steaming: but sparks came from the chimney and lit up the sky, sometimes leaving a trail of lineside fires.

The shed enginemen were the drivers and fireman who marshalled the shed, but they took on the name of turners way back in antiquity. It is probable that once they were responsible for turning engines on the turntable, but if this was so, it was beyond living memory. A set of men booked on for this job, so that the whole 24 hour period was covered every day of the year. It was a busy job, with varying periods when two pairs of hands would have been helpful. The turners were seldom men doing the job by choice or for promotion towards main line work; they were mostly drivers whose eyesight or some disability made them ineligible for main line work and were therefore relegated to this position, or perhaps to the shunting engine in one of the local yards. In some cases this applied to the fireman, but mostly it was part of a young fireman's early duties and served as part of his long apprenticeship through the various fireman's links to the rank of junior driver.

As an engine came onto the ashpit off train working, the fire was cleaned or dropped by the firedroppers; the engine was then taken round by the turners into the queue of engines on the coal road. When the coalman had done one engine, so the queue moved forward and the next engine was coaled. During this time the fireman not only coupled them together in the coal road, but attended to the fires and boilers of those still with a fire in the box.

There was a multitude of extraneous jobs for the turners.

The turners had a small wooden cabin near the turntable which was also used by the firedropper; before World War I a dingy shelter under the coal stage was their cabin, while the coalmen worked above and the water tank was above them.

Firedroppers had a filthy, sweating job. As engines arrived on the ashpit with varying depths of hot fire in the firebox, one of the two firedroppers climbed onto the footplate and laboured with a long iron dart to break the clinker, then with a long pair of heavy tongs, lifted out a few of the firebars, and pushed the fire into the ashpan. His mate would be shovelling the swirling ash from the smokebox, and then raking out the ashpan. At the busier time of day it was a question of just going from one engine to the next until it was time to go home. A bucket of hot water from an engine was always available to swill off the accumulated sweat and dirt.

The coalmen shovelled coal from a wagon into tenders and bunkers on a lower level than their wagon. All were sheltered under the engine water supply tank.

The manual coaling of engines carried on until the end of steam. Not until well after World War II did a mechanical grab come to the depot to load ashes from the ashpit and coal some engines, but it never ousted the coalmen. In fact it was under repair for nearly as much time as it was working.

The post-war period of full employment and staff shortage brought problems in finding staff for such a detestable job. A bonus scheme helped persuade men to do the job, but they were not the conscientious long-service men of early years. Those who remained coalmen for perhaps 30 years usually had to do other, lighter, labouring work in the last few years of their working life.

There has always been a 'Shed Gaffer', but at various times the status of the shed improved and a Superintendent took up residence.

There seems to have always been another foreman to cover other than the normal daylight hours. There was a night foreman many years ago, then two foremen covered these hours until World War II, and three running shift foremen covered the 24 hours with duties that kept the shed moving, while the shed foreman was responsible for the administration of the shed and the outstation sub-sheds at Cambridge, Oxford, Bedford, Banbury, Leighton Buzzard, Aylesbury and Newport Pagnell. These sheds all gradually closed: Bedford, Cambridge and Banbury were closed before World War II.

Mr McFazden was Shed Foreman in 1851 at the time of the Bicester crash. Joe Fennell recalls a Mr Middleton, when he started his railway career in the 1870s, and then Trevithick. At the end of the 19th century, Joseph Dibb was in charge and his title was carved on his gravestone in Fenny Stratford Cemetery — Chief of the Locomotive Dept at Bletchley LNWR. In 1903 Mr Tabener came from Ordsall Lane and remained until 1917.

Shed foremen came for short spells until Walter Dibb, son of the previous Dibb, was in charge at the time of the 1926 General Strike.

Mr Nelson followed with the rank of Superintendent because of the shed's improved status for the first time. After Mr Nelson there was a loss of status and shed foremen were in charge once again, with Mr Tetlow having several years in the position.

The last shed foreman was Ernie Dodd, who came in 1948 and stayed until the bitter end. Ernie had Superintendents in residence for various periods, but when Dick Tyldesley departed, Ernie reigned supreme. Ernie became the first and last with the fancy name of Shedmaster at Bletchley.

The running shift foreman was responsible for keeping the shed moving during his shift and providing the power of the correct classification for all trains to be worked. This was no mean task, as the shed was virtually bursting at the seams, the wartime traffic making hitherto undreamed of demands.

Coal was of low quality and generally small, which made the coalmen's job slow and detestable. The poor coal and the longer hours engines spent in traffic reacted also on the firedroppers, with thicker and harder clinker for them to deal with.

Looking back, it seems that only through the ingenuity of the shift foreman and the turners was the antiquated little loco shed able to cope with the wartime pressures, especially since more than eight hours a day were worked in blackout. Throughout the war the shed congestion and chaotic working continued.

Such was the shortage of firemen that young soldiers from the Railway Operating Division of the REs were billeted on the town. One unfortunate young soldier was killed when fireman to Driver Joe King. A derailment in the subway from the sidings at Wolverton into the Carriage Works was so severe, that the engine and tender buckled up, trapping the soldier fireman, to die a terrible death. Joe King escaped without serious injury.

About the end of 1943, a hostel, consisting of a road full of coaches in the carriage shed, was opened. Its administration came under the loco shed foreman and so did the problems. The inmates were mostly young firemen from northern depots who were on loan to Bletchley, but there was also a number of goods guards. Most came and went, but some had many years at Bletchley. Some young firemen stayed long enough to get over their early years, when they played cards throughout the night and were a plague to some driver next morning. Some married local girls and settled down, never losing their Lancashire or Scottish accents.

The exuberance and high spirits of these young firemen gave the Hostel coaches quite a reputation in the small town. If there were mischievous deeds performed in the town, the police would go straight to the Hostel.

Ernie Dodd came as Shed Foreman in 1948 and saw nothing but a shortage of staff until the shed closed, but was a kindly and diplomatic man. If any of the young firemen wanted leave on Saturday, their application was always granted. Ernie knew that if leave was refused, they would not come to work anyway. Some telephoned in on Saturday afternoon so regularly to say they were suddenly taken ill, but would be alright for work on Monday, that the foreman's assistant could predict before picking up the receiver who it was, and what his excuse would be.

A favourite was that the fireman was playing football for the local LMS team; Mr Dodd would grant leave for that at any time, but they often had more than eleven in a team.

The early post-war period was almost as chaotic as the war years. The Hostel was filled with a new kind of railwayman. They did not view the driver with awe, and the drivers in turn could not choose whether or not to take any particular fireman. Firemen were in short supply and there were plenty of factory vacancies, with higher wages.

In fairness, it must be said that even young firemen recruited locally had a more independent attitude than their forefathers, although very few actually followed in their fathers' footsteps.

There were also a number of displaced Europeans working in the loco as coalmen, firedroppers and various shed grades. A few lived and catered for themselves in the trainmen's lodging house at the loco entrance, and some were in a hostel in the Park, which was not connected with the railway.

After about four years, and growing complaints about the suitability of the coaches after years of constant use, the Hostel closed down, but not before the Manor at Little Brickhill had been suitably converted. Now there was a special railway'bus to bring the Hostel inmates the three miles to and from work, or into town for pleasure.

The two hostels operated for about 20 years, during which time there were some odd characters. The first stewardess in charge was the motherly Mrs King, who somehow coped with the high-spirited boys. A few young women did the domestic chores and were in the front line for some boyish pranks.

Mrs King soon gave way to Charlie Blane, who remained until the Manor Hostel closed. Charlie was an ex-footplate man, as were many of these hostel staff, and every job in the Hostel was at some time performed by an engine driver who had failed through eyesight, accident or ill health.

Three loco shift foreman in the post-war period were Joe Keen, Bill Taylor and Jim Palmer, experienced foremen with long railway service. All had their own methods of dealing with new types of railwayman. Joe Keen had the most direct approach, and would sometimes walk to the coaches and pull the bedclothes off a young fireman who would not get up. Joe had powerful hands and there was generally a loud shout of 'Alright Joe, I'll come to work'. With gradual dieselisation, the staffing problem eased a little and the Manor Hostel had rooms to spare. In 1963 it closed down.

To a young cleaner passed to act as fireman, the oldest drivers appeared formidable, grumpy and ancient. But they were reliable men who gave a lifetime to railway service and their years of experience made them conscientious in their job. They could also tell stories of old days and different ways on the railway that enthralled their younger comrades.

When a number of them had collected in the messroom with a few fitters, labourers, and the drivers' own firemen, a discussion about some recent problem would act as a cue for a story.

The scene in the messroom on one particular winter's night was typical of its appearance for several generations of locomen. Onion peel on the table denoted the remains of a departed locoman's supper; Fitter Ted Scott would voice his usual grievance about the relative worth of the fitter and driver; a discussion on rules and regulations would arise, leading to the inevitable anecdote about the sadly steaming or overloaded engine. The story teller himself could leave a more lasting impression on a young fireman than the story.

Driver Freddy Eastaff would be sitting on the stool near the blazing fire, his white hair underneath a shiny top hat that was in its usual askew positon. His pipe was in and out of his mouth as he related his story in an unhurried and deliberate fashion. 'Staffy' enriched his story by his obvious Bucks extraction with full account of the performance of a little DX in years long past. No sooner had he finished than Driver Billy Stevens enriched the tale still further in a fast talking manner that gave a clue to his nickname of Willy Wiggles. Willy talked and moved about, even on the footplate, like a Jack-in-the-box.

The Breakdown Gang assembly, when the call came for action, was a frequent ritual for the foreman on duty. The call varied in urgency according to whether the mishap or derailment was blocking running line or in a siding causing no particular problem. The immediate job was for the gang to be called out. They were all drawn from the shed's engine maintenance staff with the shed foreman or the foreman fitter, when one of this grade was allocated to the shed, in charge. To be a member of the gang one had to live near the station. Most of the gang were regular day shift workers, so a daytime call out did not take long.

While calling up was in progress the turners, or a spare set of enginemen, would be dragging out the breakdown train from its stabling road in the 'seconds' — a road between the main line and the shed yard — and marshalling it so that the crane on departure would be next to the engine.

The origin of the Breakdown Gang at Bletchley loco shed is rather obscure. A gang of 'mechanics' from Wolverton was called to the 1853 crash at Oxford and the 1851 crash at Bicester; this was just a gang of 'men and implements for repairing the line', according to *Jackson's Oxford Journal*. J. E. McConnell, Locomotive Superintendent of the Southern Divison of the LNWR located at the Locomotive Works at Wolverton, led the gang.

How long this arrangement remained can only be surmised. Mr McConnell retired in 1862 and very soon the LNWR decided to cease the manufacture of locomotives at Wolverton. It is likely that during this time the responsibility for breakdown of engines or mishaps on the line would have fallen to some degree on Bletchley Breakdown Gang.

From those early days until 1940 the Breakdown Train consisted of a van for the gang to ride, a tool van and a small ten-ton hand crane.

There was a good, sound reason for being a member of the Breakdown Gang, namely 'to get some extra money in the tin'. (A small cylindrical tin was the method of receiving wages until after World War II.) A nice, heavy derailment in the area when Christmas was approaching, was a silent wish of at least some of the gang.

Bill King, the blacksmith, was a member of the gang from World War I time and probably before, until he retired in the early 1950s, and in those inter war years there was a payment of three shillings for each call out. It was during World War II that gradual increases in the payment began. In the riding van a supply of corned beef, arrowroot biscuits and tea, sugar and milk was always carried and despite the long hours spent at major mishaps, the diet did not vary. Three meals a day of corned beef and biscuits were guaranteed. After World War II the Breakdown Gang was allowed a supply of tinned foods and a member of the gang to heat them up.

For about 20 years the Breakdown Gang and the little crane did a thriving business; although the crane mostly went with them, it was often left behind.

For another five years, a larger crane did sterling work in the area, but the aid of Rugby or Willesden was still needed when heavy lifts were required.

The closure of branch lines was also decreasing the Breakdown Area as well, but when the Great Central main line closed and Woodford Halse loco shed no longer existed, the line from Claydon Junction to Marylebone was put under Bletchley Breakdown Gang, as a substantial bonus. Before this came about the 30 ton crane had departed, and taken up peaceful residence in a Museum at Brighton.

The new crane was still a 30 ton one, but it had a longer jib, was red and had a more magnificent appearance. But now steam engine days were over and the crane had a new residence, the District Electric Depot, where it was the only steam driven machine.

Herbert Leon was a popular Squire. A knighthood came in 1911 and Sir Herbert with Lady Fanny dominated Bletchley and Fenny Stratford in various ways for about half a century. He was a former Liberal MP for North Bucks, which gave him some affinity with the working classes in those days.

He complained repeatedly of offensive smoke from engines of the Railway Company interfering with his property and seriously interfering with the amenities of the Bletchley Park Estate. The smoke nuisance got worse over the years, and then he applied to the courts for protection. Action was commenced in about early 1923. It finally reached the High Court of Justice, Chancery Division, in March 1925.

The Railway Company admitted the nuisance but decided to fight the case upon their stautory rights. A settlement was arrived at under which the Railway Company agreed to pay the cost of the action, besides entering into a covenant to effect certain alterations to mitigate the nuisance.

The first of twelve specific orders for the Railway Company to put into effect was to extend the engine shed by 56 feet by the end of the year and to heighten all chimneys of the western half of the shed, so that the top of each chimney was six feet above the roof of the shed, the chimneys on the eastern half to be heightened if required by Sir Herbert, or his successors, and to be requested in writing. The breakdown train was henceforth not to be stabled in the shed and engine repairs, except to wheels, should be performed on the west side of the shed, to leave the east side for the lighting up of engines. The practice of lighting up some outside the shed had to cease and be brought into the shed for that purpose. The lighting up of fires had to be by a coal which, in combustion, gave the minimum amount of smoke, and engines were to be fired gradually. When put into practice these caused considerable inconvenience, money and unnecessary labour for about the next fifteen years.

The incessant movement of engines on the loco had a noisy competitor in the shunting yards on the opposite or east side of the main lines.

There was a shunting engine at both the north and south end of the main shunting yard.

At the north end of the yard, No 7 Signalbox was a pointsmen's box, as it had no main line signalling: points leading out of the yard for main line departures northward were controlled by No 3 Box.

While No 7 controlled the points at the north end of the yard, the 80 lever frame No 5 Box worked the points at the south end as well as the signals on the Cambridge branch line. On the opposite side of the Cambridge line, the top yard shunting engine was equally busy with traffic for the Goods Shed and the Ballast Depot where the saw mill was situated. It was the yard that marshalled trains for the eastern direction, and for many years two evening vegetable trains departed for London out of the opposite end of the same yard. When the Gas Works was in operation in this yard, that would also have made daily shunting work.

The shunting yards at Bletchley developed over many years, and as many as five shunting engines worked during the daytime, as well as a twenty four hour station carriage shunting engine. This peak was reached about 1950, but its decline to one engine was much quicker.

Until the early 1920s there was a shunting engine and a head shunter at the north end, but there was no under shunter to assist him because it was considered that, as the pointsmen in No 7 Box pulled the points at the shunter's request, it was sufficient assistance. An engine and a shunter and undershunter continually shunted the Top yard, but the south end had a shunting engine and shunter only when it was thought necessary. This position changed as brick traffic increased.

An arrival road from Denbigh Loop around the east side of the yard was built to accept Bletchley freight trains arriving from the north, and save congestion caused by the former arrival via the up loop and slow line and waiting to get back into the yard. In 1934 the Cambridge Sidings were built on the north side of the Cambridge Branch, an extension of the short Cliffe Siding, built before World War I and named after Station Master Cliffe.

From this time the yards were busier than ever before with the signalman in No 5 Box the central figure in all this see-sawing of wagons. By tic-tac signs from the shunter at the south end, points were changed by the signalman and wagons were knocked down the appropriate roads. By night a complicated method of half red, half green and various horizontal and vertical directional swings with his oil lamp took the place of tic-tac signs. While wagons rolled towards the north end, the shunter there was shunting towards the south end. As they both shunted and marshalled trains, the possibility of wagons being knocked foul of roads at the opposite end was always a danger. In this event the signalmen conferred with the others and, if they were lucky, were able to notify the shunter before damage was done. At the best, the wagons would be pushed back into the clear.

All jobs in the shunting yard were surrounded with danger. As the examiners walked around trains on the loop, the darkness and uneven ballast made it precarious, with trains speeding past on the adjoining slow lines. In the yard, wagons silently rolled past them as they examined wagons on the next road. Over the years many an examiner or shunter had reason to regret a moment's lack of thought, as he walked through a convenient space between the buffers of two wagons, when the shunting engine appeared to be standing still. Silent rolling wagons had caused a buffering up of wagons along the road. None was so foolish as one examiner who went underneath a wagon in the yard to do a quick repair while his colleague kept watch. A rolling batch of coal-filled wagons crashed into the first wagon on that road and the instant buffering up of wagons gave the hapless examiner no chance.

The shunters, undershunters, wheeltappers and greasers had foot-weary jobs in those days, when the yard was consistently full of wagons, and freight trains waited on the loop lines or arrival road, waiting to depart after examination or out of the yard for Oxford, Northampton or Willesden. Engine fires were being partially cleaned as they waited; and there was a further hazard for those working in the yard as pieces of red hot clinker were taken without warning from the footplate.

The Yard Inspector's office was a wooden hut near No 5 Box, known as No 9 Cabin.

Right back before World War I the inspector had the assistance of a telephone boy, except at night time, in his cabin. His job was not only to contact the inspector if he was required when working in the yard, but to wire forward, through the Telegraph Office, relevant information about departing freight trains.

Telephone boys in No 9 Cabin came to an end in the late 1920s, when one of the economy schemes was to move the train recording boys from No 3 Box to No 2.

During 1934 siding space was increased on the north side of the Cambridge branch, the brick traffic correspondingly increased and was probably at its peak when World War II began. The inevitably heavy demand on the yard through extra traffic must have been foreseen early in the war, as Swanbourne Sidings was built and in use by 1942.

Throughout the war Bletchley yard was busy beyond question, and it was the dexterity of experienced shunters like Fred Butler, Jack Lewis and others, surrounded by the inexperienced hands who inevitably came with staff shortages, that enabled the yard to function effectively.

After the war, although Swanbourne continued to relieve Bletchley, the North and South end shunting engines were still busy. The top yard had considerable business with the goods shed, and the ballast depot had a daytime shunt engine. By 1952 the former refuse sidings, near the new sidings built in 1934, was sufficiently level to take into a Track Prefabrication Depot, although tell-tale smoke from various spots told of underground burning.

There was some modernisation in the tic-tac signalling system after the war. A tannoy system allowed the signalman on No 5 to broadcast all over the yard, and the shunters to talk back from certain places in the yard.

Changes came under the guise of modernisation, rationalisation and economy. The diesel shunting engine was welcomed with its cleanliness, and saving time in coaling, watering, and firecleaning. The Track Prefabrication Depot was transferred to Bedford Midland and made way for the Diesel Electric Depot some years later. The construction of the Flyover made necessary siding alterations. Dieselisation passed and electrification and modern coloured light signalling meant the demolition of No 7 and No 5 Boxes, and with them what remained of the mysteries of the tic-tac.

The new Power Signalbox opened in July 1965 and Harold Mason, the signalman, standing at the panel in a white shirt, surveying the trains entering and running on the 22 miles of four line track under his control, looked vastly different to his predecessor, the railway policeman of 116 years earlier.

The railway policeman of 1849 would have been standing where the Bedford line made a junction with the main line, dressed in a top hat, a tunic complete with whistle, flags, detonators and probably a concealed truncheon.

The rules and regulations of the LNWR dated 1849, Section 9, Rule 9, gave a clear indication of his duty:

'At the junction with the Bedford at Bletchley — where stationary signals are placed, the Policeman is to keep the Red Signal always turned on to the Branch Line to prevent an engine passing to the Main Line until he has ascertained that the Main Line is clear, when he is to turn the Signal off the Branch and on to the Main Line.'

The policemen and pointsmen held responsible jobs. The policeman alone was responsible for the departure of a train from his stationary signal, after a given time had elapsed since the preceding train departed. His duties generally were to see that his stationary signal and hand lamps were well trimmed and showed a clear and distinct light. He should not allow unauthorised people on the line and any irregularities, trespassing or damage to points, crossing or guide rails were to be reported to his inspector.

The need for care and attention was well demonstrated at Wolverton on 5 June 1847 when Pointsman Bernard Fossey appears to have mistaken an express for a goods train and switched the down mails into the siding where it crashed into some coal wagons. Seven people were killed and many injured as well as much damage to engine and carriages.

Bernard Fossey pleaded in court that he had too much to do.

The judge made it clear that if a man had too much to do he should decline the position. Two years in prison and kept in hard labour, was the Judge's answer for careless pointsmen.

Inspectors of police had four rules appertaining to them in Section 8 of the 1849 Rule Book. Their duties were to walk their district and report to the Superintendent any irregularities they might detect: see the policemen, pointsmen and gatemen in the district were at their posts, clean in their persons, sober and attentive to their duties, conversant with their orders and that all points were in good working order, cleaned and oiled. Their duties also included seeing that each police box had a copy of the standing orders relative to police signals and duties. A list of names and places of abode of every policeman in the district had to be kept by an inspector so they could be summoned if needed.

With the improvements in signalling, the policeman and pointsman gradually became known as signalmen. In August 1889 the Regulation of the Railways Act enforced the block system, the interlocking of signals and points and the provision of continuous automatic brakes on passenger trains, but they were much in evidence before the Act enforced their adoption. The grade of pointsman did not completely disappear. At such places as Bletchley north end shunting yard, a small signalbox for the pointsman who controlled the points at that end of the yard and had no main line duties, remained until more or less the end of steam engines.

Joseph Dimmock was a signalman in Bletchley No 2 in the early years of this century; he also spent some years in Fenny Stratford Box, but he had been an original policeman, his truncheon being at the present time in the possession of his grandaughter. He was once known as PC Dimmock by local people and seems to have been the last one locally in living memory with a railway police connection. His descendants have spread over the town, and his son Harry, as well as spending his working life as a railwayman, served 39 years as a Bletchley Urban District Councillor and was its Chairman for five years.

In the first decade of this century, signalmen's wages varied from 22 to 34s a week. Nos 1, 2 and 3 Signalboxes were 34s and No 5 was 32s, while a porter was 17s 6d. By 1918 a 25s a week War Bonus was added.

There was an unsatisfactory promotion system until the 1920s. The usual practice was for a form to be sent to senior men thought capable of working a larger box, giving them an opportunity to apply for the vacancy. Later a vacancy list was sent to each station or a list put in the weekly notices; sometimes the list just said 'no vacancies'.

For many years men moved home for a small increase in pay. Between the wars, a porter at 40s per week became a porter signalman for 45s; then he moved to a class 6 box for 48s, then on to class 5 at 50s; class 4 at 55s, class 3 at 60s; class 2 at 65s; class 1 at 70s; finally, if ever reached, special class at 75s. There was a class 4G at Cambridge at 57s 6d per week.

Relief signalmen lodged in the numerous little villages in the area nearly all the time. If the box was within reasonable distance he could use a cycle.

At little stations such as Morton Pinkney, Swanbourne, Ridgmont, and many others, the signlaman would find himself responsible for the booking office, weighbridge, sheeting loads of hay, cleaning horseboxes out and loading cattle; in fact he was a Jack of all Trades.

In the mid-thirties many signalboxes, that opened only when a siding was in use, were demolished and ground frames installed. An annett key from the box on either side allowed the siding to be opened and signals locked while the frame was in use. Several little stations that could boast of a station master now found that he was transferred to a larger station with a number of smaller ones under his command. The signalman was often the only man on these small stations with a little of every station job to do.

While many signalboxes disappeared or were manned by porter signalmen when required, some were actually built. Bletchley No 4 was built at the outlet of the New Cambridge Sidings to cope with the growing brick traffic. Flettons Box was built for the new siding into a new brickworks. Both of these boxes came in the mid-1930s.

Changes came with World War II. The working of long hours was the lot of most railwaymen and the shortage of staff applied to most grades. Relief signalmen were having difficulties in finding lodgings and staff shortages remained until the end of steam, and then this state of affairs dramatically changed.

Signalwomen came on the branches during the war; the first was probably Nellie Franklin at Marsh Gibbon. Her husband was a signalman on the station and they lived in one of the two nearby railway cottages. The lady's training was left to Relief Signalman Sid Sellers; Mrs Franklin, like the rest of the ladies, helped to brighten up the branches.

Miss Ethel Roberts was the first signalwoman in Bletchley No 4; the Essential Works Order had somehow landed Ethel in Bletchley from South Wales and she remained in the job until the Order was lifted in 1946, then she settled in Bletchley, married to one of the many footplate men who gave a wave as they passed her box.

Sheila Powers was a local girl who soon followed and others came from as far away as Bournemouth. Three signalwomen remained until redundancies in that grade, when a new railway, without the steam engine, was in the making. They were then found other jobs.

The ladies never went into main line boxes, but remained in Bletchley No 4, Flettons

Siding, Claydon Station and Swanbourne Sidings Boxes.

When the motor car became a possible purchase, lodging was not always necessary. Conditions of service began to improve with wages. Class 6 signalboxes were all upgraded to class 5. Later class 5 were upgraded to class 4 and by the time class 4 was abolished several branch lines were closed and the signalmen's promotional area was considerably smaller.

Denbigh Box on the main line was placed near to the historic bridge in 1899 when a loop line was placed parallel with the up slow line to No 3 Box. Prior to that date Denbigh Box was a little nearer to Wolverton. Now, with the coming of the flyover it was moved nearer to No 3 Box.

Bletchley Nos 1, 2, 3 and 5 were typical LNWR elevated signalboxes, but No 3 was very high, having three floors. Access to the top floor was via stairs, then through a trap door on each floor. Level with the box's north window was Bulldog Bridge, a private bridge connecting Sir Herbert Leon's Park with his land on the opposite side of the railway.

In 1957 some electric signals replaced the semaphore signals at the south end of patform 5 and 6 at Bletchley Station. The gantry and signals had been there for more than thirty years. This made no significant change in the manual effort involved in the 96 lever frame on No 1 Box; when the flyover was completed, the frame increased to 105 levers.

With the coming of the flyover, Bletchley No 3 50 lever frame disappeared and Denbigh took over its signalling. Bulldog Bridge was made redundant and demolished soon after World War II began.

The electrification of the main line made the most far-reaching changes in the life of the signalmen. As the gantries for the overhead wires were erected, so the new automatic colour light signalling gantries could be seen among the endless structures. Staffordshire bricks could be seen gradually forming into a new power signalbox.

Down the branch lines the mechanical signalboxes were due to remain, but as the passenger services between Oxford, Banbury and Cambridge were withdrawn, various signalboxes became redundant and signalmen became a disappearing grade.

There was an affinity between the policeman and pointsman and the gateman in the early days of British Railways. In the LNWR rule book of 1849, section ten contained six rules appertaining to gatemen. He had to signal all trains past his gates and had considerable responsibilities, in fact they were comparable to most of the policeman and pointsmen. Rule 4 illustrates his responsibilities — 'If an engine follow another within three minutes, the Danger Signal is to be shown; from three to seven minutes, the Caution Signal must be exhibited'.

Since the days of Gatemen, signalmen have emerged and in some cases such as Bicester, the crossing gates are operated by the signalman. The gatemen gradually became known as crossing keepers and finally it was made the standard name in 1921 for those who operated crossing gates which were not a block post and therefore did not control trains. There were crossings with signals that only protected the gates while they were across the railway, for road traffic to pass over, and there were crossings without signals. The normal position for all gates was against road traffic.

A grade that did remain was that of gatekeeper. These were the wives of railwaymen who lived in the railway houses situated near minor road level crossings and some farm crossings, and were on duty 24 hours a day. Very little traffic used these roads in the daytime and nothing at night, so actual work was little, but attendance was more or less permanent, and always in isolated places.

The national Agreement on wages and conditions of service in 1923 gave the rates of pay: 'gatemen (Wives of Companies Servants) at present in receipt of War Wage of 7s 6d per week should be advanced from July 1st 1920 to 8s 6d per week, and from October 1st

1920 to 9s 0d per week'. This wage would invariably cover the rent of the house, so the ladies were house-bound, isolated, and living a rent-free existence without the mods and cons of even those days.

The highest concentration of road crossings was between Bletchley and Bedford, but Fenny Stratford, Woburn Sands, Ridgmont and Millbrook were block posts and therefore worked by signalmen. Lidlington once held the same rank, but has now long been a post for a grade I porter who operates the gates and issues tickets from the booking office. The porter's wife in the station house was responsible for the gates at night. Of these level crossings, Fenny Stratford had gates operated by a large wheel in the signalbox. Woburn Sands had this luxury added in the late 1930s, which with Bicester, made them the only crossings on the branch lines that could boast wheel operated gates. The remainder were all crossings with varying degrees of traffic.

The gradual popularity of the motor car changed the life of all crossing keepers. As the cars increased, so the 9s a week crossings decreased and the manned crossing with crossing keepers paid the porter's rate, with far longer hours, and perhaps a day off once a week.

After World War II life changed dramatically and took on an element of danger.

The ladies who looked after the little-used crossings for 24 hours a day were about to disappear. To cover the eventuality of an unmanned level crossing, there was a Sectional Appendix Instruction for train crews on the Banbury branch, to open level crossing gates and close them against the railway after use, when a crossing keeper was not in attendance.

One 24 hour a day lady near Potton met her death on her own crossing, it can only be assumed familiarity bred contempt. An engine dropped off a few lumps of coal as it passed over the crossing and the lady immediately proceeded to pick it up, but she did not see or hear the approaching train in the opposite direction.

It was a long established practice to give some crossing keepers' jobs to railwaymen disabled because of an accident at work. Wally Oxford came to Bow Brickhill Crossing with an artificial leg and remained there for 26 years. He was a fireman at Stafford; but it was at Crewe in 1928 when he was struck by an express train and the serious injury resulted in the amputation of one leg.

Bob Hammond heard that a crossing keeper's position at Wooton Broadmead was vacant, and a house to go with it. It was in 1939 that he set off from his home in Lincoln with a twelve hour cycle ride in front of him, to have an interview for the job with the Station Master at Millbrook station. He got the job and the house and more money than his previous job on a farm — he worked eight hours on each alternate week day and was on call every night, for £2 5s 0d per week plus 3s for being on call at night, and extra money for an alternate Sunday duty, less 4s 6d for rent and rates.

As some of the branch lines closed down completely or were open to passenger traffic only, so some of the crossing houses were demolished or sold to those who desired to live in the isolated or the unusual. Even on the Bletchley-Bedford section, where the passenger service was still running, crossing houses still disappeared. Bow Brickhill's ornamental house was damp and too near the railway line to be sold, and was demolished. Wootton Broadmead's sturdy-looking two storey brick house had the same fate.

Automatic half barriers were installed at Marston Crossing as early as 1961 and some years later the house was sold. The barriers appear to have been successful, but not without incidents.

It has often been said that the original platelayers were the farm workers who jumped over the fence when railways first came, to earn a shilling a week more. It may have been true, for along these branch lines they were all men equally at home on the land. In the 1920s they were mostly those who had started their railway career in the previous century. They were

135

rough and tough, used to outdoor life, experts at catching rabbits and pheasants. Many had their regular customers for rabbits among the train crews.

Most were gardeners on a large scale; many kept pigs and chickens. Their whole life was manual work with a pint of beer for recreation.

Gangers with their small gang had their own length in the vicinity of their homes. A few miles away would be regarded as 'vicinity'. These lengths were the ganger's domain and he would be away all day in the quiet countryside. Old wooden cabins along the length were resting places for a midday meal. The cabins were mostly built of redundant sleepers with a brick fireplace and chimney and a look of antiquity. Coal was generally plentiful from the spillage of engines, but most drivers would kick off a few hundredweights of coal on request, and a rabbit or some plants would then be given in return if required.

The gangs on the main line had much the same life, but they not only had four lines to contend with, but more frequent and faster traffic.

The large extra gang or relayers at Bletchley had a different way of life. They did the big heavy relaying jobs which required many men. They had to go, not only along these branch lines, but along the main lines, anywhere from London to Coventry and on other branch lines. Wherever they went outside the Bletchley station area, they would have to lodge. Even when they were working as near as Stoke Hammond, Winslow or Verney Junction, lodgings had to be found. If a platelayer decided he would go to his own home because it was within walking or cycling distance, and the Timekeeper found out, he lost his one shilling or perhaps one and sixpence lodging allowance.

These lodging jobs were mostly for a week, and it was the tool nipper's job to find lodgings for the men. On arrival at the place of work he went to various houses to see if men could be lodged. Often they were the homes of other railwaymen or houses that had lodgers previously, some over many years, making them well known. Jenny Rush of Winslow was one such person. She was an eccentric old lady living in a little cottage outside the village, and one could say she lived on her own, if a house full of dogs is discounted.

Finding lodgings was only a small part of the tool nipper's job. He was responsible for the tools being on the job. He would see that a wagon of tools was loaded and despatched for the next job. In this way two wagons were in use for the gang; one was with them and the other was en route for the next relaying job.

These were all the tools required, except for the platelayer's shovel, which he took with him wherever he went. It was stamped with his number and if it was broken or worn out, an exchange could only be done if he produced his old shovel or the broken parts. It was then suitably marked, so that any enterprising platelayer could not use the same worn out shovel to acquire a second one.

The platelayer who started his railway career at the turn of the century was used to roughing it. He would sit on the grass or in the shelter of a bridge and, with a clasp knife, slice off his Bucks Clanger.

The platelayer's dress altered little for nearly a century. They all had wide and thick Scotch leather belts with a brass buckle. In the World War I period, labourer's trousers had bell bottoms, tight knees, no turnups, and under the knees, straps called Yorkers. These saved wear at the knees and held the shovel scraper. As late as 1935-36 the older men wore this same style of dress.

The Bucks Clanger was his staple diet. The original was a long pudding filled with mixed bacon and onion, but there were variations. Some had bacon one end and onion or potato in the other. Some had meat of various types and others even had meat one end and jam the other. They were cooked at home and eaten at work, either cold or warmed up.

There were five county dialects from Oxford to Cambridge, but there was one similarity;

136

they all had a rural broadness. George Windsor from Stoke Hammond would sit and eat his cold Clanger with bacon and potatoes at opposing ends. He ate them regularly and whenever anyone asked him where the bacon was in his lengthy Clanger, he always said 'I've cut past it'. Some said he had cut past it so often when asked, that it was doubtful if bacon was in it. When he had eaten it all, he always patted his well-proportioned stomach and said 'That'll stay me'. George was cutting past his bacon with a clasp knife one day, when a rat scampered past; he quickly threw his half-devoured Clanger and hit his target fair and square. The rat laid still and quiet and presumably dead while George picked up his undented Clanger and with a few criss-cross wipes on his well worn sleeve, commented in disgust 'I hate them dirty bloody things' and resumed cutting past his bacon.

Ernie Dickens, a life-long railwayman from rural Mursley, remembers when he was a young man in the 1920s, watching an old ganger slicing his Clanger with a clasp knife, when maggots appeared in the meat. He continued cutting and eating. When he saw Ernie's contorted face he said 'They et me meat, now I'll bloody et em'.

Ernie's own father, with the unexplained name of Thecker, was a tough old ganger on the Swanbourne length. He chewed tobacco and spat much and often. His trail could always be followed by the sleeper ends, which seemed his target as he walked.

Thecker was no mean drinker. He could wallop it back any time and anywhere, but he preferred it strong. On one occasion at Banbury he went across to the Great Western canteen. The first pint was tried and, after a comment about its weakness, he emptied a bottle of Daddies Sauce into it, and with one tip he downed the lot.

Fogging duty was an important part of the length gangs' life. It is only since modern colour light signalling, that this unpleasant job has become redundant.

When fog became thick, the signalman would decided that fogmen were required at the distant signals. In the daytime the men, being already on duty, would know they were required and proceed to the signals at which they would be needed. The fogmen's lamps were kept in the signalboxes and usually cleaned by the signalmen, ready for the next fog, so the fogman reported to the box for his lamp when going to his post. The one man at the position usually had a small sentry box with detonators already inside. Coal was already collected for these occasions, so that an open fire could be started immediately; detonators were placed on the lines as well as exhibiting a coloured light, according to the position of the distant signal.

One platelayer would go to the signalbox and inform the signalman that his distant signals were manned and be the signalman's tail lamp man. The lighted tail lamp denoted a train had passed complete, and he then informed the signalman accordingly. This was generally done by a whistle, a number of whistles denoting a particular running road.

When fog came down at night, the signalman would inform the Control Office and a call boy would call a designated platelayer, who in turn called out those of his gang who were available for fogging duty. Some outlying villages did have Fogmen's Cottages, where the signalman was able to actuate a bell fixed in the house.

Ganger Dickie Hawes lived in Denbigh Cottages; he was one of the conscientious old timers. As soon as fog was seen he would go out into his garden, and if the fog was too thick to see the signal gantry near Denbigh signalbox, he was soon on his way to call some of his gang, and then off to his sentry box at Denbigh distant signals, after a quick call at the signalbox.

When the war ended in 1945, the permanent way man was little different than his predecessor of the previous century. The shovel was his main tool; he used to pick and sieve to clean ballast on his length and had a long handled hammer to knock in loose chair keys as he walked the length. The relayers hauled heavy lengths of rail and sleepers about by hand.

Staff shortage and a terrific arrears of track maintenance brought in the first changes. Polish and various displaced European workers came into the gangs. Contractors began to perform work that had always been done by railwaymen. For the first time, working on Sunday could be performed 52 times a year. Money could be earned, but only by a seven day week.

Mechanical assistance was as inevitable as pay day. Soon the prefabrication of track became a practical proposition. A depot was installed on the former tipping site on the down side of the commencement of the Cambridge Branch.

Small kango hammers for packing the sleepers by vibration began to appear, and the incessant packing by shovel and small ballast was on the decrease.

Then came the big sophisticated machinery moving under its own power, and the machine operator and maintenance man was required. The Austrian manufactured Plasser-Theurer Tampers to perform the laborious sleeper packing came, as other large expensive machinery began to invade the permanent way. Regulators, tampers, liners, consolidators and Matisa machines did the work of many men. Tracklayer cranes with vertical arms to work under bridges, and overhead wires displaced the conventional cranes on prefabricated relaying. Then came the Italian-built Speno Railgrinder.

Younger men began to operate and maintain machines and night work became the lot of many permanent way men.

Bonus schemes came and many an old ganger who was as tough as old boots, shivered at the thought of using a pencil. Some found more money could be earned with a pencil than a shovel.

The branch line gangs even became mobile; a tool-equipped van moved them about their longer lengths. 'Buses hired by the Divisional Engineer carried men around the countryside to the larger and heavy maintenance jobs. The fogman disappeared with automatic coloured light signalling.

The artizan staff are seldom mentioned when railway history is written. Their job was important and had a great similarity to the permanent way men. They were the carpenters, bricklayers, plumbers and the mates to go with them.

The repairing and general maintenance of bridges, culverts, signalboxes and station buildings down to the mess room tap, was their domain, and it brought with it a rough and tough way of life. They too lodged away for a week at a time, sometimes as near as Loughton, three miles away.

Between the wars there were about 50 in this department of various grades. Their huts for offices and tools were clustered around the saw mills in the ballast yard. Wood fencing was cut in the saw mills from used sleepers, but there was little else mechanical.

If a remote bridge along the Banbury branch needed brickwork repairing, bricks, sand, cement and a few minor tools were conveyed in a wagon to the nearest siding and then ferried out on a platelayer's trolley. There were no messroom facilities for them. They could perhaps share a remote platelayer's hut if one was near the job; if not, they had to do the best they could for shelter.

Artizan staff at Bletchley gradually decreased. The saw mills disappeared to make way for the flyover. Like the permanent way men, the road motor vans came to take men and their tools from job to job. Hired machines became available for almost any former manual job, but the depot went down to just token staff of a supervisor, carpenter, plumber and bricklayer, who worked in motorised conjunction with Watford and Northampton Depots.

When the railways first came, steam locomotive was known as the Iron Horse and no doubt it made some horses redundant. When the *Bedford Times* Coach ceased its regular service immediately the Bedford-Bletchley line opened, the *Bedford Times* newspaper forecast that the roads would soon be left just for 'gipsies and the new police'.

Horses immediately began to play an enormous part in the successful operation of the railways until after World War II: in fact they were still being used in Bletchley until 1952; only 13 years before the last steam engine departed from Bletchley loco shed. They were treated affectionately by railwaymen and the travelling public.

Horses could be seen shunting the wagons detached into the siding near Launton for Bicester Aerodrome, shunting wagons in Winslow Goods Shed, the brewery traffic at Bedford and Brackley; in fact at some time or other they were at most stations where there was more than a single siding, and were used for shunting wagons. At Potton, the traders' horses and carts bringing in vegetables or carting out manure were once a scene of traffic congestion. The drayman with his horse and dray for local delivery was attached to many stations.

Bletchley had shunting horses right from the very early days of railways. These horses were trained and utilised only for shunting. To be a shunt horse driver was not anybody's job. It was certainly a responsibility and a job that needed heart; a job that one had to want. The shunt horse driver had to look after himself and the horse as he walked about the station, stepping over the rails to cross the main lines, although the horses were trained to the point of being uncanny.

The shunt horse stables were in the Railway Approach Road, next to the stables and later the garage of Cecil Hands, who ran a local taxi service. When the horse was saddled for work it would wander on its own across the roadway, through the little wicket gate opposite, and await the call from its driver. When the call came, without guide or rein tugging, it would move off to meet its driver and go to the required spot on the station. Along number one platform, across the main line near No 2 Signalbox, it would clearly and precisely step over rails and points rodding to a small 'waiting stable', where it waited for an up express with one or so vans to be detached from the rear, and then pull them over the main line to place them on the rear of the Oxford or Banbury passenger train. If there were vans or horseboxes to be detached on a down train, then the horse would proceed from the wicket gate to a 'waiting stable' at the south end of the station and await the down train.

Sometimes a 'fly shunt' was required and the horse would know the drill. With a good sturdy pull and stop, the driver quickly took off the harness hook from the moving vehicle and it would roll past the horse into the required road. This type of shunting was a daily task, but there were hazards and a great responsibility for the driver. When a vehicle was being pulled by a horse, it was always possible on a down gradient for the rolling vehicle to move faster than the horse, and it could overtake the horse walking in the six foot or cess. The driver would have to steady the wagon or throw off the hook and watch the horse if it was too near the moving traffic. This responsibility was the probable reason for a shortage of candidates for shunt horse drivers in later years.

Should a horse be killed or have to be destroyed after an accident, it was a far greater expense to the Railway Company than if its driver had suffered the fate and the horse been left to carry on. When horse shunt driver 'Itchy Coo' Clements lost his horse, it is said its hoof was caught in a diamond crossing near No 1 Box and a passing express hit it before efforts could be made to extract its foot; he held on to Ginger — as it was called — until the very last second.

Another horse also named Ginger had been a Shunt horse for many years, and had an uncanny knowledge of the lines, and no doubt had what could be called 'horse sense'. Ginger was pulling a load of cattle off one of the Banbury trains, when it fell between the loco siding and the down fast line, pulling its driver down with it. An express train was approaching, the animal had the presence of mind to turn over on its back, shoot its legs in the air and remain lying in this position until the express had passed, saving its own life as well as that of the driver.

Another dark brown horse named Bob used to light the incandescent gas lamp at the bottom of the platform slope. After turning the tap with its neck, it would carefully look round to see that the lamp was alight, then wag its tail with apparent satisfaction.

Sadly the shunt horse had to go. Young horse drivers like George Catterall and Cyril Tilley had not long taken over, and become attached to their horses when, about the beginning of World War II, the use of shunt horses ceased.

But this was not the end of railway horses at Bletchley. The drayman, with his horse attached to the dray, were familiar figures standing silent and motionless waiting for the driver while he delivered parcels.

By 1952 the last two horses departed. In earlier years the dray horses were stabled in the goods yard, but when the shunt horses became redundant and departed, the dray horses made their home in the stables in the Railway Approach.

The last horse draymen were Happy Windsor and Bert Shepherd. They gently traversed the town delivering goods. Happy Windsor and his horse were known as 'Appy and Arry', and Bert Shepherd and his horse were 'Bert and Nobby'.

Another familiar station character in those years, who was befriended by Bill Tarbox, was Buckingham Lil. She came to the Market from Buckingham every Thursday and got drunk in the Park Hotel, which enjoyed an all day opening licence on Market days. When she staggered up the Railway Approach, Bill would give her shelter and rest in the stables while she waited for the return Banbury train. That the stables were rat infested did not bother her, and she did not seem to bother the rats. At train time Bill would load her on to a four wheel barrow and take her to the train for loading into a compartment on the Banbury train. At Buckingham, her husband was generally there to help with the unloading.

Station Inspector Bugg introduced a little dignity into the stewardship of the garden when he took over after Bill Tarbox.

Arthur Marsh commenced as a boy clerk at Buckingham Goods Shed in 1899 and became Clerk in Charge in 1905 at a salary of £60 per annum, less 2½% superannuation. At 91 he was able to say with a smile 'I have no regrets at living so long; my long years on a pension are making up for the low wages I received whilst I was at work'.

ABOVE: *Erebus* near the Shed at Oxford, c1906 with Fireman Allen
holding the handrails and BELOW: an original Ramsbottom DX No 978
c1870, at Bletchley.

ABOVE: *Hardwicke* — in 1895 it averaged 67.2 mph on a record run Crewe-Carlisle, and spent its declining years at Bletchley, renumbered 5031 in 1923, and 790 when it went to York Museum. CENTRE:Driver Jonas Sinfield on a Webb Four Cylinder Compound c1901; Guard Corn holds the shunting pole. BELOW LEFT: Driver Herbert Soulster, 1902. RIGHT: *Bucephalus* No 990 in Bletchley Station during World War I; Driver Bill Eames, Fireman Charlie Worby and Carriage Shunter Teddy Green.

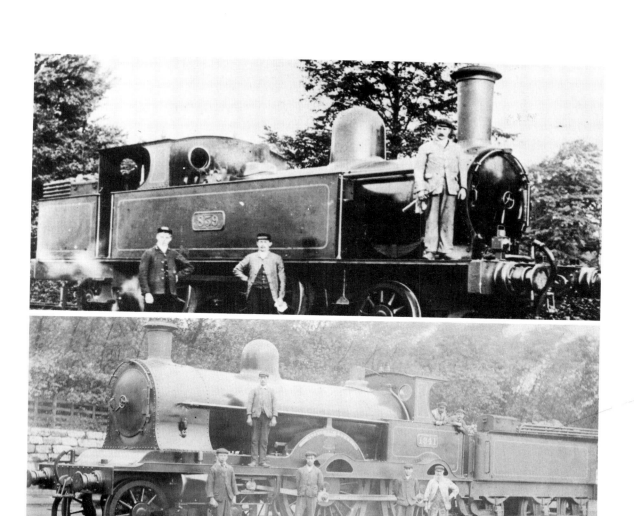

ABOVE: A 2-4-2 No 859 in the Bletchley area, c1900; CENTRE: *Alfred the Great* No 1941, early 1900s with left to right: Cleaner Billy Stevens, — , Cleaner Joe King, Cleaner George Lines and Labourer Daniel Cumberland; on the footplate Driver Joe Howe and Fireman Bill Eames. Sir Herbert Leon's trees are behind. BELOW: A quiet Sunday afternoon at Bletchley Loco Shed, 1955 — during the strike.

ABOVE: Bletchley engine cleaners in 1903 with a Lady of the Lakes class on No 5 road. BELOW: Signalman Joseph Dimmock in Bletchley No 2 Signalbox c1904, when signalmen were called constables.

ABOVE: Outside Bletchley Shed 1907, an LNWR coal tank No 119, often called a *Gadget,* with Boilersmith Pratt on footplate; CENTRE: a Cauliflower on Bletchley ashpit, and BELOW: The streamlined articulated three car Leyland oil-engined train at Bedford St John's in 1938 .

LEFT ABOVE: *Sir Gilbert Claughton* No 2222 in 1913 when it came to Bletchley and had to be turned, with the staff involved in this delicate operation, and BELOW. Bletchley Carriage Cleaners c1900. RIGHT: Bill Cox models the new Passenger Guard uniform in 1913. CENTRE LEFT: Bletchley Junior Railway Choir (Muckley's Choir after its conductor Bill Muckley) in 1927 — the choir broadcast on 2LO at Savoy Hill in Children's Hour, and RIGHT: Engine Cleaner George Judge after his return from France in World War I. BELOW LEFT: Drivers, fitters and labourers at Bletchley Shed (top left labourer Fred Cave, fourth right Sam Garner).RIGHT: Shed Cleaners c1925.

146

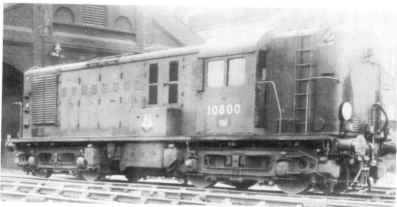

LEFT: Sidney Sellers at 14 in 1918, in his new LNWR Signalbox Lad's uniform; he retired 50 years later as a Special Class Signalman. ABOVE: Off to Bletchley Show, left to right: Goods Shed Foreman Faulkner, Fitter Dan Collier, Drivers Teddy Giltrow, George Culley and Sam Gurney, early 1920s; CENTRE: the general mixed traffic diesel loco on trials at Bletchley in 1951. BELOW: Potton Station staff 1919/20.

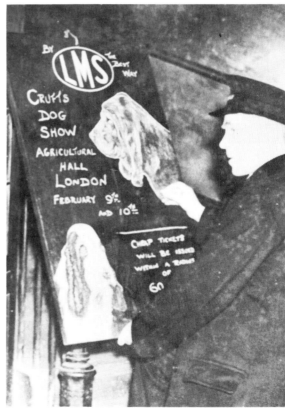

ABOVE: Bletchley Station Brass Band, 1920s; LEFT: the Railwaymen's Mission Hall altar, Banbury, and RIGHT: Bletchley Ticket Collector Albert Perry advertises Crufts Dog Show, c1934.

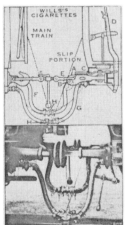

ABOVE: A failed Lizzie in Bletchley Loco Shed for repairs; the wheeldrop
is marked by two red flags; LEFT: the working of the slip coach system.
CENTRE: No 1 Permanent Way Gang outside their cabin near the
Carriage Shed. RIGHT: Firedropper Jack Millbourn and Driver Joe Long
on the ashpit.

How the Slip Coach System works: Specially equipped vehicles used as slip coaches have their coupling hooks A hinged at the lower part of the jaw B while the upper part, or tip of the hook, is held in position by a horizontal bar C. Moving a lever D in the guards compartment slides the bar. The hinged part of the hook falls and allows the coupling E to clear. As the slip parts, the vacuum brake F and the steam heating flexible connections G, both fitted with special adaptor ends H, are pulled apart. Non-return valves automatically seal the main train vacuum pipe and both portions of the steam heating pipe. The guard on the slip portion can then work the brakes until the slip is brought to a standstill.

149

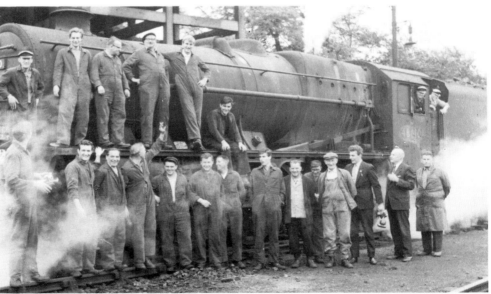

ABOVE: Bletchley No 1 Signalbox and the flyover are close neighbours for a few years; ABOVE INSET: the new power signalbox, opened June 1965. BELOW: The last steam engine leaves Bletchley Loco Shed on 5 July 1965, Driver Harold Weaver and Fireman Eddy Hancock, with a class 8 freight No 48610. The Shed staff included Shedmaster Ernie Dodd, second from right.

OUT OF STEAM

Until 1952, Bletchley Station had changed little since the 1880s. By 1953 a £20,000 improvement scheme was complete. The station frontage retained much of its Victorian character, even down to the horse-mounting stone, but this was the first facelift for 70 years. In the next 20 years, station, loco shed, goods depot, yards and the rest were to alter beyond recognition, some to disappear for good.

In 1952 the main line expresses thundered through, few stopping. The 'varsity passengers still used the Oxbridge link, but they too were dwindling. The main local customers were the three nearby brickworks, the town's three brushwork factories and the Tetley Tea blending works. The new zonal collection and delivery scheme spelt the end for the smaller wayside stations.

Bletchley's facelift did not stretch to other stations on the branch lines. Oxford closed in 1951, passengers diverted to the GWR station. Farthinghoe went in 1952. With some engine and staff changes, the branches were worked much as they were before the war. The passengers dwindled still further, and Banbury's Sunday service ceased.

In 1956 BR chose Buckingham-Banbury for an experiment with single railcars — to save rural lines. Two little olive railcars — Nos 79900 and 79901 — were allocated to Bletchley, starting in 13 August. Fast, dainty and decorative, they brought new wooden platformed halts to Radclive and Water Stratford. Loadings were so heavy on Banbury Market Days that they were coupled together to run as one train.

It was an easy-going line — if the girl at Bacon's Wood Farm wanted to get off near home, the driver simply stopped on request. There were incidents though, such as when Driver Bernard White hit a herd of cattle one winter's night at 70 mph. The farmer paid for the damage to the railcar and one bullock died. Another time, the 'car sped into Banbury with no response from the brakes, finally easing off just two yards from the stops. Despite the promising start, the experiment lost way and receipts dwindled, although the service did make considerable impact. Costs were less, and traffic more, but the railcars still lost money.

The Railway Board gave notice of closure, and in 1960 the Transport Users' Consultative Committee agreed. On 31 December 1960, the Banbury-Buckingham passenger service ceased altogether. There remained the Buckingham Push and Pull to Bletchley and the railcars maintained this for four further years, sadly with few passengers. The final train left Buckingham on 5 September 1964. Protests there were, but no sustained interest in a fight.

During the lifespan of the railcars from 1956-1964, branch line changes had been widespread and devastating. In 1957, a grand scheme was pronounced. This suggested that the cross-London freight problem would be eased if the Oxbridge line was developed, and its connections improved. Bletchley was central to this bypass scheme for freight traffic.

New works would include a new double junction at Bedford, a flyover viaduct over the main line at Bletchley, a new curve north from the Marylebone-Rugby line at Claydon, works at Oxford and at Reading.

An integral development would be a new marshalling yard west of Bletchley. But it was the flyover that came first. Next was the diversion of main line traffic to the cross-country route. Another diversionary route would be from Denbigh Hall to the flyover. Contractors moved into Bletchley in 1957. In 1958 plant arrived to tackle the flyover itself. It was then announced that the new marshalling yard would be at Swanbourne, and Horwood House and vast tracts of land were bought.

In 1959 the British Transport Commission announced withdrawal of the passenger service on the entire Oxbridge line and Banbury branch. No-one believed it could happen. Bletchley was now a town of 14,600 and in the throes of railway development; the universities would surely protest.There were protests and BTC said they would continue the service for two years with diesel traction. Steam had generated losses of over £70,000; diesel would reduce this to £26,000 pa. On 2 November 1959 twin set railcars inaugurated an imaginative service. There was little else that changed, except at Bletchley.

In mid-1960 the flyover was in business. A new approach road overwhelmed the old trainmen's lodging house. In 1961 an underbridge took shape. In 1963 passenger services were again under threat on the cross country lines. Everyone objected, from MPs to private people. The TUCC heard them all on 21 July 1964, but the Minister said that Bletchley's development would not be prejudiced by the closure. For a year the line lasted.

By 1965, the flyover complete, along with the Diesel Electric Depot, and with overhead wires only 38 miles away at Rugby, down came the old portico and the chimneys of the hotel and the Coffee Tavern. Instead, there stood the new gantries, footbridge and platform lift shafts. On 5 July the new signalbox was commissioned. One modern box controlled 33 route miles, 104 track miles, 41 controlled signals, 84 semi-automatic/automatic signals, 33 position light ground signals, 198 routes and 67 points. Bletchley Power Box came into full operation mid-day on Sunday and within an hour Bletchley No 1 was a heap of rubble. Others followed; Wolverton Nos 1 and 2, Denbigh Hall, Bletchley 2 and 5, Stoke Hammond, Flettons Sidings, Leighton Buzzard Nos 1 and 2 and Cheddington.

On the same day, the last steam engine left the shed. Instead, ten diesel electrics were stabled. The Station Master went and the Station Manager arrived. Dick Mansell stayed on as an assistant for a while. In July 1965 the Minister consented to the withdrawal of passenger services from the Oxford-Cambridge branch lines; 4 September was the due date. Yet another deferment, due to inadequate road services, saved the lines.

Just two days under two years later, the branch lines closed — all except Bletchley-Bedford, saved again through inadequate alternatives by 'bus. Banbury's link closed to freight by December 1966, and the lines were lifted in 1967. Swanbourne's vast yard never materialised — in March 1967 the siding closed for good. Horwood House was sold. On 30 December 1967 the Oxbridge passenger service ceased.

Still the Bletchley-Bedford hourly railcar defiantly ran. In 1972 BR announced closure — a new 'bus licence meant the road option was open. Seven local authorities intervened, and the service was reprieved. As 1974 dawned, Transport Minister John Peyton announced that within an £81m BR package, £212,000 would be earmarked for this service, with a review in 1975. That year came and went, with ageing railcars and an uncertain prospect.

Meanwhile, Verney-Banbury lines were torn up; bridges and culverts were demolished; Buckingham station came down; housing replaced Padbury's station and yard. Rubbish piled up at Farthinghoe.

The Bedford-Cambridge section rusted away and was pulled up over a period of years; bridges came down and grass grew over ballast. Willington station was demolished and a scrap iron dump took over the goods yard. Blunham station became offices, the pub closed and yet the lattice bridge over the Ivel survives.

Sandy station was halved; Potton station became a timber yard; Gamlingay was isolated by a factory and the infilled bridge. Old North station became a coal yard. Lords Bridge acquired a futuristic look with spruced-up buildings, saucer shapes and 'Mullard Radio Astrology Observatory' painted on the gate.

In 1973 the Bicester-Oxford section went single track and a stone depot took over the old Oxford Road Junction siding — for road building was keeping the line alive.

Islip went quickly, but Bicester only lost the down platform — scrap iron proliferated. The surviving Ordnance Siding and a rarely used petrol depot siding at Islip were all that remained on the western line.

Winslow station is boarded up, the Station Master's house in ruins; a bungalow stands in the sidings at Verney Junction — the station and railway cottages have gone. Claydon's Station Master's house has also gone; Marsh Gibbon's building remains, while at Launton, the crumbling house shelters the crossing keeper.

The once picturesque buildings at Millbrook, Ridgmont, Woburn Sands and Fenny Stratford have slipped into disrepair. An upholsterer works at Woburn Sands, and a signalman at Ridgmont, but Millbrook is deserted. Fenny Stratford is surrounded by a wilderness, and vandals have left their mark.

The story has no end. Bletchley may yet become a fine, new City, though now without the lines that once joined it to Oxford and to Cambridge. One day it may not matter, but for someone who has travelled those tracks so many times, felt their past and known their charming characters through contact or memory, the loss of the Oxbridge link is sacrilege.

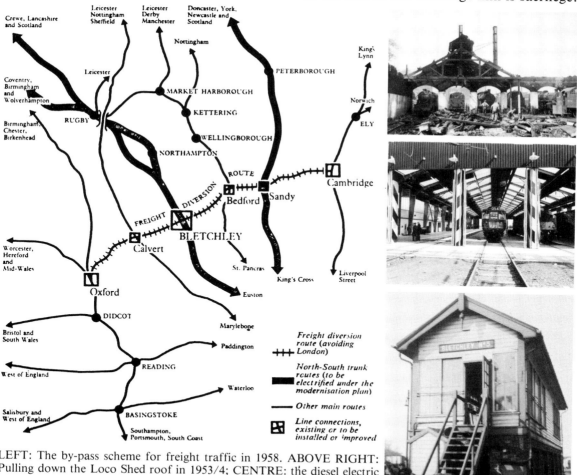

LEFT: The by-pass scheme for freight traffic in 1958. ABOVE RIGHT: Pulling down the Loco Shed roof in 1953/4; CENTRE: the diesel electric Depot Shed; BELOW: Bletchley No 5 Signalbox, now gone.

Bletchley Station — ABOVE: after the 1952 renovation and BELOW: today.

INDEX

SUBSCRIBERS

Presentation copies

1 Milton Keynes Development Corporation
2 Milton Keynes Borough Council
3 Buckinghamshire County Council
4 Buckinghamshire County Library
5 British Rail
6 National Union of Railwaymen
7 Sir Peter Parker
8 Sydney Weighell

9 A. E. Grigg
10 Clive & Carolyn Birch
11 S. J. Bragginton
12 Nick Mawson
13 Mrs W. Green
14
15 D. J. Simpson
16 J. V. Vincent
17 A. A. Grigg
18 David G. King
19 Reginald Waters
20 William Sinfield
21 M. J. Smith
22 David J. Castle
23 A. Wells
24 M. R. Brackenbury
25 The Leon School
26
27 R. Hancock
28 D. N. Ratcliff
29 Bernard Frederick Lewis
30 Peter John Alderman
31 The SMS 683 Group
32 Richard Abbey
33 Keith Mulreedy
34 William John Chalkley
35 Ian K. Hutchinson
36 Peter Chard
37 Andrew Pike
38 Leslie Patrick Bowler
39 George Peter Fishwick
40 D. P. Gibbins
41 B. Segrott
42 Trevor Mark Clarke
43 Stephen Williams
44 Mrs C. D. Duncan
45 John Hammond Soddy
46
47 Mrs D. M. Eley
48 Cedric Hoptroff
49 Bill Sinfield
50 G. J. Fenton
51
52 R. J. Ayers
53 L. Aldridge
54 Dr Peter Jarvis
55 Clifford G. O. Clarke
56 Harold Taylor
57
63 Robin Leleux
64 P. J. Stanbridge
65 G. L. Champkin
66 F. W. Harris
67 D. Sowster
68 A. W. Biggs
69 Thomas H. Read
70
72 W. H. Bowler
73 A. F. Norman
74 D. Young
75 R. G. Sear
76 Terence S. Trew
77 G. J. Yardley
78 Christopher Fogden
79 Jean Evelyn Burdett
80 D. A. L. Robinson
81 M. J. Smith
82 D. Elgie
83 R. H. Smith, JP
84 L. P. Thacker

85
86 Barry Wheeler
87 Industrial Railway Society
92 Society
93 Alan Hall
94 S. G. Sellers
95 Michael Champion
96 P. Tarbox
97 Leon Higgs
98 M. P. Seagrave
99 Gerald Sandison
100 J. E. James
101 Gordon Reginald White
102
103 Peter Clarke
104 Bletchley NUR
115 Branch
116 J. C. S. Sanders
117 M. J. Smith
118 F. J. Clare
119 R. K. McKay
120 L. S. Hawkins
121 G. F. Eckersley
122 V. G. Leyshon
123 James Brandon
124 Frederick Cotchin
125 G. C. Baker
126 R. J. Millburn
127 David W. Ford
128 Thomas Borland
129 R. Merivale
130 C. Stacey
131 Trevor James Massey
132 C. Bateman
133 E. G. Hancock
134 Robert P. Davidson
135 Christopher Lindsay
136 A. J. Johnson
137 P. G. Healey
138
139 E. Jones
140 Harold V. Hudson
141 R. G. Lawrence
142 Paul Clarke
143 G. Grigg
144 Gareth James
145
146 John D. Doggett
147 Morris Wells
148 L. Pateman
149 A. C. S. Jinks
150 Kenneth Pateman
151 A. Rollings
152 W. J. Hughes
153 Patrick Bennett
154
156 S. H. Bowler
157 Trevor S. Jennings
158 G. M. Rix
159 Brian Alderman
160 David Barrow
161 W. Duff
162 Andrew Buchanan
163 R. M. Chown
164 R. M. E. Cook

165 Philip Lingard
166
167 S. T. Green
168 R. T. P. Circuit
169 T. E. Simpson
170 A. G. Williams
171 Anthony John Mann
172 Edwin Gravestock
173 David Yewen
174 W. J. Woodward
175 A. Sinfield
176 H. G. Lovett
177 Donald Wheeler
178 Mrs Janine Turnbull
179 M. J. Martin
180 Henry Pikesley
181 James Morris
182 David Robinson
183 Ken Scanes
184 William Mountney
185
186 Anthony J. Coulson
187 C. Dell
188 Leslie Manson
189 H. A. G. Bowler
190 ASLEF Bletchley Branch
191 David Pascoe
192 J. R. Cowley
193
194 J. Mann
195 John C. Halsey
196 Percy Birtchnell
197 Kevin Dingle
198 J. E. Beckett
199 Mrs Linda Carter
200 John Harradine
201 G. W. Hitchinson
202 P. L. Pay
203 George Howe
204 Robert M. Gush
205 Ann Margaret Dearman
206
209 Alan E. Scott
210 D. W. Bodsworth
211 David Essam
212 David Bissel
213 J. W. Dicks
214 M. D. Sumner
215 R. E. B. Smith
216 Colin Wroblewski
217 W. Kevill F. Armstrong
218 Colin D. F. Smith
219
220 John Lynch
221 Donald Fraser Blane
222 Jack Blane
223 Margaret Bessie Osmond
224 Simon Laurence Tottman
225 Mrs Eileen Langley
226 Beryl Swann
227 E. S. Neal

228 Edward James Neal
229 A. C. Heady
230 M. J. Clayton
231 J. Wilbur Wright
232 G. R. Green
233 H. T. Buckingham
234
236 W. J. Goodway
237 R. Clary
238 John Draper
239 G. C. Gibbs
240 Les Jackson
241 B. E. Rocard
242 Adrian Banfield
243 Colin Green
244
245 Joc Van Es
246
247 Michael Grace
248 William L. Short
249 A. V. Pritchard
250 P. B. Morgan
251 A. L. Hill
252 D. T. Clifford
253 J. Y. Rawlinson
254 Mrs P. Stearn
255 V. I. Faulkner
256 F. J. Boaot
257 Norman Fernando
258 J. Horsley
259 P. Jaggs
260 Ian Charles Westall
261 B. Hormer
262 Mrs D. M. Johnson
263 A. Long
264 Eileen Parker
265 Ian E. James
266 Ron Mead
267 Peter Grigg
268 C. B. R. Garner
269 Nigel Aston
270 Mrs I Hitchon
271 A. J. Slope
272 Malcolm R. Simpson
273 R. A. Waldron
274 A. E. W. Naish
275
276 A. C. G. Oakley
277 John Dixon
278 Derek Hibbert
279 R. C. Pearce
280 S. J. Stollery
281 Andrew Peacock
282 D. C . Alexander
283 Gary Lucas
284 S. E. Randolph
285 Colin Tooth
286 Donald A. Stewart
287 Nigel John Gibbs
288 J. Rose
289 I. T. Leigh
290 B. Titchmarsh
291 George Alexander Black
292 Edward F. Griffin
293 Ian Windmill
294 Kevin Lane
295 D. L. Hanson
296 A. P. Tomkins
297
298 Peter Adrian Ford
299 Michael Powell
300 G. M. Sawford
301 E. R. H. Mills
302 Albert Reed
303 William A. Simpson

304	C. T. Ashton	383	C. G. Linford
305	J. Bratton	384	E. B. Hubble, BA,FRBS
306	A. M. Ford	385	S. V. Blencowe
307	R. N. Pattenden	386	R. M. Stokes
308	Charles Sedge	387	R. Unwin
309	Roger Ashcroft	388	D. J. Hattan-Bennett
310	C. B. Martindale, FRIBA	389	S. A. Cruikshank
311	David John Turley	390	John S. Spencer
312	Cecil Thomas Tilley	391	J. N. Parker
313	Robert Harper	392	L. V. Wood
314	John S. Sermon	393	Brian Stopford
315	S. E. Baker	394	M. J. Boyes
316	E. Smith	395	N. L. Stone
317	A. Waring	396	M. Zalewski
318	D. K. Plummer	397	K. Higham
319	Leighton Buzzard Narrow Gauge Railway Society	398	R. A. Brown
		399	David Allen
		400	R. W. Hill
320	Tel Airs	401	M. J. Morley
321	John H. Young	402	M. W. Kemp
322	Mrs G. C. Collons	403	A. M. Jervis
323	Adrian Shooter	404	Devon County Council
324	K. J. Cornes	405	Kevin Kingston
325		406	D. W. Edwards
326	D. E. Smith	407	Richard W. T. Carlton
327	R. E. Aston	408	Peter R. Mitchell
328	C. E. Stanley	409	J. R. Fairman
329	Charles Robert Smith	410	F. A. Blencowe
330	Mrs C. V. Wilkins	411	
331	Martin Anderssohn	412	W. M. West
332	L. J. Colby	413	W. C. Daniels
333	J. J. S. Goss	414	A. H. Thurlow
334	Malcolm P. Carvell	415	F. Moran
335	G. B. Dodd	416	Brian Harrison
336	Clive Nichols	417	J. D. Irving
337	Milton Keynes Urban Studies Centre	418	John C. Peach
		419	Nigel D. Mundy
338	Ian James Thompson	420	National Railway Museum
339	Quainton Railway Society	421	S. A. Tuffrey
343		422	R. French
344	Thomas E. Whitlock	423	S. J. Osborne
345	P. W. Price	424	L. N. Hoamond
346	Stephen M. Britt Hazard, MA, FGC	425	Dr B. D. Wheeler
		426	Donald T. Jayne
347	Judge L. J. Verney	427	Michael King
348		428	H. Evans
349	John A. Cook	429	Mrs J. Rorison
350	G. P. Crabbe	430	H. A. Jarman
351	Mrs I. Hitchon	431	P. N. Hall
352	G.E.and M.Appleton	432	L. J. Abbiss
353	T. Hitchcock	433	Christopher Charles George
354	T. F. Berreen	434	J. A. Jennings
355	David G. Fearn	435	E. E. Strang
356	Michael J. Fearn	436	A. J. Philips
357	Herbert Waine	437	D. Bruce
358	G. Fletcher	438	N. R. Deacon
359	P. Yates	439	L. G. Cooke
360	G. L. Smith	440	P. J. Monger
361	Mrs Mary Leigh	441	H. C. Casserley
362	J. V. Rigby	442	David James Godwin
363	Mr & Mrs E. Wilkins	443	Michael James Sherman
364	John Carr	444	John Lunn
365	T. J. Cook	445	E. G. Bowman
366	W. Daniell	446	Hertfordshire Railtour
367	L. W. Grigg	447	David Read
368	Robert McLean Blaikie	448	Malcolm Read
369	David Hoskins	449	Victoria and Albert Museum
370	C. R. Brooks	450	Mrs J. Stephenson
371	Daniel F. Grigg	451	David Stimson
372	Eric G. Evans	452	Frank A. Hewer
373	Christopher D. Goodwyn	453	K. Jones
374	D. A. A. Berry	454	Charles Henry Gannon
375	Mrs E. M. Bradshaw	455	G. Stevens
376	Kenneth Prince	456	Mrs D. P. Claridge
377			
378	Rosalind R. Jolley		
379	J. N. Smith		
380	D. Evans		
381	M. E. Davies		
382	Robert Zalewski		

457	Richard William Bird	543	Dr B. A. Evans, MRCP
458	T. J. Garrod	544	K. Mulready
459	Mrs B. Dark	545	D. Haley
460	R. J. Atkins	546	J. A. Curtis
461	P. Wince	547	D. Stuart Johnson
462	Mrs P. E. Hickford	548	Buckinghamshire
463	W. Croot	578	County Library
464	J. A. Wall	579	A. D. Harris
465	G. F. Willaret	580	Michael Taylor
466	D. C. Blake	581	A. S. Labrum
467	Bernard-Gil Melotte	582	Dennis A. Lovett
468	Peter Gulland	583	T. Philp
469	J. F. Atkins	584	M. Tasker
470	Peter J. Smith	585	A. P. Dransfield
471	N. R. Aston	586	Christopher Trafford
472	Frank E. Atter	587	W. Dick
473	N. Vokins	588	R. R. Roberts
474	M. J. King	589	Mrs Sylvia Black
475	B. W. Eggetton	590	Leonard C. White
476	G. C. Potts	591	C. Caines
477	P. Iles	592	Mrs B. Watson
478	David Bezzer	593	S. J. Murphy
479	W. L. Hanks	594	R. C. Gent
480	A. C. Weeds	595	F. Dimock
481	A. Foxley	596	S. Emmerton
482	D. K. Bednall	597	R. J. Williams
483	K. O'Haren	598	G. Williams
484	D. H. Graham	599	D. N. Ratcliff
485	L. F. Tilley	600	
486	J. F. Scott	601	M. J. Wagstaff
487	J. Milner	602	N. R. Deacon
488	B. A. Blackford	603	B. K. Smith
489	R. A. Ingram	604	A. W. Willis
490	J. A. Mcloud	605	D. P. Smith
491	W. Swann	606	A. E. Bowers
492	Ross Smith	607	J. R. Slater
493	J. Everett	608	Mr & Mrs K. D. Meadley
494	E. V. Maeder	609	Mr Peloake
495	J. C. Taylor	610	N. K. Peerless
496	David Jacobs	611	J. J. Bromfield
497	M. Jewell	612	J. W. Eggelton
498	Mrs J. Andrews	613	M. A. G. Hutt
499	D. C. Scott	614	Mr Kingston
500	David Slade Allard	615	D. O. Warden
501	Frank Cheney	616	J. A. Pyne
502	J. P. A. Mullineer	617	N. A. Kent
503	Alan Walker	618	A. J. Beckingham
504	L. Capron	619	Philip R. Murphy
505	R. A. B. Saxby	620	C. J. C. Hyait
506	P. N. J. Garratt	621	Ron Risbridger
507	Roland Walter Doggett	622	J. Deillon
508	A. R. Hillier	623	E. D. Baker
509	Mrs G. Ellis	624	S. P. Shane
510	G. E. Etherington	625	R. A. P. Bardsley
511	S. W. E. Daniels	626	T. Jones
512	R. Maund	627	Mr Franklin
513	W. R. Ballard	628	Matthew Mella
514	W. R. Clark	629	E. G. Hayward
515	C. R. Wright	630	Mrs P. M. Moyes
516	L. Penrice	631	Brian Baldwin
517	Industrial Railway Society	632	Mrs M. A. Metcalfe
522	J. A. Turner	633	M. W. Short
523	J. A. Turner	634	Mrs S. Woodforde
524	H. Holderness	635	Richard J. Spreckley
525	Judith Hooley	636	R. A. Davies
526	Joseph Walker	637	Mrs I. Hazlewood
527	W. P. Litchfield	638	P. L. Mortimer
528	M. A. Abbiss	639	Mr Beechey
529	M. P. Burgoyne	640	Frank Abbott
530	P. A. Rose	641	Kenneth E. Griffin
531	L. A. S. Cooper	642	Janet Wearing
532	Bletchley College of Further Education	643	A. W. T. Dilley
		644	C. R. Draper
533	E. Legg	645	F. C. Woodall
534		646	W. Skeats
536	John Wilson	647	Charles Easterbrook
537	Trevor Clark	648	G. G. Fulcher
538	B. J. Hobbs	649	Mrs B. Charlton
539	J. Hopkins	650	R. H. Harding
540	G. Dowsing	651	D. A. Rose
541	F. W. Charles	652	J. D. Robinson
542	F. J. Driscoll		

160

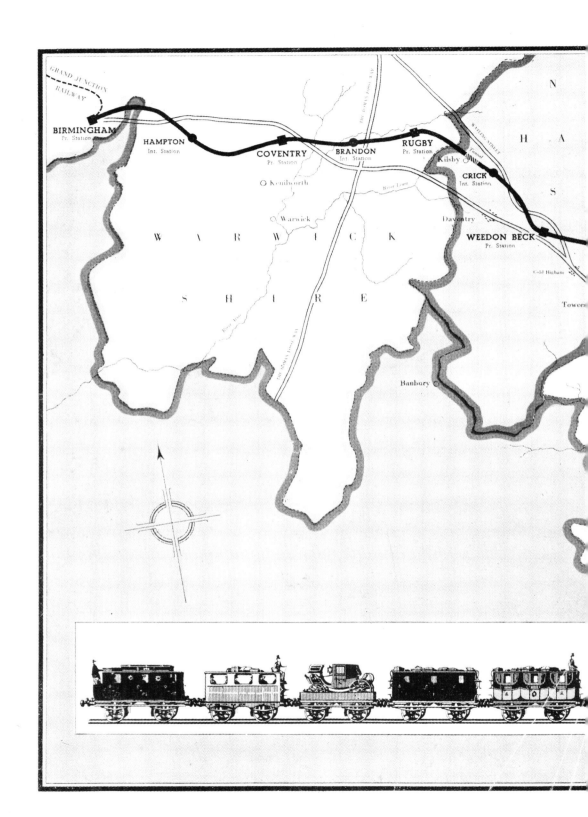